Religion
ON TRIAL

Other books in ABC-CLIO's On Trial Series
Charles L. Zelden, Series Editor

Religion
ON TRIAL

A Handbook with
Cases, Laws, and Documents

James John Jurinski

A B C ✹ C L I O

Santa Barbara, California • Denver, Colorado • Oxford, England

Library of Congress Cataloging-in-Publication Data
Jurinski, James.
  Religion on trial : a handbook with cases, laws, and documents / James
John Jurinski.
    p. cm. — (On trial series)
Includes bibliographical references and index.
    ISBN 1-85109-491-1 (hardcover : alk. paper)   ISBN 1-85109-496-2 (e-book)
1. Church and state—United States.   2. Freedom of religion—United
States.   3. Church and state—United States—Cases.   4. Freedom of
religion—United States—Cases.   I. Title.   II. Series: On trial.
KF4865.J87 2003
342.7308'52—dc22   2003020750

08   07   06   05   04   10   9   8   7   6   5   4   3   2   1

ABC-CLIO, Inc.
130 Cremona Drive, P.O. Box 1911
Santa Barbara, California 93116-1911

This book is printed on acid-free paper.
Manufactured in the United States of America

To my friend, Professor Vincent Carrafiello

Contents

Series Foreword

The volumes in the On Trial series explore the many ways in which the U.S. legal and political system has approached a wide range of complex and divisive legal issues over time—and in the process defined the current state of the law and politics on these issues. The intent is to give students and other general readers a framework for understanding how the law in all its various forms—constitutional, statutory, judicial, political, and customary—has shaped and reshaped the world in which we live today.

At the core of each volume in the series is a common proposition: that in certain key areas of American public life, we as a people and a nation are "on trial" as we struggle to cope with the contradictions, conflicts, and disparities within our society, politics, and culture. Who should decide if and when a woman can have an abortion? What rights, if any, should those with a different sexual orientation be able to claim under the Constitution? Is voting a basic right of citizenship, and if so, under what rules should we organize this right—especially when the application of any organizing rules inevitably results in excluding some citizens from the polls? And what about the many inconsistencies and conflicts associated with racial tensions in the country? These are just some of the complex and controversial issues that we as a people and a nation are struggling to answer—and must answer if we are to achieve an orderly and stable society. For the answers we find to these disputes shape the essence of who we are—as a people, community, and political system.

The concept of being "on trial" also has a second meaning fundamental to this series: the process of litigating important issues in a court of law. Litigation is an essential part of how we settle our differences and make choices as we struggle with the problems that confront us as a people and a nation. In the 1830s, Alexis de Tocqueville noted in his book *Democracy in America*, "There is hardly a political question in the United States which does not sooner or later turn into a judicial one" (Tocqueville 1835, 270). This insight is as true today as it was in the 1830s. In *The Litigious Society*, Jethro K. Lieberman notes: "To express amazement at American litigiousness is akin to professing astonishment at learning that the roots of most Americans lie in other lands. We have been a litigious nation as we have been an immigrant one. Indeed, the two are related" (Lieberman 1983, 13). Arriving in the United States with different backgrounds, customs, and lifestyle preferences, we inevitably clashed as our contrasting visions of life in United States— its culture, society, and politics—collided. And it was to the courts and the law that we turned as a neutral forum for peaceably working out these differences. For, in the United States at least, it is the courthouse that provides the anvil on which our personal, societal, and political problems are hammered out.

The volumes in this series therefore take as their central purpose the important task of exploring the various ways—good and bad, effective and ineffective, complex and simple—in which litigation in the courts has shaped the evolution of particular legal controversies for which we as a people are "on trial." And, more important, the volumes do all this in a manner accessible to the general reader seeking to comprehend the topic as a whole.

These twin goals—analytical and educational—shape the structure and layout of the volumes in the series. Each book consists of two parts. The first provides an explanatory essay in four chapters. Chapter 1 introduces the issues, controversies, events, and participants associated with the legal controversy at hand. Chapter 2 explores the social, economic, political and/or historical background to this topic. Chapter 3 describes in detail the various court decisions and actions that have shaped the current status of the legal controversy under examination. In some cases that will be done through a close examination of a few representative cases; in others by a broader but less detailed narrative of the course of judicial action. Chapter 4 discusses the impact of these cases on U.S. law— their doctrinal legacy—as well as on U.S. society—their historical, sociological, and political legacy.

Part 2, in turn, provides selective supplementary materials designed to help readers more fully comprehend the topics covered in the chapters of Part 1. First are documents aimed at helping the reader better appreciate both the issues and the process by which adjudication shaped these matters. Selected documents might include court opinions (excerpted or whole), interviews, newspaper accounts, or selected secondary essays. Next comes an alphabetically formatted glossary providing entries on the people, laws, cases, and concepts important to an understanding of the topic. A chronology next provides the reader an easily referenced listing of the major developments covered in the book, and a table of cases lists the major court decisions cited. And lastly, an annotated bibliography describes the key works in the field, directing a reader seeking a more detailed examination of the topic to the appropriate sources.

In closing, as you read the books in this series, keep in mind the purposefully controversial nature of the topics covered within. The authors in the series have not chosen easy or agreeable topics to explore. Much of what you read may trouble you, and should. Yet it is precisely these sorts of contentious topics that need the most historical analysis and scrutiny. For it is here that we are still "on trial"—and all too often, as regards these matters, the jury is still out.

Charles L. Zelden
Ft. Lauderdale, Florida

Preface

Although the United States was founded on the principle of freedom of religion, religion has been "on trial" in America almost from the first days of the republic. This is one area of the law where court cases have shaped daily life for millions of Americans. Although this volume contains an analysis of the historical and current background of many of the legal issues surrounding religion in everyday life, the book focuses most closely on six actual trials and their legacy and impact.

Rather than a treatise with hundreds of footnotes, this entire book is a reference handbook that will help users start their research. Part 1 includes a historical overview as well as chapters devoted to the cases. Part 2 of the book contains not only a chronology and A–Z listing of key people, laws, and concepts, but also a number of original documents including excerpts from a number of leading court opinions and statutes. There is also a bibliography that includes both print and Internet resources.

All of the legal opinions discussed in this volume are readily available on the Internet and readers should access the full opinions to gain a fuller understanding of the factual background to the cases, the legal issues posed, and the courts' reasoning. The views in this book are my own, and I am solely responsible for any errors.

James John Jurinski
Portland, Oregon

Part One

1
Introduction

Although the United States was founded on the principle of freedom of religion, religion has been "on trial" in America almost from the first days of the republic. It may seem ironic that the court system should be so involved in the very private matter of religion, but that involvement is almost inevitable. Because the United States is so accepting of religious practices, the diversity of religions makes for a volatile mix, and conflicts arise that must be resolved by the courts. Although most Americans agree with the concept of freedom of religion, the actual application of that guarantee has generated a lot of controversy. For example, such issues as whether prayer should be allowed in public schools or whether government funds should be given to churches to do charitable work have been hot topics at the turn of the twenty-first century. By necessity the courts have become arbiters of what kinds of restrictions the government can impose on religious practice, and what role religion will play in public life. This book provides an introduction to this complicated and important topic.

The United States is notable for its religious pluralism. Although a majority of the U.S. population describe themselves as "Christians," there are a remarkable number of individual Christian churches with varying beliefs and doctrines. Of course, there are millions of religious Americans who are not Christians. There are also millions of Americans who profess no religious beliefs. Although the United States has always had a diverse population, the trend has accelerated. The insularity of small towns is eroding, and migration and immigration have created a more heterogeneous mix of schoolchildren in many areas of the country. An increasing number of school children are non-Christian immigrants from Asian countries. These students' families not only speak a diverse number of languages but are also members of a diverse number of religions. Our governmental system is designed to protect the interests of these minorities as well as the interests of the majority.

Religion is an area where laws and court decisions can shape the patterns of daily practice. A court may decide if a minister can say a prayer at a high school graduation. A court may decide if a nativity scene can be placed in front of a municipal building at Christmas. A court may decide if a worker at a fast food restaurant can wear a cross despite the company's "no jewelry" policy, or if an employee can refuse to work on Sunday. In the United States, the ultimate arbiter of these decisions is the Supreme Court, and over the years the Court has been at the center of many of these controversies regarding religion. Congress is also an important player through its law-making power. This chapter explains how laws pertaining to freedom of religion evolve, including the roles of Congress and the Supreme Court in this area.

The First Amendment

Freedom of religion has always been recognized as an important individual right in the United States, and that right is contained in the First Amendment of the U.S. Constitution, which provides: "Congress can make no law respecting an establishment of religion, or prohibiting the free exercise thereof."

The first half of this amendment is called the Establishment Clause, and guarantees that the government will not create an "established" church. The second half, called the Free Exercise Clause, prohibits the government from enacting laws that impinge on any individual's practice of religion. The U.S. Supreme Court has firmly established that the First Amendment protections apply to state and local governments as well. Because the public school system is funded by tax dollars, it is also considered part of the government. Accordingly, the First Amendment freedom of religion guarantees apply to local school district decisions as well as to congressional acts. Many freedom of religion cases involve schools, because they are venues in which individuals with different beliefs come into close contact with one another.

The First Amendment creates an inherent tension. The Establishment Clause requires that government cannot endorse a specific religion or the practices of a specific religion, but the Free Exercise Clause requires that the government do nothing to discourage individuals' religious practice and expression. Taken literally, the first clause may appear only to limit the establishment of an "official" church. However, the courts have held that any favoritism on the part of the government can be a violation of the Establishment Clause. For example, posting the Ten Commandments in public buildings has been held to violate the Establishment Clause because it favors Christianity and Judaism over other religions. Recitation of the Lord's Prayer at public events favors Christianity. The courts have even held that schools enforcing a moment of silence in classrooms to encourage individual prayer is unconstitutional. The Supreme Court has also recognized, however, that students as individuals have a constitutional right to religious expression that does not end when they enter the school door. Therefore the Court has held that students may use school facilities for religiously oriented clubs and engage in silent prayer or prayer aloud as long as they are not required to do so by school officials.

On one hand, when the courts ban religious activity such as Bible reading from the schools in an effort to comply with the Establishment Clause, they limit the rights of the religious individuals who wish to read the Bible in school. On the other hand, if the courts permit Bible reading to promote the free exercise of religion, they implicitly endorse the practice of a particular religion in violation of the Establishment Clause. The First Amendment creates two freedom of religion goals that are not always possible to reconcile. These goals can come into conflict when the majority's religious practice offends a minority. Readers who keep this concept in mind will appreciate why the Supreme Court has such a difficult time resolving the cases to everyone's satisfaction.

The Wall of Separation

Separation of church and state is a distinguishing characteristic of the U.S. system of government. The Founding Fathers envisioned a secular government because most of them or their parents emigrated from countries dominated by state-run churches. In order for religion and politics to be separate spheres, the founders recognized that freedom of religion required that government not be involved in the promotion or protection of particular faiths or discouraging citizens from practicing the faith of their choice. However, the separation of church and state in America has never been rigid. For example, from the earliest days of the republic, the president has taken the oath of office by swearing on the Bible, and it is the custom in many courts for witnesses to do the same. U.S. currency bears the motto "In God We Trust." The pledge of allegiance has included the words "One nation under God" since the 1950s. Churches pay no local property taxes. Despite these entangled relationships, the First Amendment has been interpreted by the courts to contain a "wall of separation" between church and state.

Despite this legal precedent, many important political debates have ethical and religious implications. Some of these "entanglements" are obvious, while some are more subtle. For example, the issue of whether a city may erect a cross on city property raises the issue of whether the city is promoting or endorsing Christianity. Although the majority of the citizens may view the activity as a praiseworthy use of tax money, it may also offend those of other faiths or those of no faith. This issue is at once both a political and a religious issue. The antislavery abolitionist movement had religious roots, as did the temperance movement to ban the sale of alcoholic beverages in the early twentieth century. The legalization of abortion and the possibility of human cloning are two more recent issues that have religious implications.

The religious content of other issues may be more subtle. For example, the issue of gays in the military or recognition of same-sex unions may appear to be political or social issues, but for some, these are religious issues. Some individuals' hostility toward gay and lesbian people is rooted in their religious beliefs. These individuals may believe that the sexual conduct is condemned by the Bible and should not be tolerated or encouraged in any way. Although our political system is theoretically based on the separation of church and state, issues are not always clearly secular or religious. Because of this overlap, it is impossible to completely separate religion and politics. Not surprisingly, the issues that have both political and religious implications are the very issues that trigger the greatest controversies.

There are also differences of public opinion regarding how much government entanglement with religion is appropriate. On one hand, those who argue that the Constitution mandates a "wall of separation" between church and state believe that religion is a personal and family matter only. They would argue that when a schoolteacher or a legislator posts a copy of the Ten Commandments, it promotes Christianity and Judaism in an impermissible way. On the other side of the issue are people who believe that public life should not be a "Godless" zone. They believe that religious individuals should be free to express themselves in public. Further, they argue that if the majority desires to have a public prayer or Bible reading, then those of other religions could remain silent or be excluded. They believe that the act of erecting a cross or a crèche on public land does not constitute an endorsement of religion. Some proponents of this view also argue that the biblical account of Adam and Eve should be taught along with the theory of evolution in biology classes.

Some Americans feel that efforts to accommodate religious minorities have gone too far, and that these efforts result in discrimination against the religious majority. They argue that banning prayer from public schools and other religious activities from public buildings has resulted in discrimination against the Christian majority. Specifically they argue that the courts' approach of banning public religious activities is flawed. They argue that this enforced secularization of society in the interest of protecting the minority of believers and nonbelievers has impinged on the majority's right to religious expression. In their view, public places need not be "Godless" secular zones, but places where religious expression is tolerated and not suppressed. Their opponents argue that allowing organized prayer and other religious activity in the schools and in other public venues is an unconstitutional promotion of the majority's religion at the expense of those in the minority.

Areas of Legal Conflict

A detailed description of the many trials dealing with religion would fill many books this size. Accordingly only a small number of trials are introduced here, but they are presented in detail in Chapter 3.

That chapter includes a discussion of six trials that have interpreted freedom of religion, which are important not only because they define the contours of the law regarding religion in the United States but also because they illustrate how the U.S. legal system deals with real disputes that need to be resolved. These cases illustrate that although it is easy to devise generalized rules, it can be far harder to apply those rules to specific situations. Most of the cases in Chapter 3 generated not only majority court opinions but also dissenting opinions showing that judges and Supreme Court justices—like other Americans—do not always agree on how these issues should be resolved.

The Pledge Case

Although the pledge of allegiance may not seem to have strong religious content, it has generated some of the most intense conflicts involving religion in the schools. The patriotic pledge of allegiance is typically recited by students at the start of each school day, although currently its recitation is becoming less common in some parts of the country. Interestingly, the words "under God" were inserted in the pledge only in 1954 (and before World War II students saluted the flag using the "Nazi salute"). The pledge has been controversial because Jehovah's Witnesses prohibit their members from reciting it because they believe it to be a worship of a "graven image." Quakers also are uncomfortable with the word "pledge." An early concession was made by the courts in that the presidential oath of office allows the president the option to "affirm" or "pledge" to uphold the duties of president.

During World War II the recitation of the pledge became mandatory at the start of every school day. Parents of Jehovah's Witness students sued to allow their children to avoid recitation of the pledge on religious grounds. The U.S. Supreme Court held in *Minersville School District v. Gobitis* that Jehovah's Witnesses could not be excused from reciting the pledge of allegiance in school. Chapter 4 details the aftermath and impact of this famous case. Chapter 4 also details the 2002 Ninth Circuit Court of Appeals decision in *Newdow v. Congress,* which held that inclusion of the words "under God" in the pledge is a violation of the First Amendment's Establishment Clause.

Antievolution Statutes

Darwin's theory of evolution remains a controversial topic. Many devout Christians believe in the literal truth of the Bible including the biblical account of the creation in the Book of Genesis. These devout individuals believe that Darwin's theory is incorrect, and they object to the teaching of evolution in the public schools.

Chapter 3 also contains a detailed analysis of the famous *Scopes v. Tennessee* (1925) "Monkey Trial" and the equally important if not as famous *Epperson v. Arkansas* (1968), two remarkably similar cases, forty-three years apart, in which teachers challenged the constitutionality of state statutes banning the teaching of evolution. The *Scopes* trial garnered international publicity but did not settle the controversy. In contrast, the Supreme Court decision in *Epperson* that such statutes were illegal nationwide had a far-reaching impact. However, the controversy over teaching evolution did not end. Chapter 4 discusses the legacy of these cases up to the present time. Readers might anticipate that the antievolution movement will generate more trials in the future.

Holiday Displays

Most U.S. towns and cities put up holiday decorations during the Christmas season. Although Christmas is essentially a religious holiday, no one can argue with the fact that in the United States, Christmas has also become a commercial season for merchants, theaters, and restaurants. The inevitable question is whether public support of such displays is an endorsement of Christianity. Some argue that any support of a religious holiday is a violation of the strict separation of church and state required by the Establishment Clause. Others argue that public support is a harmless traditional accommodation of religion. Another issue involves whether secular decorations like Santa Claus and Christmas trees should get different treatment than religiously inspired decorations like crosses or nativity scenes.

This controversy has generated numerous trials. Chapter 3 discusses a 1984 case, *Lynch v. Donnelly,* that eventually made it all the way to the U.S. Supreme Court. In this curious decision, a bitterly divided Court decided that the city's financing of a crèche on public land in Pawtucket, Rhode Island, was not an entanglement with religion as long as the crèche was accompanied by other traditional holiday decorations. The case did not settle the issue. Chapter 4 discusses another case, *County of Allegheny v. Greater Pittsburgh ACLU,* in which nearly identical issues perplexed the Supreme Court.

School Prayer

The issue of religion in the schools proved to be one of the most contentious social issues in twentieth-century America, and promises to remain one in the twenty-first-century. Public schools are places where families of very different backgrounds come together. These families often have different values, and also different religious beliefs. School plays a large role on shaping children's social values and worldview, so parents and community members are concerned about the messages children receive in the classroom. Although some parents object to any religious observance in the classroom, others feel that excluding religious activities creates an atmosphere that has contributed to the moral decline of the citizenry.

Congressional and presidential candidates have taken an interest in the topic of religion in the schools because it is an issue of prime interest to voters. The issue has had a strong polarizing effect on society, with many individuals wanting to maintain the "wall of separation" erected by the courts that has banned school prayer, Christian observations, and the teaching of "creation science" in the schools. Others believe this precedent ignores the fact that the United States is a religious society, and want to return school prayer, Christmas festivals, and the teaching of the biblical account of creation alongside the theory of evolution. Some Americans even favor a constitutional amendment guaranteeing school prayer in public schools.

Chapter 3 discusses the Supreme Court decision in *Engel v. Vitale* (1962), also known as the "Regents School Prayer Case." The U.S. Supreme Court in this case banned organized prayer in public schools. The decision caused a huge uproar among Christians, some of whom started an unsuccessful campaign to impeach Chief Justice Earl Warren. Chapter 4 discusses the legacy and impact of this case. Although the school prayer case forbade organized school prayer, the ban on school prayer was not enforced in some parts of the country. Chapter 4 discusses how the ban on prayer was later extended to prayers at school graduations. The chapter also details some of the subissues, including aid to parochial schools, release-time programs, and the school voucher issue.

Refusal of Medical Care

Christian Scientists reject conventional medical care, believing in spiritual healing instead. Jehovah's Witnesses reject blood transfusions. Other religions also reject conventional medical care in favor of faith healing. These religious beliefs run directly into conflict with medical ethics, which require doctors and hospitals to save human lives. Under common law, attempting suicide was a crime, which implies that the government has an interest in saving lives as well. This rule still applies in some states.

Chapter 3 discusses the opinion in *Application of the President and Directors of Georgetown College* (1964). This opinion was written in connection with an order granted by a U.S. Court of Appeals judge allowing a hospital to administer blood transfusions to save the life of a patient. The patient and her husband had refused to give permission for the transfusions because as Jehovah's Witnesses they believed blood transfusions violate the Scriptures. Chapter 4 discusses the legacy of the *Georgetown College* case, and presents a case in which religious parents chose to decline medical care for a child with fatal results.

Accommodation of Religious Practice

More than 100 years ago, the U.S. legal system was faced with the *Mormon Cases*. Mormons lived communally and often polygamously (married multiple wives). The Supreme Court decided in these cases that although the Free Exercise Clause of the First Amendment guarantees freedom to practice religion, there are limits to what the law will accommodate. Polygamy was not accommodated despite being central to the original Mormon tenets. The Church of Latter-Day Saints no longer condones polygamy, although the practice persists within splinter groups in Utah. (In an interesting contrast, the Catholic Church was allowed to use sacramental wine in its masses throughout the Prohibition period of the early twentieth century, during which the sale of alcoholic beverages was banned.)

An equally important issue is whether individuals are exempt from a law if that law negates religious beliefs. Chapter 3 concludes with a discussion of a very important case, *Employment Division of Oregon v. Smith* (1990), in which the U.S. Supreme Court upheld Oregon's denial of unemployment benefits to an employee who had used peyote—a controlled substance—at a Native American religious ceremony. The individuals in the case claimed that they were exempt from the state's drug laws because the use of the peyote was a religious act.

Although the case involved use of an illegal drug, church leaders of all political stripes were alarmed at the Court's change of attitude toward religious rights. Justice Scalia, writing for the majority, decided to jettison the Court's compelled accommodation test—a test used to guarantee the right of religious practice. The majority opinion held that there were very few instances when a religious individual could be exempt from general laws, even when those laws conflicted with their religious beliefs and practices. Religious leaders successfully pressed Congress in 1993 to enact the Religious Freedom Restoration Act specifically to override the *Smith* decision.

The *Smith* case did not end the controversy. In another trial, *City of Boerne v. Flores,* a case involving a local zoning issue, a federal court found the 1993 Religious Freedom Restoration Act unconstitutional. That case also made its way to the Supreme Court. The case created a "separation of powers" issue. Although the Constitution guarantees the free exercise of religion, it is also clear that there are limits to what will be permitted. Which branch of government has the "last say"—Congress or the Supreme Court? This is the ultimate issue addressed by the *City of Boerne* case.

The U.S. Legal System

Many of the cases concerning freedom of religion have been heard by federal courts as well as the U.S. Supreme Court. Because many readers might be unfamiliar with both legal terminology and procedures, the following facts about the U.S. system of government will prove helpful, especially in interpreting the cases presented in Chapters 3 and 4. Definitions for many legal terms can also be found in the Key People, Laws, and Concepts section of this book.

The U.S. legal system is characterized by a dual federal and state court system. Generally, cases dealing with state laws are heard in state courts, and matters involving federal law or the Constitution are heard in federal court. Because most court cases about religion in schools involve First Amendment freedom of religion issues, the cases are almost always tried in federal court.

The U.S. Constitution

The Constitution serves a number of functions. It establishes the basic structure of the federal government, provides for the states' self-government, and limits the actions of government in a number of ways. The enumerated powers are expressly delegated to the federal government by the states. The implied powers expand the power of the U.S. Congress to legislate where it is "necessary and proper." The reserved powers of the states include the police power to look after the general health, safety, welfare, and morale of their people.

Two constitutional doctrines are often confused: federalism and separation of powers. Federalism deals with the allocation of powers among federal, state, and local governments. The United States—like most large nations—is a federal system, which allocates power among different levels of government. This allocation naturally leads to disputes over which level of government has the final say in a matter. The issue frequently comes up in religion in the school disputes. Under the Supremacy Clause of the Constitution, when federal and state laws conflict, the state statute must give way. For example, if a state legislature passes a law permitting Bible reading in the classroom, this must give way to a federal law or court decision banning the practice. Because religion in the school issues involve basic constitutionally guaranteed rights, federal laws normally hold sway.

As opposed to federalism, the doctrine of "separation of powers" deals with the allocation of governmental power among three distinct and coequal branches: the legislative, executive, and judicial. These branches are represented at the federal level by the Congress, the president, and the federal court system, respectively, with the Supreme Court at the apex. The state governmental systems normally mirror the federal arrangement. ("Separation of powers" should not be confused with the "separation of church and state," which deals only with freedom of religion.)

The Constitution consists of two major parts and several subparts. The first part contains the Preamble and seven substantive articles. Article I establishes Congress; Article II, the presidency; and Article

III, the federal court system. The second part of the Constitution contains the constitutional amendments, including the first ten amendments, which are called the Bill of Rights. (Several states had refused to ratify the original Constitution unless it included specific protections for citizens. These were included under the first ten amendments and the entire document was ratified by the states in 1791.) Although the Constitution can still be amended, there have been only twenty-six amendments in more than 200 years, and many are quite minor. The U.S. Constitution is the oldest written constitution still in use in the world.

The First Amendment guarantees a number of important fundamental rights: free speech, freedom of the press, freedom of assembly, and free exercise of religion. The First Amendment specifically protects citizens from congressional abuse of power. Since about 1900, the courts have adopted the absorption doctrine, which provides that the Fourteenth Amendment's Due Process Clause extends most of the First Amendment's protections—including freedom of religion—to citizens of state and local governments as well as the federal government. Accordingly, the constitutional right to freedom of religion applies to local school districts because they are government funded. Private and parochial schools are not part of the government and are not required to comply with the First Amendment guarantees because the Constitution only restricts actions of the government.

Judicial Review

In the United States, the Supreme Court has the power to declare a federal or state law unconstitutional if it conflicts with the U.S. Constitution. Interestingly, the Constitution itself does not give the Court power to declare laws invalid. The Court assumed this power itself in an 1803 case, *Marbury v. Madison.* Because the Court has enjoyed this power for 200 years, it is safe to say that judicial review has become part of our governmental system. For example, in 1997 the Court declared that a law passed by Congress in 1993 called the Religious Freedom Restoration Act was unconstitutional. Although Congress had passed the law with the intent of granting churches and other religious activities broad immunity from regulation, the Supreme Court found that the law was impermissibly broad.

An examination of the Constitution reveals that many of the protections are rather vague. It is often up to the Court to determine the limits of these protections. For example, the Free Exercise Clause of the First Amendment guarantees the right to practice the religion of one's choice, but almost everyone would agree that if the religion included human sacrifice, the government would have a legitimate interest in forbidding the practice.

The Federal Judicial Branch

The remainder of this chapter is excerpted from "Understanding the Federal Courts," found at www.uscourts.gov.

> The structure of the federal court system has varied a great deal throughout the history of the nation. The Constitution merely provides that the judicial power of the United States "be vested in one Supreme Court, and in such inferior courts as Congress may from time to time ordain and establish."
>
> If the federal court system is viewed as a pyramid, at the top is the U.S. Supreme Court. On the next level are the thirteen U.S. Courts of Appeals and the Court of Military Appeals. On the following level are the ninety-four U.S. district courts and the specialized courts, such as the Tax Court, the Court of Federal Claims, the Court of Veterans Appeals, and the Court of International Trade.
>
> The powers of the U.S. courts are limited first to the powers granted to the federal government by the U.S. Constitution and second to judicial powers. The courts cannot exercise powers granted by the Constitution to the legislative branch or the executive branch of the federal government. The Constitution ensures the judicial branch's equality with and independence from the legislative and executive branches. Although federal judges are appointed by the president with the advice and consent of the U.S. Senate, and the funds for the operation of the courts are appropriated by Congress, the independence of the U.S. courts is provided for in three respects:
>
> 1. Under the Constitution, the courts can be called upon to exercise only judicial powers and to perform only judicial work. Judicial powers and judicial work involve the application and interpretation of the law in the decision of real differences; that is, in the language of the Constitution, the decision of cases and controversies. The courts cannot be called upon to make laws, which is the function of the legislative branch, or be expected to enforce and execute laws, which is the function of the executive branch.

2. Federal judges are appointed for life. In the language of the Constitution, they "hold their Offices during good Behavior"; that is, they serve as long as they so desire, and they can be removed from office against their will only through "impeachment for, and Conviction of, Treason, Bribery, or other high Crimes and Misdemeanors."

3. The Constitution provides that the compensation of federal judges "shall not be diminished during their Continuance in Office." Neither the president (the head of the executive branch) nor Congress (the legislative branch) may reduce the salary of a federal judge. These three provisions—for judicial work only, for holding office during good behavior, and for undiminished compensation—are designed to assure federal judges of independence from outside influence so that their decisions can be completely impartial and based only on the laws and facts of the cases. Courts are presided over by judicial officers.

In the Supreme Court, the judicial officers are called justices. In the courts of appeals, district courts, and other courts, most of the judicial officers are called judges. Justices and judges have the authority, duties, and benefits assigned to them by law, as enacted and amended by Congress. Judges who are at least sixty-five years old and have served as active judges for a minimum of fifteen years often elect to take senior status. As senior judges, they may continue to hear cases, deal with administrative matters, and serve on special commissions and committees. Senior judges have handled 15 percent of the federal courts' caseload.

The U.S. Supreme Court

The U.S. Supreme Court consists of nine justices appointed for life by the president with the advice and consent of the Senate. One justice is appointed as the chief justice and has additional administrative duties related both to the Supreme Court and to the entire federal court system. Each justice is assigned to one of the courts of appeals for emergency responses. The Supreme Court begins meeting on the first Monday of October each year and usually continues in session through June. The Supreme Court receives and disposes of about 5,000 cases each year, most by a brief decision that the subject matter is either not proper or not of sufficient importance to warrant review by the full court. Cases are heard en banc, which means by all the justices sitting together in open court. Each year the court decides about 150 cases of great national importance and interest, and about three-fourths of such decisions are announced in full published opinions. The Supreme Court is located across the street from the U.S. Capitol Building in Washington, D.C. The nine current justices of the Supreme Court are Chief Justice William H. Rehnquist, Associate Justice Stephen Breyer, Associate Justice Ruth Bader Ginsburg, Associate Justice Anthony Kennedy, Associate Justice Sandra Day O'Connor, Associate Justice Antonin Scalia, Associate Justice David H. Souter, Associate Justice John Paul Stevens, and Associate Justice Clarence Thomas.

Lawsuits

There are various routes a case may take to a federal court. Some cases may originate in a U.S. district court, while others will come from a state court or federal agency. A person involved in a suit in a U.S. court may proceed through three levels of decision. Generally, the case will be heard and decided by one of the district courts on the first level. If a party is dissatisfied with the decision rendered, the party may have the decision reviewed in one of the courts of appeals.

In the U.S. legal system, the party bringing a lawsuit is the "plaintiff," and the party sued is known as the "defendant." There may be multiple plaintiffs and/or defendants. Defendants may also make claims against plaintiffs (counterclaims) and defendants may make claims against one another (cross-claims).

Generally the defendant has the option of having the case heard by a judge or jury. When there is both a jury and a judge, the jury is called upon to decide the facts and the judge must then apply the law to those facts. The judge must also instruct the jury regarding the law it is to use in arriving at its verdict. When there is only a judge, the judge fills both roles. After the trial, other judges who act as an appellate court provide a check on the decisions of the trial court judge by reviewing the judgment.

In the United States, a court cannot change a law on its own initiative. The court can only act when a dispute is brought before it. For example, many religion in the schools issues reach courts after a student or a student's parents complain to a federal court about a certain practice in the public schools. Most cases start in U.S. district court, the federal court system's general jurisdiction trial court. These cases may then be taken to a federal court of appeals.

The court of appeals reviews the rulings of the district court if one or both of the parties involved in the lawsuit think a decision was incorrectly made. The court of appeals may reverse the decision if the judge made an error in applying the law, but cannot reverse because the jury or judge made a mistake about the facts, unless the finding is not supported by any evidence. The appeals court can affirm, in whole or part, or reverse in whole or part. An appeals court will "remand" the case back to the district court if additional fact-finding is needed to resolve issues.

If dissatisfied with the decision of a court of appeals, the party may seek additional review in the Supreme Court of the United States; however, the Supreme Court primarily reviews only cases that involve a matter of great national importance and only accepts a small number of cases each term. This pyramid-like organization of the courts serves two purposes. First, the courts of appeals can correct errors that have been made in the decisions of trial courts. Second, the Supreme Court can ensure the uniformity of decisions by reviewing cases in which constitutional issues have been decided or in which two or more lower courts have reached different results.

2
Historical Background

Although Americans have had conflicts over religious practice almost from the start of European colonization, the issues have changed over time. Issues surrounding freedom of religion have spawned litigation that became major Supreme Court cases. Knowledge about the historical background of religion in public life is of prime importance in understanding the historical and social context of the trials discussed in this book.

The first section of this chapter concentrates on the history of Christianity. Although religious practice in the United States is increasingly pluralistic, from the start Protestants have been in the majority. Consider the fact that all but one of the U.S. presidents have been white, male, and Protestant. Legal questions about freedom of religion often involve two basic underlying issues: firstly, whether government action is endorsing the majority's Protestantism and, secondly, whether government action is limiting a minority's freedom to practice its faith. A basic knowledge of the history of Christianity will help put both of these issues in perspective.

The Christian Church in Europe

After the Christians were expelled from Jerusalem, they brought their faith to Greece and Rome as well as to other areas in the Middle East in the first century A.D. Christianity, with its emphasis on an eternal afterlife, was embraced by the poor, but it also held an appeal for the better off. The Romans generally tolerated a variety of religions, but Christians were harshly persecuted by the Roman authorities, especially in the third century A.D., as the empire declined. Christians were persecuted by the Romans less for their religious practices than for the political implications of their faith. Because Christians met in secret, they were sometimes assumed to be subversive. Christian doctrine was also thought to be politically subversive. In Rome the emperor was considered to be a god, *Divus Caesar, semper Augustus,* worthy of worship. Christians' refusal to worship the emperor was considered seditious.

Christians followed Jesus' lesson to render unto Caesar the things that were Caesar's and to God the things that were God's. Although this concept is familiar to the modern mind, it ran against established thinking at the time. This "dualism" was later refined by St. Augustine in his book *City of God.* Augustine wrote that there were really two cities—the temporal, earthly city of the state and the heavenly City of God. Augustine argued that spiritual and political authority were distinct. Augustine's duality—the separation of spiritual and political power—remains an underlying tenet in church-state relations to this day.

The persecution of Christians ended, for the most part, under the Emperor Constantine in the early fourth century. In about the year 312 A.D. the coemperors Constantine and Licinius issued the Edict of Milan, which allowed Romans freedom to choose their own religion or religions. Although there were other important centers to the east, Rome, the center of the Roman Empire, also became the center of Christendom. During this period, church and state were closely aligned. The Roman Catholic Church structure reflects to this day the structure of the late Roman Empire. Constantine, who was sympathetic to Christianity and is reputed to have converted on his deathbed, was actively involved in church affairs. He summoned a council of bishops to Nicea to resolve doctrinal issues.

Christianity flourished under Constantine in the early fourth century, and by the fifth century Christianity became the official religion of the Empire, and the older Roman temples were closed. However, the Christian Church also adopted elements of the old religion in its liturgy during this period as Christianity became increasingly "Romanized." By the end of the fourth century most of Western Europe was officially Christian. However, the patronage of the state was a mixed blessing for the church. Rather than a united faith, the "church" was in reality composed of a number of groups at odds over doctrine. During this time the Roman Empire itself divided. Constantine had founded a new imperial capital, Constantinople, on the Bosporus. After Constantine, the empire was normally administered as two separate entities—the Western half administered from Rome and the Eastern Empire administered from Constantinople.

The spread of Christianity was interrupted however. A Germanic tribe, the West Goths, led by Alaric, sacked Rome itself in 410 A.D. By 476 the last Roman Emperor in the West was deposed, although the Emperor of the East remained in Constantinople. The Christian Church too had split, with the Bishop of Rome recognized as the unofficial head of Christendom in Europe while the patriarchs presided over the church in Constantinople. In the East, the church fell more and more under the sway of the emperors. With the decline of the empire in the West, the Bishop of Rome (the Pope) consolidated power over the church in the West and was largely independent of the emperors—setting the pattern for church-state affairs in Europe. Augustine's separation of church and state became a reality. This tradition is important in understanding our modern conception of church-state relations.

With the destruction of the Roman Empire after 500 A.D., Western Europe entered what is popularly termed "the Dark Ages." Even before the fall of Rome the Germanic tribes had been largely converted to Christianity. This process accelerated after 500, and by roughly 700 A.D. Christianity again extended to the limits of what was the former Roman Empire. In 711, the Arabs conquered Spain, but their army was defeated at Tours in southern France, so Islam spread no farther than Spain.

During this period, church and state did not completely diverge. In 800 A.D. Charlemagne was crowned in Rome by the Pope as the Emperor of the West. However, a second wave of "pagan" invaders put an end to Charlemagne's Holy Roman Empire. Eventually, these invaders, too, followed the patterns of the earlier aggressors and were Christianized.

Between 700 and 1000 A.D. the Roman church and the church in Constantinople continued to drift apart. The patriarchs in Constantinople refused to acknowledge the supremacy of the Bishop of Rome. In 1054 this division became formalized in the "Great Schism," which split the church into the Roman Catholic (or Latin) Church and the Greek Orthodox Church. By roughly the year 1000

A.D. Christianity was firmly established as the official religion throughout Europe with the Pope as the head of the church.

The period between 1000 A.D. and the start of the Protestant Reformation in roughly 1500, was an eventful one for both Europe and the Christian Church. During this period Europe experienced the Crusades, the Black Death, the invention of the printing press, and the Renaissance. It was also an eventful time for the church. From 1378–1417 the "Schism of the West" resulted in two sitting Popes—one in Rome and one in France. Although space does not permit even a summary of this period, it was an era in which the nation states of Europe emerged, although Germany and Italy did not take their modern form until much later. It was also a period in which the increasing power of the church often came into conflict with the power of kings and other rulers.

The Reformation

The supremacy of the Roman Catholic Church was shattered in the 1500s by the Protestant Reformation. Martin Luther, John Calvin, and others led a movement that protested not only doctrinal issues but also the very authority of the Pope in Rome. Luther argued that man could be saved by faith alone—rather than by good deeds on earth. He also rejected the need for the sacraments. Essentially, the Protestants argued that the faithful enjoyed a direct and personal relationship with God and accordingly did not need the clergy, the bishops, or even the Pope. Branded as heretics by the church, the reformers started their own faiths. What followed was nearly one hundred years, in which the politics of Europe were largely animated by the struggle between the Catholics and Protestants, including several wars fought over religion. Many if not most of these conflicts had political as well as religious causes. Catholics and Protestants, all followers of Christ, had little toleration for one another. In Spain, Protestants were not tolerated at all, and in some parts of Germany, Catholics were given the choice of conversion or expulsion. Although the details of these events are too involved to include here, by the year 1650, the northern half of Europe had become Protestant while the south remained loyal to the Roman church.

Today people in most countries enjoy the right to practice whatever faith they choose, but that was not always the case. In seventeenth-century Europe, every nation had an established church. The

senters with mixed results. James was succeeded by his son Charles I in 1625.

Like his father, Charles wanted not only to rule England largely without the English Parliament, but he also wished to impose the Anglican religion on both England and Scotland. He ran into opposition from the Parliament on both counts. A number of the members of Parliament were Puritans—Calvinists who believed that the Church of England shared many of the vices of the Roman Catholic Church. A crisis ensued when Charles attempted to force the Scots to convert to the Church of England. The Scots rioted, and the king, who had ruled without Parliament for eleven years, convened the Parliament to raise taxes to pay for an army to put down the Scots. When the Parliament proved hostile, Charles called for new elections, and the very same members were reelected. Although they had been summoned to help Charles put down the Scottish rebellion, those in Parliament had their own agenda. Radicals in Parliament took the opportunity to state their own demands, including the execution of Charles's advisers and the abolition of bishops in the Church of England. Both of these were, of course, unacceptable to the king. This set the stage for what is termed the Puritan Revolution.

The conflict between the king and Parliament escalated into an armed conflict, and Puritans—known as the "Roundheads" for their distinctive haircuts—defeated the royalists. Oliver Cromwell, who had organized the Puritan army, the "Ironsides," promptly purged Parliament of those who disagreed with him, and this "rump" Parliament sentenced Charles to be hanged. After the king's death, Parliament established a commonwealth with Cromwell at its head. Cromwell was finally forced to disband even his "rump" Parliament and attempted to govern as Lord Protector—essentially military rule. Although the Puritans were extreme in their religious views, they did allow a measure of toleration except for Unitarians and "High Anglicans." Roman Catholics were persecuted, especially in Ireland where thousands were killed.

Two years after Cromwell's death his son was unable to maintain the Protectorate and the Puritan Revolution was over. King Charles II, the son of Charles I, took the throne. The Church of England again became England's established church. Puritans, also know as "dissenters," did not fare well. The Puritans found it harder and harder to practice their faith. When Charles's younger brother, James, converted to Catholicism, Parliament reacted by passing the

Test Act, requiring all officeholders to be members of the Church of England.

James II, brother of Charles II, became king on Charles's death in 1685. He ruled as if there were no Test Act and allowed both Puritans and Catholics to hold office. However, when he baptized his first son a Catholic, Parliament decided to depose him rather than risk a permanent Catholic monarchy. They were fearful that James would make the Roman Catholic Church the established church in England. Members of Parliament put aside their differences and invited James's grown daughter, Mary, wife of the Dutch William of Orange, to be queen. In 1699 James II left England, and Queen Mary, a Protestant, took the throne. Parliament also passed the Toleration Act, which allowed all dissenters to practice their faith, although it still excluded them from holding public office. Although Catholics were not mentioned, they too were allowed to practice their religion; however, Catholics, Jews, and Unitarians were legally barred from holding public office in England until the Test Act was repealed in 1826.

The England that the American colonists abandoned had an established church supported by the government, and English citizens enjoyed only a tenuous right to the free exercise of religion. Dissenters knew all too well that having an established church was unfair to those of other faiths. They also knew that the right to freely practice religion is an important right. These concepts would later be engrafted in the U.S. Constitution.

The Colonial Experience

Although all thirteen colonies were English, they were religiously diverse. Plymouth Colony was established by the Pilgrims, a group of dissenters who wished to practice their faith. The Massachusetts Bay Colony in Boston was founded by the Puritans, a separate group of dissenters. Repression of the dissenters in England propelled the establishment of the American colonies. Between 1630 and 1640, during the English Civil War, more than 20,000 Puritans settled in the Massachusetts Bay Colony. By 1700 there were approximately half a million Englishmen in what had become the thirteen colonies. As the number of colonists grew, so did the diversity of religious practice.

To understand the religious environment during the colonial period, it is useful to remember that the English colonization of America started at the end of the Protestant Reformation. Jamestown, Virginia, the first permanent English colony in North America, was founded in 1607, less than ninety years after Martin Luther first nailed his ninety-five theses to the door of the castle church at Wittenberg. Farther north, the Pilgrims landed at Plymouth Rock in Massachusetts in 1620, which was thirty years before Oliver Cromwell established the Puritan Commonwealth in England. Numbers of these early settlers had actively participated in the Protestant Reformation and the Puritan Revolution in England. Many of the colonists emigrated at least in part to practice their faiths without government interference.

It is also helpful to remember that most of the colonists viewed themselves as English—not Americans. No doubt, many colonists viewed their stay in America as a temporary one. They would perfect their faith in the New World and would then transplant it back to England. In large part, these settlements should be viewed as an extension of the Reformation, and for some an experiment to create a theocracy on earth. As John Winthrop of the Bay Colony wrote, " . . . we shall be a City upon a Hill, the eyes of all people are upon us." Although on the one hand colonists were starting new societies in a new world, they also couldn't escape their identities and perspectives. Colonists from England brought with them not only their religion but also their social norms, and they typically tried to replicate English society in North America. Although there were established churches in most colonies, there was also diversity of religious practice almost from the start.

Plymouth Colony was founded by the Pilgrims in 1620 by separatists who practiced Congregationalism, which replaces church hierarchies by putting each local church congregation in control of its own affairs. In England, these dissenting sects were barely tolerated, and so the Pilgrims left, settling first in Holland, not only to avoid persecution but also to set themselves up as a religious enclave that would serve as an example to their brethren back in England. Plymouth, in contrast to its neighbor, the Massachusetts Bay Colony, was known for its religious toleration.

Founded by Puritans in the 1630s, the Massachusetts Bay Colony was a religious enterprise from the start. Church and state were closely aligned in enforcing strict religious conformity. The Massachusetts Puritans believed they were servants of God—Winthrop's "City on a Hill." This left no room for those who practiced other faiths. The Puritans allowed no toleration for those of other faiths. Those who practiced other faiths faced fines, imprisonment, and expulsion from the colony. The Quakers, more formally known as members of the Society of Friends, were evangelistic, and they were subjected to especially harsh treatment. Quakers' ears were cut and their tongues burned. Four Quakers were hanged to death for returning after being expelled from the colony, including Mary Dryer. Her statute can be found outside the Massachusetts State House in Boston.

Eventually, Massachusetts recognized the Congregational Church as the colony's established church. The rest of New England followed the Massachusetts model, except for Rhode Island. Roger Williams, who was exiled from the Massachusetts Bay Colony for his tolerance of other religions, founded Rhode Island, which offered religious freedom to all. In fact, church and state were considered separate in Rhode Island from its beginning. Williams was perhaps the first person to use the phrase *wall of separation* when talking about the relationship between the government and religion.

The Dutch had founded New Amsterdam, where they established Calvinist Dutch Reformed Churches that exist to this day. The colony was a mercantile center, and the Dutch followed the model from Holland and tolerated a number of faiths. After the English conquered the colony, they changed the name to New York, but the original diversity of religious practice prevailed. Under the Dutch, the Dutch Reformed Church received financial support from the government. When the English took over the colony, the Dutch Reformed Church lost its special status. All towns were required to support a church and minister but were free to select the denomination of their choice.

Pennsylvania, founded by William Penn as a "holy experiment," became home not only to the Quakers but also to a number of minor Christian sects including the Mennonites, Brethren, Amish, and Moravians. Because of its religious toleration, Pennsylvania may have been the most religiously diverse colony.

Maryland, founded by George Calvert, the first Lord Baltimore, was a haven for Roman Catholics who were persecuted in England. The Act of Toleration was passed by the Maryland Assembly in 1649, guaranteeing all Christians the right to worship.

In Virginia, the Church of England was the established church from the start. Colonists were not allowed to practice other religions within the colony. However, dissenters soon arrived and challenged the monopoly of the Church of England. Dissenters (also called Nonconformists), including Baptists, Methodists, and Presbyterians, all argued that England's Act of Toleration (1689) allowing religious tolerance should apply to the colonies as well. It granted "free exercise" of religion—at least to Christians. It is not surprising that Virginia would be the colony where our modern view of separation of church was debated and established.

In the Carolinas, founded in 1665, there was a mix of faiths, with Church of England adherents and French Huguenots along the coast and Baptists and Presbyterians inland. In Georgia there was even a greater mix of faiths, including Catholics.

The established Church of England did not fare well in the colonies during the Revolution. Even before the outbreak of war, there was spirited debate about a proposal to bring bishops to America. The colonists observed that bishops would need to be supported, which meant new taxes. If Parliament could require a tax to support a Church of England bishop, then it might also impose the Church of England as the established church in each of the colonies.

The year 1720 marked the start of a twenty-year period of religious fervor called the Great Awakening. The movement resulted in a fragmentation of several mainstream religious denominations. Colonial Christianity was now a diverse mixture of many smaller denominations. However, the "established" church in most colonies was still supported by tax revenues, whereas the other churches generally received no funds. There was no state-run system of public education although most towns had schools that were often affiliated with the church. Early school curriculums included both moral and religious instruction including prayer and Bible reading.

Although many colonists led lives that were dominated by their religious beliefs, it would be incorrect to assume that all colonists were so devout. In fact, there is some evidence that most colonists were not even associated with organized religion. Records suggest that less than 10 percent of colonists were members of organized congregations. In some cases, this condition was due to distance—those living on the frontier were far from any church or minister. However, it also suggests that colonial America was more secular than is popularly believed.

Whatever the participation in organized congregations, it is unquestionable that religion and religious values animated not only the colonization of America but also many of the basic values embedded in both the Declaration of Independence and the Constitution. The year 1776 saw not only the signing of the Declaration of Independence, signed only a few months after the start of Revolutionary War with England at Lexington and Concord, but also the publication of Thomas Paine's *Common Sense.* This pamphlet influenced both political thinkers and the general public in the new United States. Hundreds of thousands of copies were sold in a country of just half a million citizens. Paine argued for freedom from oppression in both politics and religion. Paine's ideas, including a strong plea for the free exercise of religion, were later incorporated in the Bill of Rights. Although Paine argued that government should protect individuals' right to practice religion, he also felt that there should be no established church and that the government should avoid active participation in religious subjects.

Although few outside observers would have predicted that the rebellious American colonists could resist the British crown, the Americans, with the help of their French allies, prevailed. The former colonies became an independent federation of states—the United States. Under the original government, the Articles of Confederation, the states operated more like separate countries than one nation. Accordingly, between the peace with Britain and the ratification of the U.S. Constitution in 1791, legal affairs, including dealing with religious issues, were left to the individual states.

Many of the nation's leaders during this period were Virginians, and not surprisingly, Virginians were also the first to consider how independence would affect church-state relations. Recall that Virginia had been a stronghold of the Church of England before the war. No doubt, many in Virginia favored maintaining it as its established church.

Thomas Jefferson felt otherwise. Jefferson penned the Virginia Bill for Establishing Religious Freedom, which prohibited penalties imposed on account of religious beliefs or practices and outlawed mandatory attendance or financial support of any religious activity. However, the bill was not immediately passed by the Virginia legislature. There was substantial resistance to the proposal, especially the idea of withholding funds from an established church. Patrick Henry, another well-known revolutionary leader, firmly believed that it was appropriate for the state of Virginia to use tax money to support teachers of the Christian faith. Henry represented the traditional view that the majority had the right to use tax money to support an established church. Jefferson and James Madison, in contrast, felt that supporting an established church not only favored one church over another but also threatened the freedom of religious minorities.

In the following year, 1785, James Madison published his *Memorial and Remonstrance against Religious Assessments.* Madison attacked a bill that would allow Virginia to financially support all churches. Madison pointed out that although the bill proposed to use tax dollars to support all religions, it also had the potential to allow the state to favor one religion over another. Madison argued forcefully against any "establishment"—in other words, an "established church." This idea was later to find its way into the First Amendment. Madison was especially fearful that those of the majority religion would infringe on the rights of those who were members of minority faiths. The Virginia proposal was defeated, and the next year Virginia passed Jefferson's Virginia Bill for Establishing Religious Freedom.

The Constitution

Although the War of Independence had won independence from Britain, it did not result in a functional United States. The Articles of Confederation, drafted during the war, provided a loose confederation of the states rather than a viable nation. Sharing a continent with three major powers—Britain, Spain, and France, many Americans came to the realization that a more powerful central government was not only desirable but essential. In 1787 delegates from the thirteen states met in a Constitutional Convention in Philadelphia to fashion a new document. Among the fifty-five framers were Washington, Jefferson, Madison, and the elder statesman Benjamin Franklin. The document is notable not only for what it includes but also for what it excludes. Unlike all state constitutions, there is no reference to God or a supreme being. The U.S. Constitution does not provide for an established church or even the furtherance of Christianity.

The U.S. Constitution is also noteworthy because it only applies to government actions and not to the actions of citizens. As originally penned, the Constitution did not contain the familiar amendments. For example, there was no First Amendment guaranteeing freedom of religion. Madison, who drafted the original document, argued that since the Constitution did not specifically give the government any power over religion, there could be no abuse. However, when several states seemed unlikely to ratify the document without a Bill of Rights, the convention promptly drafted one.

When Virginia ratified the Bill of Rights in 1791, the U.S. Constitution had been ratified by a majority of the original thirteen states. The final document included the Bill of Rights consisting of ten amendments guaranteeing rights to citizens and states.

Indeed, the First Amendment includes guarantees that "Congress shall make no law respecting an establishment of religion, or prohibiting the free exercise thereof; or abridging the freedom of speech, or of the press; or the right of the people peacefully to assemble, and to petition the Government for a redress of grievances." The first two clauses are called the Establishment Clause and the Free Exercise Clause, respectively. The only other reference to religion in the document is found in Article VI, Clause 3, which prohibits religious tests for public office. This ensures that the government cannot require an individual to be a member of a particular religion—or any religion at all—as a condition of service.

It is important to know that the original Constitution with its attached Bill of Rights was only meant to apply to the actions of the federal government. Although some members of the Constitutional Convention favored including limits on state powers, that was not the approach taken. Accordingly, the First Amendment's religion clauses—protecting the free exercise of religion and prohibiting the establishment of a religion—only applied to the federal government. Accordingly, states had wide latitude in fashioning laws regarding religion. Although established churches died away in the early 1800s, other laws based on religious practice did not. Several states had laws prohibiting Jews, Catholics, and Unitarians from holding public office. Some of these laws were not repealed until later in the century. Similarly, states enacted "blue laws" limiting commercial activity on the Christian Sabbath.

Although the Constitution has a strong separation of church and state flavor, some commentators have suggested that the drafters were merely ensuring that the states, rather than the federal government, would have the power to make laws regarding the establishment and exercise of religion. In fact, at the time, a few states continued to have state-supported established churches. Massachusetts maintained a state-supported church until 1833. Some states also had laws that discriminated against members of religious minorities. For example, several states withheld full legal rights from Jews and Roman Catholics. The courts did not apply the First Amendment to the activities of state and local governments until well into the twentieth century. Although the religion clauses in the Constitution are only sixteen words long, they continue to guide the country in resolving freedom of religion issues.

The Nineteenth Century

Religion in the United States became increasingly diverse during the 1800s. Although the Anglican Church (formerly the Church of England) had predominated in many states, it was soon outdistanced by other Protestant denominations, especially the Baptists. Ever since the Great Awakening before the Revolution, Protestantism had split between the evangelical wing and the more traditional wing.

Although there was a separation of church and state during this time, the period also witnessed the development of a "civic religion." Because the majority of Americans were Protestants, this civic religion took its tenor from the mainstream Protestant churches. Many of the "public" religious traditions started in this era. Although many states had "blue laws" banning commercial activity on Sundays, in 1810 the federal government decided to initiate seven-days-a-week mail service. Because this conflicted with the views of many and the laws of some states, it was decided to have no mail delivery on the Christian Sabbath. Likewise, there is no mail delivery on Christmas Day. Coins and currency came to bear the motto "In God We Trust." The president is sworn into office by a minister using a Bible. Presidents, from the early days to the present, have invoked the help of God in securing the safety and prosperity of the nation.

The Protestant majority was weakened with the wave of immigration from Ireland and Germany, and many eastern U.S. cities had a sizable population of Roman Catholics who were often viewed with suspicion by their Protestant neighbors. Following the European example, the Catholic Church established its own school systems and colleges in larger cities to help educate these immigrants and also to combine religious and moral instruction in the curriculum. Instruction in the public schools at the time included both prayer and Bible reading. However, Catholics and other minorities recognized that the instruction had a strong Protestant influence. Catholic schools in Europe received government financial support. Although Catholic bishops in the United States lobbied to get government financial support for their parochial schools, they were unsuccessful. In fact, the Blaine Amendment, proposed in 1876 but never ratified, would have outlawed spending any state or federal monies to support religious schools.

There was a backlash against both immigrants and the Roman Catholic Church, both of which were viewed by many "nativist" Americans as pernicious foreign influences. The aptly named "Know Nothing" movement sought to exclude foreign-born persons from elected office and to require a twenty-five-year waiting period for citizenship. Its political party had nationwide support and by 1854 controlled state government in both Delaware and Massachusetts.

Friction between Protestants and Catholics over public education remained a problem for the next one hundred years. The presidential candidacy of John F. Kennedy in 1959–1960 was controversial because he was a Roman Catholic. Kennedy had to make a special statement espousing his views on the separation of church and state. In the year 2000 the election of a new chaplain for the House of Representatives revealed that an anti-Catholic bias is alive and well. Although a committee had selected a Roman Catholic as best-qualified for the post, several congressional leaders evidently thought a Catholic would not be good choice for the job and blocked his appointment.

Post–Civil War Amendments to the U.S. Constitution

The Fourteenth Amendment, enacted in 1868 to protect legal rights of ex-slaves and other African Americans, also extended the reach of First Amendment rights of due process of law and equal protection before the law to the states. In the 1940s, court decisions held that the Fourteenth Amendment also extended other First Amendment protections, including the Establishment Clause and the Free Exercise Clause to the states. Accordingly, neither the federal government nor state governments could make a law respecting an establishment of religion or prohibiting the free exercise thereof. These rulings ultimately had the result of banning most religious activity in the public schools.

Although the nineteenth century was a relatively quiet period for separation of church and state issues, there was one notable exception: the notorious Mormon cases. Joseph Smith had started his

Church of Jesus Christ of Latter-Day Saints in upstate New York af-
ter experiencing a religious revelation. Although the Mormon
Church was Christian it added The Book of Mormon to the Old and
New Testaments. Like the early Christians, the Mormons lived com-
munally sharing their property. Most controversial of all, the early
Mormon Church accepted polygamy (simultaneous marriage to mul-
tiple wives). The Mormons were persecuted as they moved from
Ohio to Missouri to Illinois. Smith was murdered in 1844. Led by
Brigham Young, the sect moved to the Great Salt Lake Basin.

Shortly thereafter in 1850, Congress established the Utah Territory and in 1862 passed a law aimed at the Mormons banning
polygamy in all federal territories. Congress followed up by disen-
franchising polygamists and making it illegal for them to hold public
office. Congress eventually moved to confiscate the Mormon
Church's property including the temple in Salt Lake City.

The Supreme Court in the (1879) case *Reynolds v. United States*
adopted the view that although the Free Exercise Clause of the Constitution protects individuals' religious beliefs, the Constitution does
not stop government interference with religiously motivated actions.
As the cases described hereafter illustrate, the issue of how far the
government can go in regulating religious practice is still very much
at issue.

In 1892, as the century closed, the Supreme Court heard the case
Church of the Holy Trinity v. United States, which concerned
whether a special exemption from immigration laws for the clergy vi-
olated the Constitution by showing favoritism toward the clergy
over other citizens. In its opinion, the Court acknowledged that
"This is a Christian nation." This statement illustrated how far the
Court—and perhaps popular opinion—had drifted away from the
Founding Fathers' conception of separation of church and state.
Even today, proponents of prayer in public schools sometimes cite
this case for support.

Although it is clear that the Founding Fathers did not desire the
government to be a "godless" zone, their experience taught them that
true religious freedom depended on true separation of church and
state. They understood that mixing government and religion had
been a failure and that separation would result in more, not less, religious liberty. As President John F. Kennedy said to the Greater
Houston Ministerial Association during his presidential campaign in
1960: "I believe in an America that is officially neither Catholic,

Protestant nor Jewish . . . where no religious body seeks to impose its will . . . where religious liberty is so indivisible that an act against one church is treated as an act against all."

By the end of the twentieth century both the Supreme Court and the country would be much closer to Kennedy's vision— an America that is not officially a Christian country, but one that accommodates religious practice by all faiths and a country in which all faiths can band together realizing that government action against one faith is a threat to all religions.

The Twentieth Century

Although there were few trials concerning religion and religious freedom in the nineteenth century, there was an explosion of litigation in the twentieth. This is an area where court decisions have shaped the law for millions of Americans on a daily basis. The following material is divided into four sections. The first section addresses issues involving the government's attempts to restrict or regulate the practice of religion. The second section examines the contentious issue of religion in the public schools. The third section deals with public aid to religious and private schools. The chapter concludes by examining some other trials involving religion as well as addressing some issues that may be litigated in the coming years.

Regulating Religious Practice

As the *Reynolds* case involving the Mormon practice of polygamy illustrates, trials challenging government regulation of religion often involve religious practice of minority faiths. In some cases the minority faith practice is offensive to the majority as was the case when the Court ruled that polygamy was unlawful despite the Mormon's sincere religious belief in its legitimacy. In other cases the issue is whether the religious practice breaks an existing law. For example, some Native Americans have used peyote in their sacraments for hundreds of years. However, peyote is a controlled substance, an illegal drug, and its use for any purpose may break the law in some states. The *Smith* case, described later, concerns whether such religiously inspired use of an illegal drug is lawful.

In other cases a person's religious beliefs may conflict with their duties as citizens. For example, the Amish and members of some other faiths are pacifists and their religion prohibits them from engaging in military combat. Their beliefs are normally accommodated by allowing them to serve in noncombat roles or avoiding military service altogether. The Jehovah's Witnesses believe that it is sacrilegious to recite the pledge to the American flag or any flag for that matter. This belief caused a national uproar in the years just before the attack on Pearl Harbor and the start of World War II. In those years children in public schools nationwide were required to recite the pledge to the flag every morning. Although Jehovah's Witness parents asked that the pledge be ended, the school districts refused. The issue at trial was whether the government could sponsor a patriotic exercise that offended certain devout students and whether the schools could force those students to either participate or be forced to listen to it even if they themselves remained silent.

The case, *Minersville School District v. Gobitis,* which is discussed in more detail in Chapter 3, reached the U.S. Supreme Court in 1940. U.S. Supreme Court Justice Felix Frankfurter wrote the opinion in *Gobitis* in which Jehovah's Witnesses asked to be excused from saying the pledge of allegiance. Frankfurter, writing for the Court, held that despite the fact that their religious precepts prohibited reciting the pledge, the government could force schoolchildren to recite the pledge of allegiance to create national unity. The case caused a mass expulsion of Witness children from school and even precipitated mob violence against Witness churches, some of which were burned. Some people viewed the Witnesses' refusals to recite the pledge as a treasonous act rather than as a sincere expression of religious belief. Witnesses were already unpopular. Mainline Christians had long mocked their beliefs and found the Witnesses' door-to-door proselytizing efforts annoying. Some of those in the majority viewed the Court's opinion as vindication of their hatred, and the unfortunate result was real oppression of this minority religious group.

This bigotry wasn't the only problem for the Witnesses. In *Cantwell v. Connecticut* (1940) the Supreme Court heard a case involving two Jehovah's Witnesses who sought to pass out religious literature in downtown New Haven, Connecticut. The city, like many others, passed a law requiring those who wished to pass out religious literature to get a license. The law's purpose was to discourage and regulate Witnesses and other groups. The Cantwells nearly incited a riot. They carried a portable, spring-loaded phonograph on which they played a record called "Enemies," a diatribe against other religions and especially the Roman Catholic Church.

The Cantwells had not applied for a license because they presumed they would be turned down on the grounds that they were not members of an established religion. In *dicta* the Court noted that freedom of religion includes the freedom to believe and the freedom to act. Although the first was an absolute right, the second was not. The *Cantwell* case was important because the Supreme Court held for the first time that the Free Exercise Clause was incorporated into the Fourteenth Amendment and accordingly applied to state and local as well as federal laws. This finding also meant that the First Amendment applied to the actions of local school districts as well. This decision generated a torrent of litigation, which will be discussed in the next section of this chapter.

The ruling against the Witnesses in *Gobitis* did not last long. In *West Virginia State Board of Education v. Barnette* (1943), heard just three years later, the Supreme Court invalidated a West Virginia law requiring mandatory recitals of the pledge of allegiance and flag salutes in public school rooms. In *Gobitis,* an almost identical case, the Court had upheld just such a statute. There were three new members on the Court, and two justices had changed their minds about the issue.

In 1954 Congress added the words *under God* to the pledge. This happened during the Cold War period in which tensions with the Soviet Union were at their height. The reference was added to distinguish the religious United States from the "godless" and officially atheistic USSR. In 2002 the U.S. Ninth Circuit Court of Appeals ruled in *Newdow v. Congress* that the words *under God* were a violation of the Establishment Clause when the pledge is recited in public school. The Jehovah's Witnesses pledge cases and the *Newdow* case are detailed in Chapters 3 and 4, respectively.

During the twentieth century the courts have also had to determine how to accommodate the Sabbath in an increasingly pluralistic country. In the early nineteenth century most states had "blue laws" prohibiting commercial activity on Sundays. These laws were religiously inspired. Although Sunday is the traditional Christian Sabbath, Saturday is the Sabbath for those of other faiths, including Seventh-Day Adventists and Jews. Members of these faiths have complained that state laws requiring them to close their businesses on Sunday is a violation of the Establishment Clause, the Free Exercise Clause, or both. The plaintiffs did not succeeded in challenging the status quo.

In 1961 the U.S. Supreme Court heard four separate cases involving state blue laws. In *McGowan v. Maryland* the Court upheld Maryland's blue law mandating the closing of businesses on Sundays. Eight justices found no problem in Maryland's declaring the Christian Sabbath as a day of rest for all citizens. Although Sunday-closing laws had a religious origin, the Court reasoned that Sunday closing had long since become secular.

Justice William O. Douglas, in dissent, found the Maryland law a violation of both the Establishment Clause and the Free Exercise Clause of the First Amendment. Dissenting in another case, *Braunfeld v. Brown,* challenging New York's law, Douglas wrote that Sunday-closing laws violated both the Establishment Clause and the Free Exercise because the laws imposed a criminal penalty "on those who, unlike the Christian majority . . . worship on a different day or do not share the religious scruples of the majority."

Sabbath observances can also cause problems for employees who want to refrain from working on that day. In *Sherbert v. Verner* (1963) the Supreme Court recognized that the Free Exercise Clause of the Constitution protects both religious actions as well as religiously motivated actions from government discrimination. The Court held the government could not deny unemployment benefits to a Seventh-Day Adventist who refused to work on Saturdays. The employee refused to work on Saturdays, which prevented her from finding work. Although the case involved only one employee and a few thousand dollars of unemployment benefits, the case was significant because it also established that the Free Exercise Clause sometimes required an exemption from general laws when the law places a substantial burden on religious practice. In other words, although most out-of-work people would be denied unemployment benefits if they refused for whatever reason to work on Saturday, Mrs. Sherbert was given an exemption from this law because her reason for not wanting to work was religiously motivated.

Under the Equal Employment Opportunity Act, an employer may not discriminate against employees or potential employees on the basis of religion. Employers must try to accommodate an employee's religious Sabbath. However, an employer may also terminate an employee who refuses to work on a particular day if the employer is not able to make reasonable accommodation.

After *Sherbert* the courts reasoned that the Free Exercise Clause requires that religious practices be accommodated and that exemptions be granted when a law imposes a substantial burden. However, it is not always clear when or how much accommodation is appropriate. The Supreme Court case that went the farthest in protecting a sect's practices despite a general law was *Wisconsin v. Yoder* (1972). In *Yoder* the Supreme Court held it unconstitutional to require compulsory education for Old Order Amish children whose parents object on religious grounds.

In *Yoder* the Court upheld the right of Amish parents to withhold their children from public school despite the state of Wisconsin's compulsory schooling law. Although the state had a strong interest in requiring Amish children to attend school, it did not overbalance the burden on religious freedom of compelling them to do so. The *Yoder* decision is unusual because it granted the Amish the free exercise of their beliefs despite a clear state law compelling school attendance. It is also a curious decision because it favored one particular religious group.

Another Free Exercise Clause case involved an Orthodox Jewish Air Force officer who wanted to wear his yarmulke (skullcap) on duty to show his devotion to his faith. The case, *Goldman v. Weinberger* (1986), eventually reached the U.S. Supreme Court. Air Force regulations did not allow any nonofficial garments, but Goldman argued that wearing the yarmulke did not create a clear danger to military discipline or performance. It seemed likely that the military regulation would fail the *Sherbert* test. However, the Court ruled that the *Sherbert* test should not apply to the military, which could continue to ban any religious dress to maintain order and discipline. Interestingly, after this case Congress responded by passing a law specifically permitting Goldman and others to wear religious dress in the Air Force. Of course, Orthodox Jews are not the only sect who may desire accommodation from dress restrictions. A Christian may want to wear a cross, and a Sikh may desire to wear a turban. There have been a number of cases over the years regarding whether schools or private companies can ban religious dress or jewelry. Some courts have held that employers have the right to insist that employees wear no jewelry and only authorized uniforms. Some courts have also held that schoolteachers cannot wear religious dress or jewelry in the classroom because it endorses a particular religion. What employees do on their own time is another matter.

At the end of the twentieth century the Supreme Court rethought its "compelled accommodation test." In *Employment Division, Oregon Department of Human Resources v. Smith* (1990) the Supreme Court held that religious belief could not excuse commission of a crime (use of peyote by Native Americans). The *Smith* case is detailed in Chapter 3. Religious leaders were alarmed by this decision, because it appeared that if a state criminalized a religious practice the Free Exercise Clause would have to give way to the state law. They reasoned that the holding could presumably be applied against any religious practices, such as receiving sacramental wine at communion services. Religious groups asked Congress for additional protections. Congress responded by passing a new federal law.

This law, the Religious Freedom Restoration Act (1993), provided among other things that federal, state, and local "Government[s] shall not substantially burden a person's exercise of religion even if the burden results from a rule of general applicability . . . except that Government may substantially burden a person's exercise of religion if it demonstrates that application of the burden to the person (1) is in furtherance of a compelling government interest; and (2) is the least restrictive means of furthering that compelling interest."

Generally, the new law made churches and other religious organizations exempt from most state and federal laws unless the government could show some "compelling government interest" in enforcing the law. Many churches used the law to protest city and county zoning rules that limited church building and parking lot expansions. One of these cases made it all the way to the Supreme Court.

In 1997 the U.S. Supreme Court in *City of Boerne v. Flores* overturned the 1993 Religious Freedom Restoration Act in a case involving a church that wanted to expand its building despite city zoning rules prohibiting the expansion. The Court ruled that the statute was unconstitutional because it did not merely enforce the right to practice religion, but in legislatively overruling the *Smith* decision, the law also attempted to make an unconstitutional substantive change in that constitutional protection. By overturning the law, the Supreme Court opened the door to more regulation of religion by Congress. The *City of Boerne* case is discussed in detail in Chapter 4. Congress responded by passing the Religious Land Use and Institutional Persons Act, which once again attempted to legislatively overrule *Smith* in zoning issues. The law requires local governments to demonstrate a compelling interest before they can block church expansions and building alterations. Although a few lower courts had upheld the law, by the middle of 2003 the Supreme Court had not yet ruled on the new law's constitutionality. Unless personnel on the Supreme Court change, the new law will likely share the same fate as the original Religious Freedom Restoration Act and will be declared unconstitutional.

Social Issues

In the nineteenth century the *Reynolds* case approved the criminalization of polygamy. The finding was based not only on the "common law," which recognized only monogamous marriages but also on unspoken religious precepts that underlie that law. Jewish and Christian church law allows only a single spouse. Although many non-Western societies have tolerated or encouraged such "plural marriages," European society has been based on monogamy, and the common law in England and North America reflects that cultural norm. The law that made polygamy a crime reflected the social expectations of the majority even though it impinged on the Mormons' free exercise of their religion. It is unlikely that the outcome of the *Reynolds* case would be any different if it were tried today.

The law bans other nonviolent activities as immoral and therefore unlawful. The rationale for such laws is also moral and religious. Until recently most states banned cohabitation by unmarried couples, and a few still do. Many states had laws criminalizing "sodomy," although such laws were seldom enforced. The antisodomy laws also reflect religious teachings that homosexuality is a deviant behavior. In 2003 the U.S. Supreme Court heard arguments in favor of decriminalizing sodomy nationwide.

The Supreme Court in June of 2003 struck down a Texas law that criminalized sodomy. The Texas statute, like others in four states, criminalized sexual behavior between same-sex partners. Criminal sodomy statutes in nine other states applied to both same-sex and unmarried opposite-sex couples. Although only a minority of states had similar statutes and prosecutions were few, the decision was significant because of its breadth. The Court held that governments cannot label gay and lesbian private sexual conduct a crime (*Lawrence and Garner v. Texas* [2003]). The three justices who dissented predicted that the case could lead to same-sex marriage, an issue that was not before the Court. Gays and lesbians still do not enjoy full legal rights because they are banned from serving in the military. Also, federal fair housing and employment statutes do not protect gays and lesbians from discrimination although some local statutes do.

Many devout Christians believe that homosexuality is sinful. Accordingly, they object to laws that give protections to homosexuals from employment and housing discrimination and from hate crimes. Gays and lesbians have successfully lobbied for both government and private employers to provide health care and other benefits for same-sex partners. On the other hand, the religiously motivated anti-gay bias persists. The Boy Scouts gained unfavorable publicity when the pubic discovered that the group rejects scout leaders who are either openly homosexual or atheist. However, because the Boy Scouts is a private organization and not part of the government, they are free to discriminate against both atheists and homosexuals. Gay rights activists have successfully challenged laws barring homosexuals from adoption, and they are also pressing for legal recognition of same-sex marriages, which are recognized in several European nations as well as in Canada. Conservative Christians are staunchly opposed to legalizing same-sex marriages.

Medical Issues

Although medical issues at first seem to involve ethical rather than religious issues, a closer examination reveals that many "ethical" views are really faith-based. Although most religions recognize the sanctity of human life, most also recognize numerous exceptions to this precept. Most religions recognize that killing by police officers and soldiers can be justifiable.

The religious recognition of the sanctity of human life is also reflected in the law. Of course, taking another's life is usually a criminal act, as is attempting to kill another. In common law, attempting suicide was also a crime, although some states have decriminalized it.

A surprising number of religious sects believe in "faith healing" or some variation of it. Christian Scientists believe that they have no need for doctors but can be cured by "spiritual healing." Other faiths believe that healing comes from prayer, not pills. Somewhat surprisingly, most states recognize that adults who rely on faith healing are not committing suicide. However, when religious parents decide that their children should be healed by faith healing rather than conventional medicine, most states take the opposite view and hold parents criminally liable if a child dies after receiving no medical treatment. These issues are discussed in both Chapter 3 and Chapter 4 of this book.

Another legal-religious issue involving the sanctity of life involves capital punishment. There is no consensus on this issue. The Roman Catholic Church's position is that capital punishment is morally wrong. The Church believes that this view is consistent with their pro-life policy. However, other religious individuals in the pro-life movement who believe abortion is sinful also believe that it is not a sin for the state to kill a convict sentenced to death. Euthanasia and doctor-assisted suicide have similar opponents and proponents.

The right to life movement (antiabortion movement) is also religiously inspired. In 1973 the Supreme Court, in *Roe v. Wade,* decided that women have the right to an abortion—a right based in their right to privacy and the right to select an appropriate medical procedure. Foes of abortion believe that an abortion murders the fetus. Evangelicals, Roman Catholics, as well as individuals who are not members of a particular faith oppose abortion based on their religious beliefs. The Roman Catholic Church has taken a position not only against abortion but also against capital punishment, reasoning that both are the taking of human life.

The Catholic Church has also taken the position that individuals should not use birth control devices, including condoms. One can argue that it is hypocritical to be against abortion and still use birth control devices. In fact, birth control devices were not always freely available and some religious leaders feel they should not be. They would like to ban both abortion and the use of birth control devices.

Justification for *Roe v. Wade* relies heavily on the Supreme Court ruling in *Griswold v. Connecticut* that established a right to privacy by making birth control available. These cases conclude that reproductive questions are private medical questions for the individual, not the state or a particular religion, to decide. Others argue that the government has a legitimate interest in protecting human life from the time of conception and can constitutionally ban both abortion and artificial birth control.

Since 1973 opponents of abortion have waged a political and publicity campaign. In the past, religious individuals have been behind many political movements including the antislavery abolitionist movement, as well as Prohibition, the temporarily successful effort to ban the sale of alcoholic beverages throughout the United States.

Although *Roe v. Wade,* the case invalidating state restrictions on abortion, has never been reversed, it has been eroded as the Supreme Court has upheld state parental consent laws, and recently late-term abortions have been banned by Congress. Additionally, members of the right to life movement have used pressure and publicity to dissuade doctors from offering abortion services and to dissuade women from seeking abortions.

Like the abolitionist movement before the Civil War, the antiabortion movement has its radical and violent side. After an activist Christian group, "Operation Rescue," distributed "wanted posters" with abortion doctors' names, addresses, and faces, abortion clinics were bombed and doctors were murdered all in the name of saving human life. Responsible members of the movement repudiated this violence. After juries awarded large damage awards against abortion clinic bombers, the violence slowed. However, in 2003 the Supreme Court announced that the RICO Act, the Racketeer Influenced and Corrupt Organizations Act, which was originally aimed at organized crime, could not be used against abortion clinic bombers.

Other medical issues lie ahead. Stem cell research, which uses the tissues of fetuses, is a promising area of medical research. However, many individuals have strong religious objections to this type of research, and current federal regulations limit such research in the United States. Looking ahead, human engineering, including genetic manipulation and human cloning, raises a number of legal-religious issues that will eventually find their way into a courtroom.

Religion in Public Schools

Families of very different backgrounds come together in U.S. public schools, often bringing very different values and religious beliefs. But schools also play a large role in shaping children's social values and worldview, and parents are rightfully concerned about the messages they receive in the classroom. Although some parents object to any religious observance in the classroom, others feel that excluding religious activities and observances creates a "godless" atmosphere that contributes to the moral decline of the children.

When pubic schools were established in the early nineteenth century, the country was predominantly Protestant, and, not surprisingly, daily classroom activities included prayer and Bible reading. Problems arose as immigration made the nation's population more diverse. When large numbers of Roman Catholics started attending public school, their parents objected to the Protestant prayers. In 1908 the Illinois Supreme Court banned in-class reading of the King James Bible in Chicago public schools (*People ex rel. Ring v. Board of Education),* because district Roman Catholics complained about their children reading daily in the classroom from the Protestant Bible. The court agreed with the complaining parents that even exclusion of the students from the Bible reading would subject the Catholic students to an unacceptable religious stigma. Although some states followed the lead of Illinois in banning Bible reading, other states let local school districts decide, and still other states, mostly in the South, required Bible reading in the schools as a means of moral instruction.

Until the *Cantwell* case in 1940, nearly everyone assumed that the First Amendment protections only applied to federal laws or federal actions. *Cantwell* opened the courtroom doors to parents who wished to complain about religion in the public schools. In 1948 the Supreme Court handed down the first in a line of major cases that would change the contours of U.S. society by largely eliminating religious activities in the public schools. The case, *People of Illinois ex rel. McCollum v. Board of Education,* banned use of public school buildings for release-time religious instruction.

Vashti McCollum gained the national spotlight when she filed a lawsuit objecting to the religion classes being given in her son's school. A local group, the Council on Religious Education, was formed to provide religious instruction in the Champaign, Illinois, school system. The students were released early from class, and children with parental permission attended religion classes in the schools. Nearly all the children participated and instruction was available for Jews, Catholics, and Protestants. Although Vashti had given Terry permission to attend the classes when he was in fourth grade, she grew uncomfortable with the instruction and did not give permission the next year. Although her son was not compelled to attend, he was required to sit alone in a small anteroom outside the teacher's rest room or to sit alone in the hall. He was the subject of teasing from his fellow students and disapproval from his teachers. When the school district failed to improve the situation, Vashti McCollum sued.

The U.S. Supreme Court in *McCollum v. Board of Education* (1948) agreed with Mrs. McCollum, holding that the teaching of religion on the school grounds violated the First Amendment's Establishment Clause. Following on the footsteps of *Everson v. Board of Education* the previous year, which held that state and local governments, including the public schools, were subject to the Establishment Clause, the Court used its power of judicial review to invalidate the state law that established the release-time program. No federal or state law can be contrary to a constitutional provision. Although declaring laws contrary to the Constitution is a judicial power, it also gives the Supreme Court a vast power to control how the law is applied in a particular area. The effect of this decision was not only to outlaw Illinois' program but any existing or potential programs that suffered from the same defects.

McCollum's case set the stage for all of the later cases that banned religious expression in the public schools. Vashti McCollum paid a personal price for her beliefs. She later revealed that she and her family were harassed all during the legal proceedings and she was called "an emissary of Satan, a Communist, and a fiend in human form."

In *Zorach v. Clauson* (1952), the Supreme Court upheld a release-time program taking place outside public school grounds. Earlier release-time programs, in which religion classes were taught in public school classrooms during the release-time period, were struck down in 1948 by the Supreme Court as a violation of the Establishment Clause. The Court clearly felt more comfortable with the classes being held off the school premises. That the school system assisted the programs by helping with registration and permitting the students to leave school early did not seem important to the Court. In any event, any entanglements were outweighed by the general benefits of the program. Justice William O. Douglas's opinion noted that although it was clear that the First Amendment required a separation of church and state, it was equally clear that the Establishment Clause did not require "a philosophy of hostility to religion," but one which "respects the religious nature of our people and accommodates the public service to their spiritual needs." Three justices wrote dissenting opinions noting that there was not much to distinguish this case from the 1948 *McCollum* case that had disapproved of release-time programs. In *Zorach,* the fact that the children attended the classes at church rather than in the school itself seemed trivial to the dissenters.

One of the most important and far-reaching cases ever heard by the Supreme Court was *Engel v. Vitale* (1962). In this case the Court found that the nondenominational school prayer written by the New York State Board of Regents offended the Establishment Clause. The nondenominational prayer had been composed to be inoffensive to those who were compelled to recite it. Justice Black, writing for the Court, felt that it is "no part of the business of government to compose official prayers."

Engel v. Vitale is an interesting decision for a number of reasons. Although six judges agreed with the result, there was one dissent and two justices did not participate. Generally, decisions with less than the full Court participating create a less powerful precedent. This case proved the exception to the rule: it created a powerful precedent for the Supreme Court and lower federal and state courts as well.

The case was a virtual bombshell triggering banner headlines worldwide. The political firestorm the case brought about should not have been unexpected. Prayer and Bible reading was an established routine in many if not most schools, and many people couldn't comprehend why the Court would ban the practice if a majority of the community wanted it. In fact, a majority of Americans might have wanted prayer in the public schools. However, constitutional protections are not for the majority; they are present to protect minority interests.

Generations of Americans had grown up with school prayer. Religious Americans took the decision as a personal rebuke. The decision also had a tremendously polarizing political effect. Those who supported the rights of minorities—especially non-Christians—hailed the decision as progressive. They pointed out that the decision did not eliminate any students' right to pray silently in school. It merely banned public schools from composing and compelling the recitation of prayers. Critics of the decision labeled the Court and its justices as "godless" or "communists."

The Supreme Court heard another major school prayer case, *Abington School District v. Schempp* (1963), and again declared that organized prayer had no place in the public schools. The case went even further than *Engel v. Vitale,* decided the prior year. That case concerned a prayer penned by an administrative body. The 1963 school prayer case banned both the recitation of the Lord's Prayer and Bible reading in public schools.

As in the prior year the decision caused a furor. This reaction was fueled in part because one of the companion cases before the High Court—*Murray v. Curlett* (1962)—was brought by Madalyn Murray, an avowed atheist, communist, and Castro supporter. The timing could not have been worse. The United States had just emerged from the Cuban Missile Crisis—a showdown between President Kennedy and Soviet Premier Nikita Khrushchev over the placement of hostile missiles in Cuba—just ninety miles from Florida. President Kennedy had just committed troops to South Vietnam to combat communist incursions. Many were ready to believe the school prayer case was more evidence of godless, communist influences within United States.

Despite the ruling, many public schools—especially in the South—continued to have either Bible reading or a school prayer at the start of the day in defiance of the Court's ban. Such practices continue to this day. In *Stone v. Graham* (1980), the Supreme Court banned the posting of the Ten Commandments in public schools, even when financed with private funds. The Court found that the purpose was religious and therefore prohibited by the Establishment Clause. The fact that the display was paid for with private funds made no difference.

Opposition to the banning of school prayer was swift. Criticism was leveled at the Supreme Court's opinion from politicians and from the pulpit. Groups such as the right-wing John Birch Society organized a campaign to impeach Chief Justice Earl Warren, who wrote the majority opinion in the school prayer case. More seriously, an amendment to allow school prayer was submitted before Congress. In fact, this one or a similar amendment to allow school prayer has been introduced in almost every Congress for twenty-five years but none of them has ever come close to being enacted. President Ronald Reagan became the first president to endorse an amendment allowing prayer in the public schools. Reagan told Congress that it is time to "allow prayer back in our schools."

After both organized prayers and Bible reading were banned from the public schools, school districts responded by allowing periods of silence so children could pray silently. These fared no better with the Court. In *Wallace v. Jaffree* (1985), the Supreme Court invalidated an Alabama law allowing a one-minute period of silence at the start of each school day "for meditation or voluntary prayer." A divided Court (6–3) concluded that this mandated moment of silence amounted to "the State's endorsement of prayer activity" that transgressed the proper wall of separation between church and state. Merely allowing students to be excused was held insufficient to save the law.

The Court did say, however, that it was possible for a moment of silence to pass muster if it was not solely for sectarian purposes. The problem with the Alabama law was that it was avowedly for prayer. Presumably, a statute that required a moment of silence for no reason would have avoided the constitutional problems. Of course, the Supreme Court has never prohibited prayer in the public schools. Students are free to pray silently or out loud. However, the school cannot conduct religious ceremonies including the recitation of prayers in the classroom.

Despite the ban on daily prayers, prayers were still in evidence at special events such as graduations, awards presentations, and athletic events. The Court ruled that organized prayer is not appropriate in these venues either. A divided Supreme Court, in *Lee v. Weisman* (1992), found that an invocation at a public school graduation ceremony in Providence, Rhode Island, violated the Establishment Clause. Justice Kennedy, writing for the majority, argued that the public atmosphere created an improper coercion of students, which amount to proselytizing. The majority felt that since the graduation ceremony was a required event, a prayer at the graduation was no more acceptable than a prayer in the classroom at the start of the school day. Justice Scalia wrote a bitter dissent accusing the majority of "laying waste" to traditional nonsectarian prayers at public events and accused the majority's using the concept of "coercion" as a "bulldozer of its social engineering."

As was the case with the original school prayer case in the 1960s, the Supreme Court decision was widely disregarded. Several years later Mississippi enacted a law allowing student-initiated voluntary prayer at all assemblies, sporting events, commencement exercises, and other school-related events. The law was immediately challenged by the ACLU arguing that the "voluntariness" was a sham. A Mississippi federal district judge upheld the section of the law allowing prayers at commencement exercises but struck down the parts of the act allowing prayer at assemblies and other school-related events (*Ingebretsen v. Jackson Public School District* [1990]). In Idaho one school district allowed student leaders to say a prayer at graduation if a majority of the graduating seniors agreed. A federal court of appeals in this case held that the compulsory nature of graduation made the graduation prayer improper and that school officials could not sidestep their responsibilities by delegating the decision to the students (*Harris v. Joint School District No. 241* [1995]). These lower court trials illustrate that Supreme Court decisions do not always end the controversy when religion is the issue.

Although states try to accommodate religious practice, too much accommodation can result in an entanglement that will violate the Establishment Clause. In 1994 the U.S. Supreme Court in *Board of Education of the Kiryas Joel Village School District v. Grumet* struck down New York State's creation of a special public school district to provide state-funded special education services for a community of Hasidic Jews. The community of approximately 8,500, the Satmae Hasidim sect of Orthodox Jews established a private school based on the needs of their religious students including gender segregation, a special dress code, and speaking Yiddish. In order to obtain state aid to the village's handicapped children, the state legislature allowed the village to establish a separate public school district that would only deal with the problems of the village's handicapped children. All children in the village attended private parochial schools except handicapped children who attended the public school, which provided services exclusively to the special needs children. The public school was staffed by secular teachers and had a purely secular curriculum.

The Supreme Court held that this was a violation of the Establishment Clause. Because New York had created the school district along religious lines, it had violated the Constitution's requirement that government maintain its impartiality toward religion. A few years later the Supreme Court revisited the case but again struck down the creation of a special public school district at Kiryas Joel to provide state-funded special education services for the community of Hasidic Jews. The Court held that the new state statute allowing the district still offended the Establishment Clause.

In 1995 the U.S. Department of Education issued guidelines on the extent to which religious activity is allowed in public schools. The guidelines allow student prayer and Bible reading by individuals or groups, which is not disruptive. The wearing of religious clothing or symbols is permitted as well as limited proselytizing and the distribution of religious literature. Prohibited activities include prayer that is endorsed by a teacher or the school authorities. Teachers may teach about religion but may not teach the tenets of a particular religion and may not encourage either religious or antireligious activity. These guidelines were later reissued under George W. Bush's administration, allowing more leeway for religious observances.

Teaching Evolution

Although fundamentalist Christians want to keep prayer in the public schools, they want to keep evolution out. Although many people would assume that the battle over teaching evolution in Biology classes was finished years ago, nothing could be further from the truth.

Charles Darwin's book *On the Origin of Species by Means of Natural Selection* was published in Britain in 1859 and gained worldwide attention. His second book, *The Descent of Man,* created a sensation. Darwin concluded that God did not create man in his own image and that the physical fossil record had the potential to disprove Scripture. In conclusion he wrote: "the main conclusion arrived at in this work, namely that man is descended from some lowly-organized form, will, I regret to think, be highly distasteful to many." If anything, Darwin underestimated the reaction to his book. He was reviled both at home and abroad, although he was eventually buried in Westminster Abbey alongside many other British notables.

Fundamentalist Christian parents in the United States, alarmed that the teaching of evolution might threaten their children's faith, lobbied for state laws banning the teaching of evolution. Oklahoma passed the first such law in 1923. The last such law was declared unconstitutional in 1968, although teaching evolution remains controversial in many areas. In 1925 the world watched the "Scopes Monkey Trial" in which noted attorney Clarence Darrow represented high school biology teacher John Thomas Scopes, who was charged with violating a Tennessee law prohibiting the teaching of evolution in the public schools. This case is described in detail in Chapter 3.

In the widely publicized trial William Jennings Bryan defended the law for the state. Although Scopes was convicted and fined $100, the fine was thrown out on appeal. Bryan, a prime backer of antievolution laws, died just days after the trial. Although the "Monkey Trial" is perhaps the most famous U.S. trial of the twentieth century, few people understand its consequences. Although the media portrayed the antievolution forces as buffoons, the fundamentalists won not only the trial but the war as well. After the trial several southern states enacted laws banning evolution from the classrooms.

These laws remained on the books until the Supreme Court decision in *Epperson v. Arkansas* (1968), which also is discussed in Chapter 3 of this book. In a replay of the *Scopes* trial forty-three years earlier, the U.S. Supreme Court invalidated an Arkansas law banning the teaching of evolution in public schools. The Court held the law violative of the Establishment Clause. The Court reasoned that the ban was enacted entirely to "aid, foster, or promote one religious theory" over another and thereby offended the Establishment Clause of the First Amendment. Arkansas could not require that its school curriculum be shaped to conform to the beliefs of the Christian religion.

Although the Supreme Court made a ruling, it did not change people's religious beliefs or opposition to Darwin. The antievolution forces did, however, change their tactics. After the U.S. Supreme Court prohibited states from banning the teaching of evolution in *Epperson,* creationists started labeling their body of information supporting the biblical version of creation as "creation science." The Court had thrown out the biblical account because it wasn't "scientific." Accordingly, fundamentalists chose to depict the biblical account from a scientific viewpoint. Fundamentalist Christians formed the Creation Research Society to help combat the spread of the belief in evolution and its teaching in the public schools.

On another front, fundamentalists worked to keep evolution out of the biology books. In Texas all school districts adopt textbooks recommended by the state. Fundamentalist Christians have lobbied hard and long to persuade states not to adopt textbooks that accept evolution as fact. The goal is to get "balanced treatment," equal time for Darwin and Genesis.

In 1981 the Louisiana legislature passed a law, Balanced Treatment for Creation-Science and Evolution-Science in Public School Instruction, that mandates that any school teaching evolution must also provide equal classroom time to the teaching of so-called creation science, based on the biblical account of creation. Religious leaders applauded the law; however, parents immediately challenged it and in 1987 the Supreme Court in *Edwards v. Aguillard* invalidated Louisiana's balanced treatment law requiring public schools to provide equal time for the teaching of evolution and creation science. The Court found that the primary purpose for the law was to promote the teachings of Christianity. This favoritism violated the Establishment Clause.

Rebuffed in court, the antievolution movement has had more success at the grassroots level. Those opposed to teaching evolution have secured seats on local and state school boards.

Fundamentalists have also worked to add a "Parental Rights Amendment" to each state constitution and eventually the U.S. Constitution as well. The amendment would forbid the government—including the public schools—to interfere with or usurp the right of parents to direct the upbringing of their children. The amendment would make it easier for parents to challenge classroom material that they find objectionable. Some argue that the amendment would compel the government to pay tuition for parents who want their children educated in church-affiliated schools.

Equal Access

Although conservative Christians have lamented the loss of Bible reading and organized prayer in pubic schools, Christians have had more success in gaining equal access for religious clubs in public schools. After the original school prayer case, many school districts assumed that all religion was banned from the schools. Christian parents have successfully challenged this view.

The Supreme Court declared that a state university cannot deny use of its facilities to a religious club. The Court, in *Widmar v. Vincent* (1981), reasoned that it would be a violation of the student' First Amendment rights and would get the university embroiled in excluding groups that the university deemed religious although at the same time granting use to groups that it perceived as not religious. The equal access language in the *Widmar* case led to legislative action in 1984. Congress passed the federal Equal Access Act, which prohibits discrimination against student groups on the basis of religious, political, or philosophical views. If a public school allows "non-curriculum related groups" like clubs to use its facilities, then the school must give equal access to those facilities to religious groups.

Using the "*Lemon* test," the Supreme Court, in *Board of Education of the Westside Community Schools v. Mergens* (1990), upheld the constitutionality of the federal Equal Access Act, enacted to give equal access to public school facilities for religious groups and clubs. The Court held that although there was some involvement of school officials in the appealed case, this did not amount to prohibited entanglement with religion or an endorsement of any particular religion. Clearly, changes of personnel on the Court over the years had made a difference. It is likely that if this case had been brought two decades earlier, the Court would have found the entire act unconstitutional.

In *Lamb's Chapel v. Center Moriches Union Free Public School District* (1993), the Supreme Court decided that a school district could not deny access to school facilities to a church group that wanted to show a film on child rearing. The film was only shown to the church group after school hours, and the Court held that any benefit to the group was merely "incidental." Similarly, the Supreme Court in *Rosenberger v. Rector and Visitors of University of Virginia* (1995) held that a state university that used student funds to support a number of campus clubs and organizations could not withhold funds from a religious group to publish their Christian magazine *Wide Awake.* The Court reasoned that this would be improper viewpoint discrimination.

Aid to Parochial and Religious Schools

During the last half of the twentieth century, a number of trials have considered direct and indirect aid to parochial and religious schools. In some cases the courts have approved the aid because the aid went to the schoolchildren rather than the schools. In other cases the courts have decided the opposite. These cases illustrate that court-made law does not always provide "bright lines" that can be easily followed.

Although most people assume that there is a "right" to attend a parochial school, this was not always clear. In the 1920s Oregon voters, alarmed at the growing number of Catholics and Catholic schools in their midst, passed a referendum that amended the state constitution to require all schoolchildren to attend only public schools. The law was aimed directly at Catholic schools in the state. Under the law, all private and parochial schools were to be outlawed in Oregon. Several private schools challenged the law. A unanimous U.S. Supreme Court, in *Pierce v. Society of Sisters* (1925), held that the Fourteenth Amendment protected students' rights to attend private schools. Although the state of Oregon had authority to regulate its public schools, it could not require all students to attend only the state-funded school system.

Many of the cases in this area have concerned "incidental" aid. In *Everson v. Board of Education* (1947) the Supreme Court upheld New Jersey's subsidy of bus service to parochial schools. The Court decided that provision of bus service was not a direct subsidy of the parochial schools but peripheral or incidental, similar to providing the school fire and police protection. The majority opinion focused on the fact that the aid went to the students or their parents and not directly to the school. The Court found no constitutional problem with "a general program to help parents get their children, regardless of their religion, safely and expeditiously to and from accredited schools." Accordingly, the wall of separation between church and state was not violated. The *Everson* decision is notable also because this was the first time the Supreme Court announced that the Establishment Clause of the First Amendment of the Constitution also applies to the states, and therefore, it applied to the actions of local school districts.

Justice Black wrote the majority opinion in *Everson*. Black believed that the Constitution's Establishment Clause demanded an absolute wall of separation between church and state. In *Everson,* he explained that his conception of the Establishment Clause echoed Jefferson's earlier view: "The First Amendment has erected a wall between church and state. That wall must be kept high and impregnable. We [The Supreme Court] could not approve the slightest breach." Surprisingly, Black's opinion held that there was no breach in the *Everson* case where New Jersey had paid the bus fare of children riding public transit to parochial schools. Although Black would not countenance the "slightest breach" of the wall of separation, he reasoned that the reimbursement of the bus fare benefited the schoolchildren and their families rather than the parochial schools.

In *Board of Education of Central School Dist. No. 1 v. Allen* (1968), the Supreme Court upheld a "loan" of textbooks to a parochial school. This subsidy was upheld on the grounds that the books aided the students rather than the school. The Supreme Court allowed a state program, which loaned textbooks on secular topics to private and parochial school students. The divided Court upheld the practice reasoning that the aid went to the students or their parents rather than to the schools. The Court has also approved reimbursement of the costs of state-mandated standardized tests but disapproved of providing free teaching materials other than textbooks.

In a major case in 1971, *Lemon v. Kurtzman,* the Supreme Court prohibited salary supplements for lay teachers in parochial schools. The majority opinion, written by Chief Justice Warren Burger, was especially critical of the religious indoctrination in parochial schools, writing that: "parochial schools involve substantial religious activity and purpose." The case also established a three-prong test to see if a law offends the Establishment Clause. All three prongs must be met.

1. The statute must have a secular purpose.
2. Its primary effect must neither advance nor inhibit religion.
3. It must avoid excessive governmental entanglement with religion.

The "*Lemon* test" was used by the Court for approximately twenty-five years, and it also found its way into the Religious Freedom Restoration Act. Although the *Lemon* case has not been overruled, the Supreme Court has been reluctant to use the test since the mid-1990s.

Later cases were no more consistent. In *Meek v. Pittenger* (1975) the Supreme Court struck down state payment of auxiliary services, such as the purchase of AV equipment at parochial schools. Curiously, this case involved the same law that was upheld in the 1968 *Allen* case. But the Court also approved a program whereby the public school employees provided both speech and hearing and psychological testing services for parochial school students at their schools. The Court reasoned that such services had no "educational content" and the Court saw no danger in proselytizing.

Despite earlier rulings, in 1977 the Supreme Court held in *Wollman v. Walter* that a school district cannot provide instructional materials such as maps, magazines, tape recorders, and buses for field trips to parochial school students even though these are all used for secular, rather than religious, instruction. The Court held that the Establishment Clause was violated because of the "impossibility of separating the secular education function from the sectarian."

More recently, the Supreme Court in *Aguilar v. Felton* (1985) struck down a program that used federal funds to pay the salaries of public school guidance counselors and teachers providing remedial and clinical help to disadvantaged parochial school students. The Court held that the plan created an excessive government entanglement with religion and therefore failed the Lemon test. Yet, the Supreme Court found no Establishment Clause violation in *Zobrest v. Catalina Foothills School District* (1993), in which a California school district provided a sign language interpreter for a deaf student at a Catholic high school. The Court reasoned that there was no constitutional violation when the parochial school received only an "attenuated financial benefit" from the educational program that provided benefits neutrally without reference to the student's religious affiliation. Compare this case with the earlier case, *Wollman* (1977), in which the Court found that payment for instructional materials in parochial schools violated the Establishment Clause.

The U.S. Supreme Court in *Agostini v. Felton* (1997) overturned its 1985 holding in *Aguilar v. Felton,* finding that remedial education funded by federal aid under Title 1 could not take place in parochial school buildings. In the 1985 case, a divided Supreme Court decided that remedial education funded by federal aid under Title 1 and performed by public school teachers could not take place in parochial school buildings. The 1997 case held that the Establishment Clause did not prohibit public school teachers from giving remedial instruction in a parochial school. This was a major change in policy by the Supreme Court that had uniformly held for more than thirty years that public school teachers could not teach in parochial schools even when there was no religious instruction involved.

Since 1980 the issue of "school vouchers" has become a major Establishment Clause issue. In *Mueller v. Allen* (1983) a closely divided Supreme Court upheld a Minnesota law allowing parents of private and parochial school students to take a tax deduction for tuition and other educational expenses. The case is significant because the Court had struck down a similar law. What saved the Minnesota law was that the deduction was also "available" to parents of public school students. The Court conveniently sidestepped the issue that parents of public school students do not actually pay tuition and thereby would not benefit in real terms. Nevertheless, Justice Rehnquist, writing for the Court, found the tax scheme to be neutral. The fact that the bulk of the benefits would go to the parents of private and parochial school students was held to be irrelevant. The majority opinion stressed the value of supporting private schools not just for those students attending the schools but for the public in general. Rehnquist noted that the public benefited because each student educated in private school reduced the taxpayer's burden of educating the student. Further, the private school system provided a benchmark for the public school system and provided educational diversity.

Wisconsin was one of the first states to establish a voucher plan for religious schools. Under the state plan, the state would pay the tuition for disadvantaged children in both private nonsectarian schools and also parochial schools. The program was challenged as a violation of church and state and the program was put on hold until court arguments were heard. Meanwhile an Ohio state court struck down the Ohio Pilot Scholarship Program that provided vouchers of up to $2,500 to Cleveland public school students to attend private and parochial schools. The state court in *Simmons-Harris v. Goff* (1999) held that the voucher program violated the Establishment Clause because it provides direct and substantial, not neutral, government aid to sectarian schools.

After the Wisconsin Supreme Court split on the issue of the validity of Milwaukee's voucher program in 1996, the case was sent back to the trial court. The trial court decided that the program was an unconstitutional violation of the church-state provisions of the Wisconsin state constitution. Although many hoped that the Supreme Court would decide the legitimacy of vouchers, the Court declined to accept any voucher cases until the 2002 term.

Finally, in 2002 the Supreme Court heard a major voucher case, *Zelman v. Simmons-Harris,* and upheld the Ohio school voucher plan despite arguments that it violates the Establishment Clause. The Ohio plan gives a state-paid voucher to a family that can be used to pay tuition in private or religious schools. Relying on precedents in which the Court has allowed aid to parochial school students, the Court reasoned that the public money was supporting children and their parents, not private religious schools. Proponents of vouchers lost little time in proposing school vouchers in other states. Opponents of school vouchers argue that vouchers may be unconstitutional under many state constitutions, which have more exacting separation of church and state provisions than the federal Constitution. A few state courts have already ruled vouchers unconstitutional under state constitutions. The future of vouchers lies in the courts.

Entanglements

Although much of the late-twentieth-century freedom of religion litigation has focused on free exercise and school issues, there are a number of other conflict areas. One such area involves "entanglements." Over the years the country has accommodated a number of Christian religious practices as a part of a so-called civic religion. Prayers are recited at public events. Sunday, the Christian Sabbath, became a national day of rest. Cities maintain Christmas displays. The country also adopted "In God We Trust" as the national motto and added the words *under God* to the pledge of allegiance. Although these practices seem benign, there can be no doubt that they endorse religion and a belief in God. A majority of Americans may be comfortable with public endorsement of Christianity, or religion in general; however, a significant minority of Americans believe that these entanglements are not only improper but also unconstitutional. Many of these practices are being challenged. For example, Bible reading and school prayer and graduation invocations have all been ruled violations of the Establishment Clause.

Consider the case of government-funded Christmas decorations. No one can argue with the fact that Christmas is a religious holiday. However, it is also clear that Christmas has become a commercial event. Local governments have a interest in promoting business activity, and public Christmas decorations have the mixed purpose of celebrating a Christian religious holiday and at the same time helping merchants attract customers. The courts have had to resolve the issue of whether publicly financed Christmas decorations are an Establishment Clause violation.

The first case to reach the U.S. Supreme Court was *Lynch v. Donnelly* (1984), detailed in Chapter 3. This case upheld the display of a crèche in a park in Pawtucket, Rhode Island. A divided Supreme Court found that the practice was not an endorsement of religion as long as the crèche was accompanied by other traditional holiday decorations. The majority opinion, written by Chief Justice Warren Burger, held that the so-called wall of separation is "not a wholly accurate description of the practical aspects of the relationship that in fact exists between church and state because the Constitution affirmatively mandates accommodation, not merely tolerance, of all religions and forbids hostility towards any." The opinion also observed that Christmas was no longer an exclusively religious holiday. Justice Brennan dissented, observing:

> To suggest as the Court does that such a symbol is merely "traditional" and therefore no different from Santa's house or reindeer is not only offensive to those for whom the crèche has profound signifi-

cance, but insulting to those who insist for religious or personal reasons that the story of Christ is in no sense part of "history" . . . nor of
our national "heritage."

Supreme Court observers who read Justice Brennan's bitter dissent would not have been surprised that the Christmas decoration issue had not been laid to rest in *Lynch*. Just a few years later, the
Court accepted a similar case from Pittsburgh, but this time the decorations did not fare as well. The case was *County of Allegheny v.
Greater Pittsburgh ACLU* (1989). The local chapter of the American
Civil Liberties Union brought the case alleging that a holiday display
violated the Establishment Clause. This time the divided Court outlawed Pittsburgh's holiday display.

Conclusion

The Supreme Court's decisions that the First Amendment applied to
the states opened a floodgate of litigation over religion during the
twentieth century. Although nineteenth-century courts were reluctant to hear cases involving religion and churches, this reluctance has
disappeared. There is no reason to think that this trend will reverse
itself. The courts will continue their role in deciding the precise location of the wall of separation between church and state.

In the years ahead one would expect courts to continue to hear
cases involving the free exercise of religion by minority sects. As the
United States accommodates more non-Christian immigrants, these
cases should be expected to increase. Similarly, the Court should be
expected to hear more Establishment Clause cases if the government
moves forward with President George W. Bush's proposal to financially aid "faith-based" organizations that provide basic social services.

The flood of pedophilia lawsuits against the Catholic Church may
propel church members to sue their churches over other grievances.
Although it was once very rare for a church to be sued, today such
cases are commonplace. Courts have traditionally been reluctant to
meddle in internal church affairs, yet more lawsuits are being
brought against ministers and their bishops by their congregations.

In the twenty-first century, many lawsuits over social and scientific issues may be religiously inspired. Many devout Christians object to the gay rights movement and oppose expansion of the antidis-

crimination laws to cover homosexuals. They also oppose legalizing gay marriages. Although it might be possible to define marriage as the union of two heterosexuals, at least one major faith believes that civil divorces are invalid. In their eyes, second and third marriages are invalid. If churches become involved in providing basic social services, some may argue that the churches have to end their prejudice against homosexuality. In the late twentieth century a college lost its tax exempt status because it practiced racial discrimination in admissions and prohibited interracial dating (*Bob Jones University v. United States* [1983]). In the years ahead, churches' rights to income tax and property tax exemptions may be challenged if they discriminate against women or homosexuals.

The expansion of biotechnology is already creating issues that have religious implications. Basic questions, such as when exactly is a person dead or alive, have scientific, religious, and legal implications. For example, the courts continue to grapple with issues of when life support should be discontinued for a person in a persistent vegetative state. If a person has a legal right not to take life-prolonging medicine, is it logical and ethical to deny them medical help to end a life that promises only intense pain? Cloning and genetic manipulation should be expected to trigger the same kinds of passions in the twenty-first century as abortion did in the twentieth. Conflicts will undoubtedly arise between those who want to "reengineer" human life and those who feel that the government should place limits on such research. Although it is unclear which of these issues may be the most contentious, what is clear is that religious issues will remain "on trial" for the foreseeable future.

3

Cases

This chapter covers a number of the notable court cases that have produced strong national interest as well as a significant mark on the legal system. The legacy and aftermath of these cases is discussed in Chapter 4.

The cases were also chosen to illustrate the diversity of legal issues that face religious practice in the United States. They include:

Minersville School District v. Gobitis (1940)—In a wartime case, the U.S. Supreme Court decided that a local school district can force students to salute and pledge allegiance to the flag. Jehovah's Witnesses believe that such behavior is banned by the Bible as a form of idolatry and had asked that their children be excused.

Scopes v. Tennessee (1925) and *Epperson v. Arkansas* (1968)—Two remarkably similar cases, forty-three years apart, in which teachers challenged the constitutionality of state statutes banning the teaching of evolution. The *Scopes* "Monkey Trial" garnered international publicity but did little to change the law. In contrast, the Supreme Court decision in *Epperson* had a far-reaching effect.

Lynch v. Donnelly (1984)—In this curious decision, a bitterly divided U.S. Supreme Court decided that financing of a crèche on city-owned land in Pawtucket, Rhode Island, was not an entanglement with religion as long as the crèche was accompanied by other traditional holiday decorations.

Engel v. Vitale (1962)—Also known as the "Regents School Prayer Case," this U.S. Supreme Court decision banned all organized prayer in the public schools. The case caused a huge uproar among

Christians, some of whom started an unsuccessful campaign to impeach Chief Justice Earl Warren.

Application of the President and Directors of Georgetown College (1964)—This opinion was written in connection with an order granted by a U.S. Court of Appeals judge allowing a hospital to administer blood transfusions to save the life of a patient. The patient and her husband had refused to give permission for the transfusions because, as Jehovah's Witnesses, they believed blood transfusions violated the Scriptures.

Employment Division v. Smith (1990)—The U.S. Supreme Court upholds Oregon's denial of unemployment benefits to an employee who had used peyote, a controlled substance, at a Native American religious ceremony. Although the case involved use of an illegal drug, church leaders of all political stripes were alarmed at the Court's cavalier attitude toward religious rights. They successfully pressed Congress to enact the Religious Freedom Restoration Act specifically to overrule the *Smith* case.

Minersville School District v. Gobitis

Although the pledge of allegiance may not seem to have a strong religious content, it has led to trials that have generated some of the most intense conflicts involving religion.

The patriotic pledge of allegiance is typically recited by students at the start of each school day. Although these days its recitation is becoming less common in some parts of the country, some state statutes require daily recitation of the pledge by children attending public school. Interestingly, the words *under God* were inserted in the pledge only in 1954 (and before World War II, students saluted the flag using the straight-armed "Nazi salute"). Even before the words *under God* were inserted, the pledge was controversial. Jehovah's Witnesses prohibit their members from reciting the pledge because they believe it to be worship of a "graven image." Quakers also are uncomfortable with the word *pledge,* and an early concession was made. The presidential oath of office allows the president the option to "affirm" or "pledge" to uphold the duties of the office.

During the 1930s the United States was still mired in the economic doldrums of the Great Depression. Meanwhile, totalitarian regimes, including the Nazis, were rising in Europe. In this unstable environment a number of states made the flag salute and pledge recitation mandatory at the start of each school day.

The Jehovah's Witnesses was a small but vocal faith known for its aggressive preaching. Because of their "extreme" views and door-to-door preaching, they were an unpopular group. As the Witnesses gained converts, they became more unpopular with the leaders of older mainline churches. Many towns enacted licensing statutes aimed directly at keeping Witnesses from preaching door-to-door. (Resistance to the Witnesses persists. A 2002 U.S. Supreme Court case declared unconstitutional a local statute aimed at them.)

Earlier in the same year, as the *Gobitis* pledge case was heard, the Supreme Court had accepted another case, *Cantwell v. Connecticut* (1940), involving two Jehovah's Witnesses who sought to pass out religious literature in downtown New Haven, Connecticut. The city, like many others, passed a law requiring those who wished to pass out religious literature to get a license. The law's purpose was to discourage and regulate Witnesses and other groups. The Cantwells did not apply for a license because they presumed they would be turned down on the grounds that they were not members of an established religion. In *dicta* the Court noted that freedom of religion includes the freedom to believe and the freedom to act. Although the first was an absolute right, the second was not. The *Cantwell* case is also notable because for the first time the Supreme Court announced that the Free Exercise Clause of the First Amendment of the Constitution not only applies to the federal government but also to the states.

The Cantwells had nearly incited a riot. They had carried a portable spring-loaded phonograph on which they played a record called "Enemies," a diatribe against other religions and especially the Roman Catholic Church. They purposely picked a Catholic neighborhood and played the record. A few Catholic passersby were incensed by the anti-Catholic tirade and threatened the Cantwells with physical violence if they didn't leave. Although they left without incident, the local police arrested them, charging them with inciting a breach of the peace and evangelizing without the required license.

The Supreme Court found the license requirement a prohibited prior restraint. The local law put the local authorities in charge of determining if a group was a religion. Although New Haven could control street activity, allowing local authorities to decide what speakers and activities to permit was an impermissible burden on the free exercise of religion. This was a big victory for the minority sect that often faces local laws aimed at stopping its evangelizing efforts. However, Witnesses continued to be viewed unfavorably by a number of people.

Parents of Jehovah's Witness students were outraged that public schools wanted to force their children to salute the flag and recite the pledge despite their strong and well-known religious objections. Parents sued school districts to allow their children to avoid recitation of the pledge on religious grounds. The case that made headlines was *Minersville School District v. Gobitis,* which made its way to the Supreme Court in 1940, when the United States was on the verge of entering World War II.

Lillian Gobitis, aged twelve, and her brother William, aged ten, were expelled from the public schools of Minersville, Pennsylvania, for refusing to salute the national flag as part of a daily school exercise. The local board of education required both teachers and pupils to participate in this ceremony. The Minersville flag salute ceremony is a familiar one, with the following words at the time recited in unison: "I pledge allegiance to the flag, and to the Republic for which it stands; one nation indivisible, with liberty and justice for all." In those days, both teachers and pupils extended their right hands in salute to the flag.

The Gobitis family (who actually spelled their name "Gopitas") were members of the Jehovah's Witnesses, who believe the Bible as the Word of God to be the supreme authority. The Gobitis children had been brought up conscientiously to believe that such a gesture of respect for the flag was forbidden by command of the Scriptures. Chapter 20 of Exodus provides:

> 3. Thou shalt have no other gods before me.
> 4. Thou shalt not make unto thee any graven image, or any likeness of any thing that is in heaven above, or that is in the earth beneath, or that is in the water under the earth.
> 5. Thou shalt not bow down thyself to them, nor serve them.

Walter Gobitis, the children's father, on behalf of the children and himself, brought a suit with help from his church against the local public school his children attended. He sought to enjoin school authorities from continuing to force his children to participate in the flag-salute ceremony as a condition of his children's attendance at the Minersville School.

At the trial both William (age ten) and Lillian (age twelve) testified that saluting the flag violated their religious beliefs and quoted from Scripture to support their testimony. After trial of the issues, Judge Maris in the district court found that the compelled flag salute and recitation of the pledge violated the children and parent's First Amendment rights. The U.S. Circuit Court of Appeals affirmed this decision. The school district appealed to the U.S. Supreme Court, which agreed to hear the case because this decision ran counter to several per curium dispositions of the Court.

The Supreme Court was confronted by a stark choice. A forced recital of the pledge was offensive to members of a minority religion and, according to the two lower courts, offensive to the Establishment Clause of the First Amendment. On the other hand, recital of the pledge was a patriotic act endorsed by the Pennsylvania state legislature. There was no way to reconcile the two.

The Supreme Court voted 8–1 to require all students to salute the flag and recite the pledge. Justice Felix Frankfurter wrote the majority opinion. Frankfurter was himself an immigrant and was extremely patriotic. Although Frankfurter acknowledged the sincerity of the Gobitis children's religious beliefs, he concluded that they must give way to the fostering of patriotism:

> The question remains whether school children, like the Gobitis children, must be excused from conduct required of all the other children in the promotion of national cohesion. We are dealing with an interest inferior to none in the hierarchy of legal values. National unity is the basis of national security . . . . We live by symbols. The flag is the symbol of our national unity, transcending all internal differences, however large, within the framework of the Constitution. This Court has had occasion to say that " . . . the flag is the symbol of the nation's power, the emblem of freedom in its truest, best sense. . . . It signifies government resting on the consent of the governed; liberty regulated by law; the protection of the weak against the strong; security against the exercise of arbitrary power; and absolute safety for free institutions against foreign aggression."

Perhaps unsure of his ground in downplaying the importance of the Establishment Clause violation, Frankfurter also argued that in matters of education, the Court should defer to the Pennsylvania legislature, which had written the law. He also argued that the legislature was in the best position to write an exception for individuals who had religious objections.

> The case before us must be viewed as though the legislature of Pennsylvania had itself formally directed the flag-salute for the children of Minersville; had made no exemption for children whose parents were possessed of conscientious scruples like those of the Gobitis family; and had indicated its belief in the desirable ends to be secured by having its public school children share a common experience at those periods of development when their minds are supposedly receptive to its assimilation, by an exercise appropriate in time and place and setting, and one designed to evoke in them appreciation of the nation's hopes and dreams, its sufferings and sacrifices. The precise issue, then, for us to decide is whether the legislatures of the various states and the authorities in a thousand counties and school districts of this country are barred from determining the appropriateness of various means to evoke that unifying sentiment without which there can ultimately be no liberties, civil or religious.
>
> The wisdom of training children in patriotic impulses by those compulsions which necessarily pervade so much of the educational process is not for our independent judgment . . . the court-room is not the arena for debating issues of educational policy. It is not our province to choose among competing considerations in the subtle process of securing effective loyalty to the traditional ideals of democracy, while respecting at the same time individual idiosyncrasies among a people so diversified in racial origins and religious allegiances. So to hold would in effect make us the school board for the country. That authority has not been given to this Court, nor should we assume it.

The 8–1 U.S. Supreme Court decision in *Gobitis* held squarely that Jehovah's Witnesses could not be excused from reciting the pledge of allegiance in school. Despite the fact that their religious precepts prohibited reciting the pledge, the government could force schoolchildren to recite the pledge of allegiance to create national unity. The date of the case is important. Frankfurter, a brilliant ex–law professor had immigrated to the United States as a child with his Jewish parents. Frankfurter was fervently patriotic and undoubtedly thought saying the pledge was a small price for the privilege of living in the United States despite the Witnesses' objections on religious grounds.

Justice Harlan Fiske Stone wrote an impassioned dissent. Stone argued that although the promotion of patriotism was an important national value, no citizen should be compelled to "bear false witness to his religion."

The *Gobitis* decision caused a mass expulsion of Witness children from school and even precipitated mob violence against Witness churches, some of which were burned. With the country ready to enter World War II, many people viewed the Witnesses' refusals to recite the pledge as a treasonous act rather than as a sincere expression of religious belief. Witnesses were already unpopular. Mainline Christians had long mocked their beliefs and found the Witnesses' door-to-door proselytizing efforts annoying. Some in the majority viewed the Court's opinion as vindication of their hatred, and the unfortunate result was real oppression of this minority religious group. The Court's decision was also strongly criticized by both the press and mainline clergy who came to the defense of the Witnesses. Although many of these supporters were not in sympathy with the Witnesses' views, they recognized that protection of religious rights is an important value.

The Supreme Court's ruling in *Gobitis*, which stated the pledge was mandatory despite the Jehovah's Witnesses' religious beliefs, didn't stand for long. In just three years Stone's lone dissent was to become the majority view. The legacy of *Gobitis* is discussed in Chapter 4.

The Antievolution Statute Cases

One of the best-known trials of the twentieth century was the *Scopes* "Monkey Trial" in which noted attorney Clarence Darrow represented high school biology teacher John Thomas Scopes, who was charged with violating a Tennessee law prohibiting the teaching of evolution in the public schools. Many people are familiar with the trial because of the Hollywood movie *Inherit the Wind*. Those wishing to get a firsthand view of the trial should consult Edward Caudill's *The Scopes Trial: A Photographic Essay*, which includes nearly forty period photographs of the trial and the participants. The book also includes many little-known details that are included in this book's discussion.

Religious fundamentalists believe that Darwin's theory of evolution is contrary to the Bible's teachings. They believe the literal truth of the creation—that God created the heavens and earth in six twenty-four-hour periods. The concept of "inerrancy" is the belief that the Bible is without error with regard to history and science. Darwin's revisionism—that "man is descended from some lowly-organized form"—was not only shocking but also blasphemous. Fundamentalists did not want their children exposed to such ideas in the public schools or elsewhere.

Outraged by Darwin's book and his radical theory, fundamentalists turned to their state legislatures to stamp out the heresy. Oklahoma was the first state to act, declaring that no public school textbooks should teach Darwinism instead of the account in the Book of Genesis. Florida followed suit with a nonbinding resolution suggesting a balance between Darwin and the biblical account of creation. In 1924 the Tennessee General Assembly considered the Butler Act, named for John Washington Butler, a devout member of the Primitive Baptist Church. Butler proposed a bill to the assembly banning the teaching of evolution. He later explained that he viewed Christianity as the foundation of the government and that by espousing Darwinism and denying Christianity, the foundation of government and society would be undermined. The bill, which was praised by many religious groups, was passed and signed into law by Governor Austin Peay. During this time, the Ten Commandments could typically be found in schoolrooms, and students also engaged in prayer and heard readings from the Bible as part of their moral instruction. This was the law that would gain international attention in the little town of Dayton, Tennessee. In fact, the genesis of the trial had more to do with small-town boosterism than any religious convictions.

John Scopes, the defendant in the trial, was a young teacher in his first year of teaching. He coached high school football in addition to teaching both math and science and reputedly was well liked. Although he is remembered as the biology teacher who challenged the antievolution law, Scopes had only taught biology for one day, when he substituted for the regular biology teacher, and he had not actually taught evolution that day. Although the fact that Scopes had not taught evolution should have resulted in a dismissal of the charges, he never even testified in the trial and the trial was really about the legitimacy of the theory of evolution, not whether John Scopes had violated the law.

One day Scopes was invited to the local drugstore where a few of Dayton's citizens were playfully arguing about Darwin as well as the recently passed Butler Act. They asked Scopes his opinion of the law, and he responded that he didn't think he could teach biology without teaching evolution. At this point the locals showed Scopes a newspaper article describing how the American Civil Liberties Union (ACLU) was looking for a test case to see if the antievolution law was constitutional. All present thought it would be a big boost to the local economy if they could stage the test case in Dayton, with Scopes as the defendant. John Scopes was skeptical but was eventually persuaded to join in the fun. He was arrested for violating the Butler Act but was quickly released so he could play tennis. The ACLU was contacted and the trial was set in motion and took on a life of its own.

The test case was largely controlled by two organizations, the ACLU, which defended Scopes, and the World's Christian Fundamentals Association, a leading organization whose members included many of the most important fundamentalists of the day, including William Jennings Bryan, who volunteered to try the case for the state of Tennessee.

William Jennings Bryan was an unsuccessful Democratic presidential candidate in 1896, 1902, and 1908. A renowned orator, Bryan gained a national reputation and the Democratic nomination in 1896 after making his famous "Cross of Gold" speech, aimed at eliminating the gold standard. Bryan was also an active fundamentalist Christian. After he resigned as Woodrow Wilson's secretary of state, he delivered lectures on the religious circuit. He was staunchly opposed to the teaching of evolution in the schools and a longtime backer of antievolution laws. Bryan was also a populist—a supporter of the common man. He viewed the social implications of Darwinism with alarm. He saw Darwinism not only as an assault on religion but also as an assault on democracy and the common good. Bryan was a master politician and knew how to present his cause to garner maximum publicity. Although Bryan was trained as a lawyer, he had not been in a courtroom in decades.

The ACLU had started as an organization to help pacifists during World War I and had expanded into helping form labor organizations and eventually challenged attacks on civil liberty and academic freedom. One goal of the ACLU's test case was to maximize national publicity.

The ACLU selected Clarence Darrow to defend John Scopes. Darrow was perhaps the best-known trial attorney of his day, defending mobsters and businessmen but also Eugene Debs, the socialist labor leader. Darrow volunteered to help the ACLU defend Scopes, reputedly the only time he ever took a case for free. Darrow was an agnostic and a longtime foe of fundamentalists. It has been suggested that he also harbored a grudge against Bryan for keeping the Republican Party in power by losing three consecutive presidential elections. Like Bryan, Darrow also knew how to garner publicity, and the subject matter of the trial gave him the opportunity to maximize press exposure. Darrow's trial strategy was to put fundamentalism and Bryan on trial. In this, Darrow was at least partially successful, although Bryan won the trial.

The trial took place in a circus-like atmosphere. The local boosters, who had concocted the scheme to get the trial as a business opportunity, took full advantage of the hundreds of reporters and visitors who poured into Dayton. The townspeople set up carnival games and booths selling refreshments and monkey-related souvenirs. People paid to have their photos taken with monkeys and chimps that several opportunists had brought to Dayton for the occasion. The local druggist had a monkey dressed in a suit and bow tie to greet customers. Itinerant evangelists preached on street corners, warning about the evils of Darwinism. Although the crowds were less than the town boosters had hoped for, the international attention definitely put Dayton on the map.

The trial was held in a huge courtroom with 200 spectator seats, and many more people were allowed to stand in the rear of the courtroom. The entire trial was broadcast by a Chicago radio station, WGN, throughout the Midwest. The rest of the nation followed the trial in newspaper headlines and sensational stories. The weather during the trail was sweltering, with temperatures in the courtroom soaring above 100 degrees. Both Bryan and Darrow took off their coats and worked in shirtsleeves.

Darrow's defense team brought a number of scientists who were to serve as expert witnesses about the theory of evolution and the need to include it in high school biology classes. But Darrow's plan to put evolution on trial was stymied by the trial judge who excluded any expert testimony. Bryan's trial strategy—which ultimately proved successful—was to narrow the issue to whether or not Scopes was guilty of violating the Butler Act by teaching evolution. Day by day the entire nation followed the proceedings in the newspapers.

The weight of the spectators proved too much for the old Dayton courthouse and cracks appeared in the ceiling beneath the court-room. The judge decided to move the closing arguments to the out-of-doors benches that had been set up for overflow crowds.

This move allowed a much wider audience to view the end of the trial. In a surprise move, Darrow did not make a traditional closing argument but called Bryan to testify as an expert witness on the Bible. Darrow and Bryan went one-on-one for almost two hours. In the following dialogue, Darrow questioned Bryan about the literal interpretation of the Bible, trying to play him for the fool:

Darrow: "Upon thy belly thou shall go, and dust shalt thou eat all the days of thy life." Do you think that is why the serpent is compelled to crawl up on its belly?

Bryan: I believe that.

Darrow: Have you any idea how the snake went before that time?

Bryan: No, sir.

Darrow: Do you know whether he walked on his tail or not?

Bryan: No, sir, I have no way to know.

The following was an exchange about the seven days described in the Book of Genesis:

Darrow: Have you any idea of the length of the periods?

Bryan: No, I don't.

Darrow: Do you think the sun was made on the fourth day?

Bryan: Yes.

Darrow: And they had evening and morning without the sun?

Bryan: I am simply saying it was a period.

Darrow: They had evening and morning for four periods, without the sun, do you think?

Bryan: I believe in creation, as there told, and if I am not able to ex-plain it, I will accept it.

Bryan had never taken the Bible completely literally, but he must have felt compelled to do so for his supporters. In the end he had to admit that the days in Genesis might be longer than twenty-four hours. Those who supported the teaching of evolution probably came away with the impression that Bryan had been discredited. Those that opposed evolution probably thought he did the best he could. Although the examination made great courtroom drama, it probably changed few minds.

In his final summation to the jury, Darrow asked the jury to convict Scopes so Darrow could appeal the case to a court that could rule the Butler Act unconstitutional. After just a few minutes the jury returned. The jury voted to convict, and the judge promptly fined Scopes $100—the minimum allowed under the statute. The conviction was later overturned, because the judge and not the jury fixed the amount of the fine. Accordingly, there was no appeal, and the Tennessee statute remained on the books. No other teacher was ever charged with a violation of the Tennessee law, which was finally repealed in 1967.

Although the big city press had painted Bryan as a buffoon, his supporters were undeterred. But Bryan died just days after the trial, probably from exhaustion. However, the conflict of evolution versus creationism lived on. Various states allowed—or even required—the teaching of the biblical account of creation alongside evolution or in place of it.

The *Scopes* "Monkey Trial" brought national attention to the battle to allow evolution to be taught in the schools. Although many people know that William Jennings Bryan won a conviction (which was later thrown out on a technicality) against the biology teacher, John T. Scopes, many people assume that the adverse publicity after the trial put an end to the antievolution fight. Those who have watched the movie *Inherit The Wind* about the trial might come away with the conclusion that the trial marked the beginning of the end for antievolution forces. Nothing could be further from the truth.

In fact, the *Scopes* trial triggered a number of southern legislatures to pass antievolution statutes of their own. Although these laws were in force for decades, they were not regularly enforced. Most biology textbooks included a chapter on evolution or at least a few references to it. In some rural communities biology teachers merely refrained from teaching evolution because they knew it violated the religious beliefs of many families. In more urban areas biology teachers did teach evolution but none were prosecuted.

Arkansas was one of the states that passed an antievolution statute. The Arkansas statute, enacted by a state referendum that passed by a vote of nearly 2–1 in 1928, prohibited any state-supported school, college, or university "to teach the theory or doctrine that mankind ascended or descended from a lower order of animals." The statute carried a $500 fine for each violation. Teachers who violated the statute faced firing by their local school boards. Interestingly, there was never a single case in which an Arkansas teacher was charged with violation of the statute. It is possible that the law was never really enforced. However, it is also possible that biology teachers were well aware of the statute and avoided teaching evolution for fear of offending the statute and offending the sensibilities of students, parents, school administrators, and school boards.

More than thirty-five years after the antievolution law was enacted, the Arkansas Education Association wanted a test case to see if the statute would be thrown out. This test case would be *Epperson v. Arkansas,* which reached the U.S. Supreme Court in 1968. Up until this case, the U.S. Supreme Court had never ruled on the constitutionality of antievolution statutes because no court case had made its way up to the Supreme Court.

The Arkansas Education Association was motivated by the fact that the Supreme Court could, in effect, make a ruling banning such statutes that would apply nationwide. If the U.S. Supreme Court ruled that the Arkansas statute banned the teaching of evolution because evolution was contrary to certain religious beliefs, this would violate the Constitution's Establishment Clause. The Court could then go on to declare not only the Arkansas statute but also similar statutes in other states as unconstitutional.

Susan Epperson, the named plaintiff in the test case, was a twenty-four-year-old biology teacher at Central High School in Little Rock, Arkansas. Interestingly, this is the very school that spawned the 1954 case *Brown v. Board of Education,* which outlawed segregated public schools in the United States. Susan Epperson, who was in her second year of teaching at Central High School, agreed to bring a test case against the Arkansas antievolution statute.

In 1965 Central High School adopted a new biology textbook—the most popular high school biology text nationwide. Interestingly, various editions of the textbook had contained references to evolution starting in 1926 but they disappeared until 1964 to help sales in southern states. However, in 1965 the textbook once again included a chapter on evolution, which discussed Charles Darwin's theory of natural selection. The theory of evolution had become the majority theory about how life evolves, but the theory also runs directly counter to the literal interpretation of the Bible, which provides that

God created the Earth and all of the species in six twenty-four-hour periods. Proponents of this view had urged passage of the twenty state statutes that prevented the teaching of evolution in public schools or universities. Of course, some but not all Christians reconcile the Bible and Darwin, arguing that the "days" referred to in the Bible were not literal days but eras.

Susan Epperson, supported by the Arkansas Education Association, brought an action for a declaration that the Arkansas antievolution statute was void and enjoining her dismissal for violation of the statute. They alleged not only an Establishment Clause violation but also a violation of the First Amendment's freedom of speech guarantee. Their position was that the state statute banning the teaching of evolution was a threat to academic freedom.

Although the case did not gain the national attention given the *Scopes* case, Arkansas Attorney General Bruce Bennett did his best to see that it did. Bennett, a potential candidate for governor, requested a two-week trial and evidently planned to put Darwin's theory on trial. The trial judge did not want a repeat of the *Scopes* circus and scheduled only a one-day trial to be held on April Fool's Day 1966. Although Bennett tried his best to inject religion into the trial, his tactics proved unsuccessful.

The Arkansas Chancery Court, in an opinion by Chancellor Murray O. Reed, held that the statute violated the Fourteenth Amendment to the U.S. Constitution. The court noted that this amendment encompasses the prohibitions upon state interference with freedom of speech and thought, which are contained in the First Amendment. Accordingly, he held that the challenged statute was unconstitutional because, in violation of the First Amendment, it "tends to hinder the quest for knowledge, restrict the freedom to learn, and restrain the freedom to teach." In this perspective, the act was an unconstitutional and void restraint upon the freedom of speech guaranteed by the Constitution.

On appeal, the Supreme Court of Arkansas reversed in a two-sentence opinion. It sustained the statute as an exercise of the state's power to specify the curriculum in public schools. It did not address itself to the competing constitutional considerations of the teacher. Epperson and the Arkansas Education Association appealed to the U.S. Supreme Court, which accepted the case.

When the *Epperson* case reached the Supreme Court, the cast of characters had changed. Bruce Bennett, the Arkansas attorney general who appeared at the original trial, was missing. The trial did not win him enough publicity to become governor. In fact, he was voted out of office largely because of the *Epperson* trial. Joe Purcell took his place as attorney general, and his assistant Donald Langston argued the state's case before the Court. Langston reportedly made a less than spirited defense of the law. He did argue that the law was a valid exercise of power by the Arkansas legislature. He also argued that the law was not a violation of the Establishment Clause because it was neutral—both Darwin and the Bible would be kept out of biology classrooms. He also argued that local school boards were in a better position to decide what should be taught in local schools. When questioned why the statute didn't violate the Establishment Clause, Langston had no response.

Although the Court was likely to declare Arkansas's antievolution statute unconstitutional, there were certain problems with the case. At trial there had been no evidence that the law had ever been enforced or that any child was deprived of hearing about the theory of evolution. Likewise, Susan Epperson was not fired for teaching evolution. By the time the case reached the Supreme Court, she no longer lived in the state. Although the Court could have decided there was no real controversy on which to rule, they did rule against the statute.

Justice Fortas wrote the opinion for the Court, and Justice Black wrote a concurring opinion. Fortas wrote that the Court's decision was not due just to the vagueness of the statute . . . [but because of the] "constitutional prohibition of state laws respecting an establishment of religion or prohibiting the free exercise thereof. The overriding fact is that Arkansas' law selects from the body of knowledge a particular segment which it proscribes for the sole reason that it is deemed to conflict with a particular religious doctrine; that is, with a particular interpretation of the Book of Genesis by a particular religious group."

Justice Fortas marshaled almost a dozen prior precedents in which the Court had struck down laws or practices that favored Christianity. The Court had already struck down school release-time programs, organized prayer in the schools, and Bible reading in the schools concluding, "These precedents inevitably determine the result in the present case. The State's undoubted right to prescribe the curriculum for its public schools does not carry with it the right to prohibit, on pain of criminal penalty, the teaching of a scientific theory or doctrine where that prohibition is based upon reasons that violate the First Amendment. It is much too late to argue that the State may impose upon the teachers in its schools any conditions that it chooses, however restrictive they may be of constitutional guarantees."

Fortas then discussed the religious motives behind the law and traced its origin back to the *Scopes* case. He wrote that there could be no doubt that Arkansas had sought to prevent its teachers from discussing the theory of evolution because it was contrary to the belief of some citizens that the Book of Genesis must be the exclusive source of doctrine as to the origin of man. He wrote that it was clear that fundamentalist sectarian conviction was and is the law's reason for existence. Its antecedent, Tennessee's "monkey law," candidly stated its purpose: to make it unlawful "to teach any theory that denies the story of the Divine Creation of man as taught in the Bible, and to teach instead that man has descended from a lower order of animals." He suggested that the sensational publicity attendant upon the *Scopes* trial induced Arkansas to adopt less explicit language. The Arkansas statute differed from the law in the *Scopes* case by eliminating Tennessee's reference to "the story of the Divine Creation of man" as taught in the Bible. Fortas argued that there still was no doubt that the motivation for the law was the same—to suppress the teaching of a theory, which, it was thought, "denied" the divine creation of man.

Fortas also concluded that Arkansas's law couldn't be defended as an act of religious neutrality. Arkansas did not seek to excise from the curricula of its schools and universities all discussion of the origin of man. The law's target was the theory of evolution, because of its supposed conflict with the biblical account, literally read. For this reason, the Arkansas antievolution statute law was contrary to the First Amendment and in violation of the Fourteenth Amendment to the Constitution.

At its core, the *Epperson* decision reasoned that the ban was enacted entirely to "aid, foster, or promote one religious theory" over another and thereby offended the Establishment Clause of the First Amendment. Arkansas could not require that its school curriculum be shaped to conform to the beliefs of the Christian religion. After the U.S. Supreme Court prohibited states from banning the teaching of evolution in *Epperson,* creationists started labeling their body of information supporting the biblical version of creation as "creation science."

Although school prayer cases make headline news, curriculum issues draw less attention but have also created their share of controversy. Religious parents are extremely concerned about the content of school curricula, whereas nonreligious parents get alarmed when a school curriculum contains religious content. No issue has generated more controversy than the teaching of evolution. Many Christians deny the validity of Darwin's theory of evolution. These parents believe in the literal truth of the biblical account of the creation, and they object strongly to the teaching of evolution in the schools. On the other hand, many parents strongly object to the teaching of the biblical account as the inappropriate teaching of religious dogma in the public schools. This is one issue where there is little middle ground. Today the pendulum has clearly swung in favor of evolution.

Although some people may assume that the antievolution issue has long been settled, in fact the battle pitting the theory of evolution against the biblical account is as contentious as ever. Individual school districts and state governments continue to try to devise ways to allow the teaching of creationism in the schools. The impact of the antievolution cases is detailed in Chapter 4.

Lynch v. Donnelly

Although the First Amendment's Establishment Clause mandates separation of church and state, there has always been some intermingling. Americans have always been a religious people, and individuals do not discard their religious beliefs when they assume public office. In times of war and crisis, individuals often invoke divine guidance. Many political speeches have had overt or subtle references to Scripture. Over the years the government has adopted certain practices that reflect the religious beliefs of the wider society. Our currency bears the motto, "In God We Trust." Patriotic songs include references to God. Government offices close on the Christian Sabbath as well as Christmas Day. On the other hand, Bible reading in school goes too far. Where the line between permissible and impermissible entanglement with religion is hard to draw. In 1984, in *Lynch v. Donnelly,* the U.S. Supreme Court considered a case involving Christmas decorations. Although the decorations only cost about $200, the decision triggered a bitter dissent and remains one of the most controversial religion cases ever decided.

The facts in the case were simple. Each year, in cooperation with the downtown retail merchants' association, the city of Pawtucket, Rhode Island, erected a Christmas display as part of its observance of the Christmas holiday season. The display was situated in a park owned by a nonprofit organization and located in the heart of the shopping district. The display was essentially like those to be found in hundreds of towns or cities across the nation—often on public grounds—during the Christmas season. The Pawtucket display included many of the figures and decorations traditionally associated with Christmas, including, among other things, a Santa Claus house, reindeer pulling Santa's sleigh, candy-striped poles, a Christmas tree, carolers, cutout figures representing such characters as a clown, an elephant, and a teddy bear, hundreds of colored lights, a large banner that reads "Season's Greetings," and a crèche. All components of this display were owned by the city.

The crèche, which had been included in the display for forty or more years, consisted of the traditional figures, including the infant Jesus, Mary and Joseph, angels, shepherds, kings, and animals, all ranging in height from five inches to five feet. In 1973, when the crèche was acquired, it cost the city $1,365; at the time of trial it was valued at $200. The erection and dismantling of the crèche cost the city about $20 per year and nominal expenses were incurred in lighting the crèche.

A few Pawtucket residents and individual members of the Rhode Island affiliate of the ACLU, as well as the national ACLU, brought an action in the U.S. District Court for Rhode Island, challenging the city's inclusion of the crèche in the annual Christmas display. The district court held that the city's inclusion of the crèche in the display violated the Establishment Clause. The district court found that, by including the crèche in the Christmas display, the city had "tried to endorse and promulgate religious beliefs" and that "erection of the crèche has the real and substantial effect of affiliating the City with the Christian beliefs that the crèche represents." This "appearance of official sponsorship," it believed, "confers more than a remote and incidental benefit on Christianity." Last, although the court acknowledged the absence of administrative entanglement, it found that excessive entanglement has been fostered as a result of the political divisiveness of including the crèche in the celebration.

The district court permanently enjoined the city from including the crèche in the display. The city appealed the decision, and a divided panel of the Court of Appeals for the First Circuit affirmed. The city appealed to the U.S. Supreme Court, which reversed, finding in favor of the city.

Chief Justice Burger penned the majority opinion himself. In the opinion he explained that although the Court had held that the purpose of the Establishment and Free Exercise Clauses of the First Amendment was to prevent, as far as possible, the intrusion of either the church or the state into the "precincts of the other," at the same time the Court had also recognized that total separation was not possible in an absolute sense. In every Establishment Clause case, the Court had to reconcile the inescapable tension between the objective of preventing unnecessary intrusion of either the church or the state upon the other, and the reality that, as the Court has so often noted, total separation of the two is not possible.

Burger noted that while the Religion Clauses were often viewed as erecting a wall between church and state, the concept of a wall of separation might be a useful figure of speech but the metaphor itself was not a wholly accurate description of the practical aspects of the relationship that in fact exists between church and state.

Burger then quoted some *dicta* from other cases that observed that "the Constitution requires complete separation of church and state; it affirmatively mandates accommodation, not merely tolerance, of all religions, and forbids hostility toward any."

To bolster his "accommodationist" argument, Burger marshaled some historical facts about the Founding Fathers. He cited as his first example the fact that in the very week that Congress approved the Establishment Clause as part of the Bill of Rights, it also enacted legislation providing for paid chaplains for the House and Senate. Burger argued that this clearly illustrated that neither the draftsmen of the Constitution, who were members of the First Congress, nor the Congress of 1789 saw any establishment problem in the employment of congressional chaplains to offer daily prayers in the Congress, a practice that continues today. It would be difficult to identify a more striking example of the accommodation of religious belief intended by the framers. Burger also cited as evidence the day of Thanksgiving that was celebrated as a religious holiday to give thanks for the bounties of Nature as gifts from God.

Executive orders and other official announcements of presidents and of the Congress have proclaimed both Christmas and Thanksgiving national holidays as well as days when federal employees are released from duties. He also cited the national motto "In God We Trust," printed on our currency, the words "One nation under God," in the pledge of allegiance to the American flag, and the hundreds of oil paintings with religious themes to be found in public galleries as evidence of government accommodation of religion.

The chief justice then agreed that the city of Pawtucket had demonstrated that inclusion of the crèche was in fact "secular" rather than "religious."

The chief justice reasoned that the display of the crèche was no more an advancement or endorsement of religion than the congressional and executive recognition of the origins of the holiday itself as "Christ's Mass," and concluded that the city had a secular purpose for including the crèche:

> The display engenders a friendly community spirit of good will in keeping with the season. The crèche may well have special meaning to those whose faith includes the celebration of religious masses, but none who sense the origins of the Christmas celebration would fail to be aware of its religious implications. That the display brings people into the central city, and serves commercial interests and benefits merchants and their employees, does not, as the dissent points out, determine the character of the display.

The chief justice concluded by saying that, notwithstanding the religious significance of the crèche to some individuals, the city of Pawtucket had not violated the Establishment Clause of the First Amendment.

Justice Brennan wrote a blistering dissent, heavy on both historical facts and case precedents. Brennan was frankly astounded not only by the majority's conclusion but by its reasoning or rather, in his view, the lack of it.

In Brennan's mind the majority opinion simply could not be squared with the Court's prior cases. He accused the majority of pretending that the otherwise secular setting of Pawtucket's nativity scene somehow diluted the crèche's religious meaning. Nor did he accept the argument that the city's annual display reflected nothing more than an "acknowledgment" of our shared national heritage. He noted that during the trial the city's mayor's had testified that for him, as well as others in the city, including the crèche in its display would serve to "keep Christ in Christmas."

Finally, and most importantly, the crèche was somehow rendered nonreligious because it appeared near Santa Claus and the Christmas tree: "I refuse to accept the notion implicit in today's decision that non-Christians would find that the religious content of the crèche is eliminated by the fact that it appears as part of the city's otherwise secular celebration of the Christmas holiday."

Brennan pointed out that unlike such secular figures as Santa Claus, reindeer, and carolers, the nativity scene represented far more than a mere "traditional" symbolism for Christians: "Contrary to the Court's suggestion, the crèche is far from a mere representation of a 'particular historic religious event' . . . . To suggest, as the Court does, that such a symbol is merely 'traditional' and therefore no different from Santa's house or reindeer is not only offensive to those for whom the crèche has profound significance, but insulting to those who insist for religious or personal reasons that the story of Christ is in no sense a part of 'history' nor an unavoidable element of our national 'heritage.'"

The *Lynch* case was probably wrongly decided but remains the law today. Governments may display the crèche as long as it is displayed alongside other traditional holiday displays like Frosty the Snowman, the Cinnamon Bear, or Santa. Of course, this restriction only applies to the government—private individuals and businesses may display any holiday decorations they prefer, religious or not. Chapter 4 details how traditional religious symbols and practices have fared in later court cases.

Engel v. Vitale (The "Regents School Prayer Case")

The issue of religion in the schools proved to be one of the most contentious social issues in twentieth-century America, and the issue promises to remain contentious well into the twenty-first. Public school is one place where families of very different backgrounds come together. These families often have different values and also different religious beliefs. School plays a large role in shaping children's social values and worldview, and parents and others are rightfully concerned about the messages that children receive in the classroom. Although some parents object to any religious observance in the classroom, others feel that excluding religious activities and observances creates a "godless" atmosphere that has contributed to the moral decline of the citizenry.

The issue of religion in the schools has also become an important national political issue, and senators, representatives, and presidential candidates have taken an interest in the topic, because it is an issue of prime interest to voters. Evidence suggests that Americans are apathetic and not very interested in political issues. Fewer than half of all eligible voters vote in most elections. Many Americans perceive that they have little control over decisions made in Washington, D.C. However, Americans do get more concerned over local issues that directly affect themselves and their families. No issue hits closer to home than the issue of religion in the schools.

This issue of religion in the schools has a strong polarizing effect on society, with many individuals believing that religion has no place in public schools, whereas other individuals believe that its exclusion ignores the reality that Americans are a religious people. The first group wants to maintain the wall of separation, erected by the courts, that has banned school prayer, Christian observations, and the teaching of "creation science" in the schools. The second group wants to return to school prayer and Christmas festivals, and many also want the teaching of the biblical account of creation to be given equal treatment when teachers discuss the theory of evolution. Many Americans favor a constitutional amendment guaranteeing school prayer in public schools.

One of the most important and far-reaching cases ever heard by the Supreme Court was *Engel v. Vitale* (1962). This case, decided by a 6–3 vote, declared unconstitutional a nondenominational school prayer written by the New York State Board of Regents. The nondenominational prayer had been composed to be inoffensive to those who were compelled to recite it. The short, innocuous-sounding prayer was written by the administrative body overseeing quality in the New York State public schools: "Almighty God, we acknowledge our dependence upon Thee, and we beg Thy blessings upon us, our parents, our teachers and our Country."

The author of this book remembers reciting the prayer in public school. Before the regents' prayer was introduced, children in that school recited the Lord's Prayer, including the last sentence, which is typically not recited by Roman Catholics. Of course, non-Christians do not recite Christian prayers at home. When these children came to school, they recited the prayers along with everyone else.

The New York State Board of Regents composed the prayer, which they recommended and published as a part of their "Statement on Moral and Spiritual Training in the Schools," saying: "We believe that this Statement will be subscribed to by all men and women of good will, and we call upon all of them to aid in giving life to our program." The New York State Regents' prayer no doubt was written to be more "nondenominational" so it wouldn't be as offensive to the parents of non-Christian students.

Shortly after the practice of reciting the regents' prayer was adopted by the New Hyde Park, New York, School District, the parents of ten pupils brought this action in a New York State court insisting that use of this official prayer in the public schools was contrary to the beliefs, religions, or religious practices of both themselves and their children. Among other things, these parents challenged the constitutionality of both the state law authorizing the school district to direct the use of prayer in public schools and the school district's regulation ordering the recitation of this prayer as violations of the First Amendment's Establishment Clause.

The state trial court upheld the power of the state of New York to use the regents' prayer as a part of the daily procedures of its public schools so long as the schools did not compel any pupil to join in the prayer over her or his parents' objection. The New York Court of Appeals, the state's highest court, agreed that the prayer was proper, although two judges dissented.

The parents appealed the decision to the U.S. Supreme Court, which accepted the case. The majority opinion, written by Justice Hugo Black, ruled the prayer a violation of the Establishment Clause. Four other justices joined in his opinion. Justice Douglas wrote a concurring opinion, two justices dissented, and two took no part in the decision. Black's opinion noted that there could be no doubt that daily recitation of the regents' prayer was a religious activity. Indeed, the Board of Regents conceded the religious nature of prayer, but sought to distinguish this prayer because it was based on our spiritual heritage.

The parents contended, among other things, that the state laws requiring or permitting use of the regents' prayer violated the Establishment Clause because that prayer was composed by governmental officials as a part of a governmental program to promote religious beliefs. The majority agreed with the parents: "We think that the constitutional prohibition against laws respecting an establishment of religion must at least mean that, in this country, it is no part of the business of government to compose official prayers for any group of the American people to recite as a part of a religious program carried on by government."

The majority opinion went on to review the origin of the Establishment Clause and the purpose behind it. The majority noted that by the time of the adoption of the Constitution there was a widespread awareness among many Americans of the dangers of a union of church and state. These people knew, some of them from bitter personal experience, that one of the greatest dangers to the freedom of the individual to worship in his own way lay in the government's placing its official stamp of approval upon one particular kind of prayer or one particular form of religious service.

The Court still had to confront the state's defense that the regents' prayer was permissible because it was nondenominational. The state argued that although the prayer was religious, it didn't promote any religion in particular. Christians and Jews alike could recite the prayer without feeling uncomfortable. The state also argued that even those few who might still feel uncomfortable with any prayer were not required to recite the prayer; students could remain silent or even be excused from the room. The Court was unimpressed by these defenses. The Court concluded that neither the fact that the prayer may be denominationally neutral nor the fact that it was voluntary cured the Establishment Clause violation.

The Court noted that the requirements under the Establishment Clause are even more exacting than the requirements under the Free Exercise Clause and explained the more exacting requirements under the former:

"Although these two clauses may, in certain instances, overlap, they forbid two quite different kinds of governmental encroachment upon religious freedom. The Establishment Clause, unlike the Free Exercise Clause, does not depend upon any showing of direct governmental compulsion and is violated by the enactment of laws which establish an official religion whether those laws operate directly to coerce nonobservant individuals or not . . ."

The Court reminded readers that the Founders knew all too well the evils of government entanglement with religion: "a union of government and religion tends to destroy government and to degrade religion . . . whenever government had allied itself with one particular form of religion, the inevitable result had been that it had incurred the hatred, disrespect and even contempt of those who held contrary beliefs [and that] many people had lost their respect for any religion that had relied upon the support of government to spread its faith. . . . Another purpose of the Establishment Clause rested upon an awareness . . . that governmentally established religions and religious persecutions go hand in hand."

The *Engel* case is an interesting decision for a number of reasons. Although six judges agreed with the result, there was one dissent and two justices did not participate. Generally, decisions with less than the full Court participating create a less powerful precedent. This case proved the exception to the rule: it created a powerful precedent for the Supreme Court and lower federal and state courts as well.

The case was a virtual bombshell triggering banner headlines worldwide. The political firestorm the case brought about should not have been unexpected. Prayer and Bible reading were part of an established routine in many if not most schools, and many people couldn't comprehend why the Court would ban the practice if a majority of the community wanted it. In fact, a majority of Americans might have wanted prayer in the public schools. However, constitutional protections are not for the majority, they are present to protect minority interests.

Generations of Americans had grown up with school prayer. Religious Americans took the decision as a personal rebuke. The decision also had a tremendous polarizing political effect. Those who supported the rights of minorities—especially non-Christians—hailed the decision as progressive. They pointed out that the decision did not eliminate any students' right to pray silently or aloud in school. It merely banned public schools from composing and compelling the recitation of prayers. Critics of the decision labeled the court and justices as "godless communists."

A year later the Supreme Court heard another major school prayer case, *Abington School District v. Schempp* (1963), and again declared that organized prayer had no place in the public schools. The case went even further than *Engle v. Vitale,* decided the prior year. That case concerned a prayer penned by an administrative body. The 1963 school prayer case banned both the recitation of the Lord's Prayer and reading of the Bible in public schools.

As in the prior year, the decision caused a furor. This was fueled in part because one of the companion cases before the high court, *Murray v. Curlett,* was brought by Madalyn Murray, an avowed atheist, communist, and Castro supporter. The timing could not have been worse. The United States had just emerged from the Cuban Missile

Crisis—a showdown between President Kennedy and Soviet Premier Nikita Khrushchev over the placement of hostile missiles in Cuba— just 90 miles from Florida. President Kennedy had just committed troops in South Vietnam to combat communist incursions. Many were ready to believe the school prayer case was more evidence of godless, communist influences within the United States.

Opposition to the banning of school prayer was swift. Criticism was leveled at the Supreme Court's opinion from politicians and the pulpit. Groups such as the right-wing John Birch Society organized a campaign to impeach Chief Justice Earl Warren who wrote the majority opinion in the school prayer case. More seriously, an amendment to allow school prayer was submitted before Congress. In fact, this amendment, or a similar one, to allow school prayer has been introduced in almost every Congress for twenty-five years, but none has ever come close to being enacted. Despite the ruling, many public schools—especially in the South—continued to have either Bible reading or a school prayer at the start of the day in defiance of the Court's ban. Such practices continue to this day.

Application of the President and Directors of Georgetown College

Many devout individuals have religious objections to blood transfusions, and others believe that all medical conditions can be cured through faith and prayer. On the other hand, doctors and hospitals have an ethical obligation to save lives, and the government has a similar interest. In the following case, these interests came into conflict.

Attorneys for Georgetown Hospital applied for an emergency writ at 4:00 P.M., September 17, 1963, seeking relief from the action of the U.S. District Court for the District of Columbia denying the hospital's application for permission to administer blood transfusions to an emergency patient. The application stated that "Mrs. Jesse E. Jones is presently a patient at Georgetown University Hospital," "she is in extremis," and according to the attending physician, "blood transfusions are necessary immediately in order to save her life," and neither the patient nor her husband would grant consent to the blood transfusions. The patient and her husband based their refusal on their religious beliefs as Jehovah's Witnesses. The order the Georgetown

Hospital sought provided that the attending physicians might administer such transfusions to Mrs. Jones as would be "necessary to save her life."

The hospital's application for the order was filed with the U.S. District Court for the District of Columbia, a federal trial court. The application sought a decree to determine the legal rights and liabilities among the hospital and its doctors and the patient, Mrs. Jones, and her husband. The treatment proposed by the hospital was not a single transfusion but a series of transfusions. The hospital doctors sought a court determination before undertaking either this course of action or some alternative. The temporary order issued by the district court judge was more limited than the order the hospital asked for, in that the phrase *to save her life* was added, thus limiting the transfusions in both time and number. Such a temporary order to preserve the life of the patient was necessary if the cause were not to be mooted by the death of the patient. Neither the patient, her husband, nor the hospital, however, undertook further legal proceedings during the succeeding days while blood was being administered to the patient.

Mrs. Jones was initially brought to the hospital by her husband for emergency care, having lost two-thirds of her body's blood supply from a ruptured ulcer. She had no personal physician and relied solely on the hospital staff. Her care was solely the responsibility of the hospital. It appeared that the patient, age twenty-five, mother of a seven-month-old child, and her husband were both Jehovah's Witnesses, a sect whose teachings, according to their interpretation, prohibited the injection of blood into the body. When death without a blood transfusion became imminent, the hospital sought the advice of counsel, who applied to the district court in the name of the hospital for permission to administer blood. Judge Tamm of the district court denied the application, and counsel immediately applied to Judge Skelly Wright, who, as a member of the court of appeals, could issue a writ ordering the district court to issue the order compelling the blood transfusions.

Judge Wright called the hospital by telephone and spoke with Dr. Westura, chief medical resident, who confirmed the representations made by the hospital's lawyers. The judge, together with the hospital's lawyer, proceeded to the hospital, where the judge spoke to Mr. Jones, the husband of the patient. He advised the judge that, on religious grounds, he would not approve a blood transfusion for his wife. He said, however, that if the judge ordered the transfusion, the responsibility was not his. The judge advised Mr. Jones to obtain legal counsel immediately. He went to the telephone and returned in ten or fifteen minutes to advise that he had taken the matter up with his church and that he had decided that he did not want to hire a lawyer.

The judge asked permission of Mr. Jones to see his wife, and he agreed. Prior to going into the patient's room, the judge again conferred with Dr. Westura and several other doctors assigned to the case. All confirmed that the patient would die without blood and that there was a better than 50 percent chance of saving her life with it. Unanimously, they strongly recommended it. The judge walked into the patient's room. Her appearance confirmed the urgency of her condition. The judge tried to communicate with her, advising her again as to what the doctors had said. Her only audible reply was, "Against my will." The judge concluded that the woman was not in a mental condition to make a decision. He explained later that he was reluctant to press her because of the seriousness of her medical condition and because he also believed that to suggest repeatedly the imminence of death without blood might place a strain on her religious convictions. The judge asked Mrs. Jones whether she would oppose the blood transfusion if the court allowed it. She indicated, as best he could make out, that it would not then be her responsibility.

The judge returned to the doctors' room where some ten to twelve doctors were congregated, along with the patient's husband and the lawyer for the hospital. The president of Georgetown University, Father Bunn, appeared and pleaded with Mr. Jones to authorize the hospital to save his wife's life with a blood transfusion. Mr. Jones replied that the Scriptures said that we should not drink blood, and consequently his religion prohibited transfusions. The doctors explained to Mr. Jones that a blood transfusion is totally different from drinking blood in that the blood physically goes into a different part and through a different process in the body. Mr. Jones was unmoved. At that point the judge signed the order allowing the hospital to administer such transfusions as the doctors should determine were necessary to save Mrs. Jones's life, despite the couple's religious objections to the blood transfusions.

Later, the judge wrote an opinion about the incident that has become the leading case in the area, *Application of the President and Directors of Georgetown College.* In explaining his reasoning, Judge

Wright thought it useful to state what this case does not involve. He noted that the case did not involve a person who, for religious or other reasons, had refused to seek medical attention. It did not involve a disputed medical judgment or a dangerous or crippling operation. Nor did it involve the delicate question of saving the newborn in preference to the mother. Mrs. Jones sought medical attention and placed on the hospital the legal responsibility for her proper care. In its dilemma, not of its own making, the hospital sought judicial direction.

The judge then reviewed prior precedents. He concluded that these precedents established that the courts can order compulsory medical treatment of children for any serious illness or injury and that adults, sick or well, also can be required to submit to compulsory treatment or prophylaxis, at least for contagious diseases. The case law revealed that there are no religious exemptions from these orders.

Although there was no sick child or contagious disease in the case of Mrs. Jones, the judge felt that the sick child cases might provide persuasive analogies, because Mrs. Jones was in extremis and hardly compos mentis at the time in question; she was as little able to decide competently for herself as any child would be. Under the circumstances, it may well be the duty of a court of general jurisdiction, such as the U.S. District Court for the District of Columbia, to assume the responsibility of guardianship for her, as for a child, at least to the extent of authorizing treatment to save her life. And since under the law a parent has no power to forbid the saving of a child's life, the husband of the patient in this case had no right to order the doctors to treat his wife in a way so that she would die.

The judge also argued that the child cases point up another consideration. The patient, twenty-five years old, was the mother of a seven-month-old child. The state, as *parens patriae*, will not allow a parent to abandon a child, and so it should not allow the patient to effectively commit suicide, which would result in a voluntary abandonment of her child. The patient had a responsibility to the community to care for her infant. Thus the people had an interest in preserving the life of this mother.

The judge then considered the legality of refusing medical treatment as a form of suicide. He noted that some have argued that an individual's liberty to control himself and his life extends even to the liberty to end his life. Thus, "in those states where attempted suicide has been made lawful by statute or the lack of one, the refusal of necessary medical aid to one's self, whether equal to or less than attempted suicide, must be conceded to be lawful." And, conversely, it would follow that where attempted suicide is illegal by the common law or by statute, a person may not be allowed to refuse necessary medical assistance when death is likely to ensue without it. Only quibbles about the distinction between misfeasance and nonfeasance, or the specific intent necessary to be guilty of attempted suicide, could be raised against this latter conclusion.

The judge reasoned that if self-homicide is a crime, there is no exception to the law's command for those who believe the crime to be divinely ordained. The Mormon cases in the Supreme Court involving the unlawfulness of polygamy establish that there is no religious exception to criminal laws and that a religiously inspired suicide attempt would be within the law's authority to prevent. But the judge noted that whether attempted suicide is a crime is in doubt in some jurisdictions, including the District of Columbia where Georgetown Hospital is located.

The judge however pointed out that although refusal of medical treatment could amount to suicide, in Mrs. Jones's case it might not do so because Mrs. Jones did not want to die. She voluntarily came to the hospital as a patient seeking medical help. Death, to Mrs. Jones, was not a religiously commanded goal but an unwanted side effect of a religious scruple. There was no question here of interfering with one whose religious convictions counsel his death, like the Buddhist monks who set themselves afire. Nor was this a case that involved a question of whether the state should intervene to reweigh the relative values of life and death after the individual has weighed them for himself and found he or she no longer wanted to live. Mrs. Jones wanted to live.

Finally, the judge's opinion looked at the position of the doctors and the hospital that had a responsibility to treat Mrs. Jones. The judge pointed out that the hospital doctors had the choice of administering the proper treatment or letting Mrs. Jones die in the hospital bed, thus exposing themselves, and the hospital, to the risk of civil and criminal liability in either case. It was not certain at the time that Mrs. Jones had any authority to put the hospital and its doctors to this impossible choice. The normal principle that an adult patient directs her doctors is based on notions of commercial contract, which may have less relevance to life-or-death emergencies. It is not clear under either the law or medical ethics that a patient can command her doctor to treat her under limitations that would produce death.

The patient's lawyer suggested that this authority is part of constitutionally protected liberty. However, the judge concluded that neither the principle that life and liberty are inalienable rights, nor the principle of liberty of religion, provides an easy answer to the question whether the state can prevent martyrdom. Moreover, Mrs. Jones had no wish to be a martyr. And her religion merely prevented her consent to a transfusion. If the law undertook the responsibility of authorizing the transfusion without her consent, no problem would be raised with respect to her religious practice. Thus, the effect of the order was to preserve for Mrs. Jones the life she wanted without sacrifice of her religious beliefs.

The judge's final and compelling reason for granting the emergency writ was that a life hung in the balance. There simply was no time for research and reflection. The judge had visited the hospital and had to make an on-the-spot decision. Without the blood transfusion, Mrs. Jones's death was just a few minutes away. At the time, the judge was unsure whether the law required him to order the transfusion or not. He determined to act on the side of life.

As this case illustrates, religious beliefs often come into conflict with medical treatments. A sizable number of devout individuals believe that Scripture bars certain procedures such as blood transfusions. Others believe that prayer alone is sufficient to heal themselves and their families and they refuse to use doctors and hospitals or even get inoculations or let their children get inoculations. These beliefs obviously run squarely against modern scientific medicine and medical ethics. Most states require children to get shots before they are allowed to attend public schools in order to protect public health. Some states have granted religious exemptions to these parents although it may put the children and the community at risk of an epidemic.

The case also illustrates that there are other areas where religious beliefs can come into conflict with both the law and medicine. Although attempted suicide is a crime in many states, it is not clear if failing to take lifesaving medicine would also be a crime. When a parent commits this type of suicide, it might also constitute child abandonment, which is against the law. When parents refuse medical treatment for their children and rely on faith healing, a state protective agency may charge the parents with neglect of their child.

Families, doctors, and hospitals face a similar dilemma when a family member is in a coma or is in a persistent vegetative state and is kept alive artificially by life support machines. In the past it was unclear if the hospital staff or the family would be committing homicide by unplugging the life support machinery. Today the issue is often resolved by "medical advance directives." These are legal documents executed in advance by patients that determine how these life-and-death issues will be handled. The advance directive could direct doctors to disconnect life support if there was no hope of recovery. The advance directives can also give a family member or friend the responsibility for making this decision. Some of these issues are discussed Chapter 4, which examines the legacy of the Georgetown Hospital case.

Employment Division v. Smith

Although practitioners of mainline religions have faced little restriction in their practice, members of minority faiths in number in the United States, such as the Amish, Christian Scientists, Jehovah's Witnesses, and those who practice non-European religions have faced more problems in free exercise of their faith.

A good example of the problems encountered by members of smaller religious groups are Native Americans who utilize peyote, a controlled substance, as part of their religious ritual. In fact, an Oregon case in 1990 made its way to the U.S. Supreme Court, *Employment Division v. Smith.* In *Smith,* the Court considered a Free Exercise Clause claim brought by members of the Native American Church who were denied unemployment benefits when they lost their jobs because they had used peyote.

Oregon law prohibited the knowing or intentional possession of a controlled substance unless the substance had been prescribed by a medical practitioner. The Oregon statute defined a controlled substance as a drug classified in Schedules I–V of the Federal Controlled Substances Act. Schedule I contains the drug peyote, a hallucinogen derived from the plant *Lophophora williamsii Lemaire.*

Alfred Smith and Galen Black were fired from their jobs with a private drug rehabilitation organization because they ingested peyote for sacramental purposes at a ceremony of the Native American Church, of which both were members. When the respondents applied to the Oregon Employment Division for unemployment compensation, they were denied benefits because they had been discharged for work-related "misconduct." Smith and Black went to court to secure the unemployment benefits, and the Oregon Court of Appeals reversed that determination, holding that the denial of benefits violated respondents' free exercise rights under the First Amendment. The state appealed the decision to the Oregon Supreme Court, but that court also found for Smith and Black, reasoning that the criminality of respondents' peyote use was irrelevant to resolution of their constitutional claim because the criminal misconduct was inadequate to justify the burden that disqualification imposed on respondents' religious practice.

Oregon appealed to the Supreme Court. The Court did not initially hear the case because the Oregon courts never established whether "religiously inspired" use of peyote was actually illegal under Oregon law. The case was remanded (sent back) from the U.S. Supreme Court so the Oregon Supreme Court could answer this question. The Oregon Supreme Court concluded that although religiously inspired use of peyote was illegal under the Oregon statute, the prohibition in the statute was invalid under the Free Exercise Clause of the First Amendment. The state of Oregon again appealed to the U.S. Supreme Court, which agreed to hear the case.

The precise issue before the Court was whether the Free Exercise Clause of the First Amendment permitted the State of Oregon to label religiously inspired peyote use as a criminal violation and thus permit the state to deny unemployment benefits to persons dismissed from their jobs because of such religiously inspired use.

Justice Scalia wrote the majority opinion for the Court. He first examined the Court's traditional distinction in its Free Exercise jurisprudence between religious "belief" and religious "practice." He pointed out that the "exercise of religion" often involves not only belief and profession but the performance of (or abstention from) physical acts: assembling with others for a worship service, participating in sacramental use of bread and wine, proselytizing, abstaining from certain foods or certain modes of transportation.

Scalia opined that he thought that a state would be prohibiting the free exercise of religion if it sought to ban such acts or abstentions only when they are engaged in for religious reasons or only because of the religious belief that they display. It would doubtless be unconstitutional, for example, to ban the casting of statues that are to be used for worship purposes or to prohibit bowing down before a golden calf.

He went on to distinguish Smith's and Black's use of peyote. They had argued (and convinced the Oregon court) that their religious motivation for using peyote placed them beyond the reach of the state's criminal drug law. Oregon's law, unlike the laws in about half of the states, did not allow a dispensation for peyote used in religious practice. Scalia reasoned that at a most basic level Smith and Black were arguing that individuals should be free to violate any law, so long as the individual is following the dictates of his or her religion.

Scalia forcefully pointed out that the Court had never held that an individual's religious beliefs excuse him from compliance with an otherwise valid law prohibiting conduct that the state is free to regulate. On the contrary, the record of more than a century of our free exercise jurisprudence contradicts that proposition, citing *Gobitis* for the proposition that "[c]onscientious scruples have not, in the course of the long struggle for religious toleration, relieved the individual from obedience to a general law not aimed at the promotion or restriction of religious beliefs. The mere possession of religious convictions which contradict the relevant concerns of a political society does not relieve the citizen from the discharge of political responsibilities."

Justice Scalia noted that the Court applied this principle to a Free Exercise case in *Reynolds v. United States* (1879), in which the Court rejected the claim that criminal laws against polygamy could not be constitutionally applied to Mormons because their religion commanded the practice. The *Reynolds* case established the "beliefs and practice distinction: while laws cannot interfere with mere religious belief and opinions, they may interfere with practices."

Subsequent decisions have consistently held that the right of free exercise does not relieve an individual of the obligation to comply with a "valid and neutral law of general applicability on the ground that the law proscribes (or prescribes) conduct that his religion prescribes (or proscribes)."

Smith and Black also argued that even though exemption from generally applicable criminal laws need not automatically be extended to religiously motivated actors, at least the claim for a religious exemption must be evaluated under the balancing test set forth in *Sherbert v. Verner* (1963). Under the *Sherbert* test, governmental actions that substantially burden a religious practice must be justified by a "compelling" governmental interest. In other words, Black and Smith argued that a court should imply a religious exemption whenever the government cannot find a compelling reason for burdening or banning the religious practice. Scalia was unwilling to apply this sort of balancing to a criminal statute.

Scalia argued that it would be impractical to use the "compelling state interest" only when the conduct prohibited is central to the individual's religion, because there was no clear principle of law or logic that can be brought to bear to contradict a believer's assertion that a particular act is central to his personal faith. The religious could merely assert that their conduct was religiously motivated to escape punishment for violating the law. Scalia viewed this with alarm, saying

> Any society adopting such a system would be courting anarchy, but that danger increases in direct proportion to the society's diversity of religious beliefs, and its determination to coerce or suppress none of them. . . . The rule respondents favor would open the prospect of constitutionally required religious exemptions from civic obligations of almost every conceivable kind—ranging from compulsory military service, to [health and safety regulations, manslaughter and child neglect laws, compulsory vaccination laws, drug laws, and traffic laws; social welfare legislation such as minimum wage laws, child labor laws, animal cruelty laws, environmental protection laws; and laws providing for equality of opportunity for the races]. The First Amendment's protection of religious liberty does not require this.

In fact, most free exercise claims will be made against "valid and neutral" state and local laws. Accordingly, the *Smith* case has the potential to severely limit the use of the Free Exercise Clause to challenge any state or local law.

The majority opinion concluded by noting that it was not surprising that a number of states have made an exception to their drug laws for sacramental peyote use, even though Oregon had not. If Smith and Black had lived in one of these other states, they would have received unemployment checks despite the peyote use. However, Scalia was unwilling to say that such an exemption was mandated by the U.S. Constitution.

Prior to *Smith* the Court would have employed a balancing test asking whether Oregon's drug law substantially burdened a religious practice and, if it did, whether the burden was justified by a compelling government interest. However, the Court was obviously uncomfortable condoning a "nonmainstream" religion's sacramental use of a controlled substance. Although commentators now view *Smith* as a religious Free Exercise case, the Court may have viewed it more as a "drug case."

If the Court suspected that its *Smith* decision would have little impact, it was sorely wrong. The Court was vilified by a wide variety of religious groups with a fervor not seen since the school prayer cases of the 1970s. Leaders of both mainstream and fringe faiths were appalled by the Supreme Court's cavalier treatment of the Free Exercise Clause. The wrongheadedness of the *Smith* decision was one of the few things that could unite all of these disparate groups.

Religious leaders petitioned Congress to overturn *Smith* legislatively, and in 1993 Congress passed the Religious Freedom Restoration Act, specifically for that objective. The act's stated purposes were "(1) to restore the compelling interest test as set forth in *Sherbert v. Verner* (1963) and *Wisconsin v. Yoder* (1972) and to guarantee its application in all cases where free exercise of religion is substantially burdened; and (2) to provide a claim or defense to persons whose religious exercise is substantially burdened by government" (sec. 2).

The act provided a statutory right to challenge state and local laws under the Free Exercise Clause. The state would allow religion to be burdened only if this strict scrutiny test was met: "Government shall not substantially burden a person's exercise of religion even if the burden results from a rule of general applicability, except . . . government may substantially burden a person's exercise of religion only if it demonstrates that application of the burden to the person (1) is in furtherance of a compelling government interest, and (2) is the least restrictive means of furthering that compelling governmental interest" (sec. 2000bb–1a and 1b).

Although passage of the Religious Freedom Restoration Act seemed to have settled the threat to religious practice raised in *Smith*, its passage was not the end of the story. The act and the legacy of the *Smith* case are discussed in more detail in Chapter 4.

4

Legacy and Impact

Chapter 3 examined several important trials that have shaped freedom of religion in the United States. In *Minersville School District v. Gobitis* (1940), the U.S. Supreme Court decided that a local school district could force students to salute and pledge allegiance to the flag despite their religious objections. In *Scopes v. Tennessee* (1925), the famous "Monkey Trial," a local court upheld a Tennessee law banning the teaching of evolution. In *Epperson v. Arkansas* (1968) the U.S. Supreme Court outlawed such statutes. In *Lynch v. Donnelly* (1984) a bitterly divided U.S. Supreme Court decided that Pawtucket, Rhode Island, could display a crèche in a holiday display. However, the Supreme Court also outlawed organized school prayer in *Engel v. Vitale* (1962), also known as the "Regents School Prayer Case."

Chapter 3 also investigated the case *Application of the President and Directors of Georgetown College* (1964) in which a judge issued an order allowing a hospital to administer blood transfusions to save the life of a patient, over the patient's religious objection. Finally, in *Employment Division v. Smith* (1990), a case involving Native American religious use of peyote, the Supreme Court decided there was no automatic accommodation of religious practice from laws of general application.

This chapter scrutinizes the impact and legacy of the cases discussed in Chapter 3. In some instances the original case established a rule that has been followed by later courts. In other instances courts have rejected the original ruling and announced a new rule or modified the old one. In still others the legislative branch has stepped in to deal with the freedom of religion issues in the original case.

The one common thread in all of the cases discussed in this chapter is the fact-specific nature of the "common law" system. Although the First Amendment guarantees citizens both free exercise of religion and freedom from the establishment of religion, it is far more difficult for the courts to apply those broad guarantees in a religiously pluralistic country. The courts have the responsibility for determining when the government can legitimately limit an individual's free exercise of his or her religion. Similarly, the courts determine when the government becomes too entangled with religion. What is clear is that freedom of religion issues will continue to be litigated, and religion will remain "on trial" throughout the new century.

The Pledge Cases

Chapter 3 analyzed the trial in *Minersville School District v. Gobitis* regarding Jehovah's Witnesses' refusal to recite the pledge of allegiance. When that case reached the U.S. Supreme Court, the Court held that Jehovah's Witnesses could not be excused from reciting the pledge of allegiance in school, even though reciting the pledge is contrary to their religious beliefs. Justice Frankfurter, writing for the Court, held that despite the fact that their religious precepts prohibited reciting the pledge, the government could force schoolchildren to recite the pledge of allegiance in order to create national unity. The decision in *Gobitis* that the pledge was mandatory, despite the Jehovah's Witnesses' religious beliefs, was wrong and did not stand for long. In *West Virginia State Board of Education v. Barnette* (1943) the Supreme Court invalidated a West Virginia law requiring mandatory recitals of the pledge of allegiance and flag salutes in public school classrooms. In *Gobitis,* heard by the Supreme Court only three years earlier, the Court had upheld a nearly identical statute. There were three new members on the Court, and two justices had changed their minds about the issue.

In 1954 Congress added the words *under God* to the pledge. This change was made during the Cold War when many in the United States were fearful of the Soviet Union, which was officially atheistic. Congress inserted the words to point out the difference between the religious United States and the "godless" USSR. Mindful of the possible Establishment Clause problem, the congressional record was careful to include language that attempted to disclaim any religious purpose.

Although parents challenged Bible reading and organized prayer in the classroom, recitation of the pledge with its new *under God* language did not get a serious challenge until nearly fifty years later. In 2002 the case *Newdow v. Congress* made its way to the Ninth Circuit Court of Appeals and onto the front page of every newspaper in the United States.

Michael Newdow was an atheist whose daughter attended public elementary school in the Elk Grove Unified School District (EGUSD) in California. In accordance with state law, teachers in the school district began each school day by leading their students in a recitation of the pledge of allegiance. The California Education Code, a state statute, required that public schools begin each school day with "appropriate patriotic exercises" and provided that reciting the pledge of allegiance to the flag of the United States of America would satisfy this requirement. The school district required each elementary school class to recite the pledge of allegiance to the flag once each day. This was typically done at the start of the school day.

Newdow did not complain that his daughter's teacher or school district required his daughter to participate in reciting the pledge. Rather, he claimed that his daughter was injured when she was compelled to "watch and listen as her state-employed teacher in her state-run school led her classmates in a ritual proclaiming that there is a God, and that ours is 'one nation under God.'" Newdow argued that both the 1954 addition of the words *under God* to the pledge and the daily recitation of that version were violations of the Establishment Clause.

Newdow's complaint in the district court challenged the constitutionality, under the First Amendment, of the 1954 act adding the words *under God* to the pledge, the California statute effectively requiring recitation of it, and the school district's policy requiring teachers to lead willing students in its recitation. He sought declaratory and injunctive relief but did not seek any money damages. Specifically, Mr. Newdow wanted the district court to order then President Bill Clinton to "alter, modify or repeal the Pledge" and to order the Congress to remove the words *under God* from the federal statute that defines the pledge.

The local school district filed a motion to dismiss the case, which was joined by the federal defendants. A magistrate judge reported findings and a recommendation, and the district judge approved the recommendation and dismissed the case. Mr. Newdow appealed the dismissal to the federal Circuit Court of Appeals.

The circuit court decided that the federal courts really lacked jurisdiction over either the president or the Congress. The president, of course, has no power to either amend or repeal a statute. The court noted that while courts can find a law unconstitutional, courts have no particular power to "enjoin the president in the performance of his official duties." Neither did the court enjoy the power to order the Congress to enact or amend a law. This left the state of California and the school district as defendants.

Although the court of appeals dismissed the president and the Congress as defendants, the court determined that it had the power to determine the constitutionality of the 1954 act adding the words *under God.* Although the court correctly dismissed the claim against those parties, after determining that Mr. Newdow had "standing" as a parent to challenge the law, the court proceeded to consider whether there was an Establishment Clause violation.

Noting that over the last three decades the Supreme Court had used three interrelated tests to analyze alleged violations of the Establishment Clause in the realm of public education, the court felt free to apply any or all of the three tests and to invalidate the act adding the *under God* language if the amendment failed any one of them.

The court started its analysis by looking at how the district court had reached its conclusion to dismiss. The record indicated that the magistrate judge found that "the ceremonial reference to God in the pledge does not convey endorsement of particular religious beliefs." The circuit court, however, found that the Supreme Court precedent did not support the magistrate's conclusion.

The court of appeals' opinion stated that "[in] the context of the Pledge, the statement that the United States is a nation 'under God' is an endorsement of religion. It is a profession of a religious belief, namely, a belief in monotheism. The recitation that ours is a nation 'under God' is not a mere acknowledgment that many Americans believe in a deity."

The court did not accept the notion that the phrase is merely descriptive of the undeniable historical significance of religion in the founding of the republic: "the phrase 'one nation under God' in the context of the Pledge is normative. To recite the Pledge is not to describe the United States; instead, it is to swear allegiance to the values for which the flag stands: unity, indivisibility, liberty, justice, and—since 1954—monotheism." Accordingly, the court felt compelled to conclude that the current pledge impermissibly takes a position with respect to the purely religious question of the existence and identity of God, writing, "A profession that we are a nation 'under God' is identical, for Establishment Clause purposes, to a profession that we are a nation 'under Jesus,' a nation 'under Vishnu,' a nation 'under Zeus,' or a nation 'under no god,' because none of these professions can be neutral with respect to religion."

The court also took issue with the school district's practice of teacher-led recitation of the pledge, which amounts to state endorsement of these ideals, including the *under God* pronouncement. Although students could not be forced to participate in recitation of the pledge, the school district was nonetheless conveying a message of state endorsement of a religious belief when it required public schoolteachers to recite and lead the recitation of the current pledge.

Although the school district allowed children to refuse to participate in the recitation of the pledge, the court noted that this policy put the children in the uncomfortable position of choosing between participating in an exercise with religious content or protesting. In a case with similar circumstances, a prayer at a graduation ceremony, the Supreme Court had observed, "What to most believers may seem nothing more than a reasonable request that the nonbeliever respect their religious practices, in a school context may appear to the nonbeliever or dissenter to be an attempt to employ the machinery of the State to enforce a religious orthodoxy."

The school district had argued that the religious content of the words *one nation under God* was so minimal that it wouldn't really cause any harm. The court answered that argument, noting that to an atheist or a believer in certain non–Judeo-Christian religions or philosophies, it may have reasonably appeared to be an attempt to enforce a "religious orthodoxy" of monotheism and was therefore impermissible. The coercive effect of the policy was particularly pronounced in the school setting, given the age and impressionability of schoolchildren and their understanding that they are required to adhere to the norms set by their school, their teacher, and their fellow students. The court also agreed with Michael Newdow that the mere fact that his daughter was required to listen every day to the statement *one nation under God* had a coercive effect.

The court examined the circumstances under which the *under God* language was added to the pledge. President Eisenhower, during the act's signing ceremony, stated, "From this day forward, the millions of our schoolchildren will daily proclaim in every city and town, every village and rural schoolhouse, the dedication of our Nation and our people to the Almighty." The court saw that this was clearly state promotion of Judeo-Christian religion.

The defendants also claimed that the pledge has the secular purpose of "solemnizing public occasions, expressing confidence in the future, and encouraging the recognition of what is worthy of appreciation in society." The flaw in this argument, according to the court, was that it looked at the text of the pledge "as a whole" and glosses over the 1954 act. The legislative history of the 1954 act reveals that its *sole* purpose was to advance religion, in order to differentiate the United States from nations under communist rule. The court reiterated that "the First Amendment requires that a statute must be invalidated if it is entirely motivated by a purpose to advance religion." The purpose of the 1954 act was to take a position on the question of theism, namely, to support the existence and moral authority of God, while "deny[ing] . . . atheistic and materialistic concepts."

The court reasoned that this purpose runs counter to the Establishment Clause, which prohibits the government's endorsement or advancement not only of one particular religion at the expense of other religions, but also of religion at the expense of atheism. Although sponsors of the 1954 act expressly disclaimed a religious purpose, the court thought the language was merely a hypocritical attempt to prevent future constitutional challenges.

Lastly, the court opined that given the age and impressionability of schoolchildren, recitation of the pledge with the words *under God* was highly likely to convey an impermissible message of endorsement to some and disapproval to others of their beliefs regarding the existence of a monotheistic God, failing the Supreme Court's *Lemon* test. Accordingly, two members of the three-judge panel decided the current pledge offended the Establishment Clause. Schoolchildren in the Ninth Judicial Circuit, comprising most of the western United States, could no longer be compelled to say the pledge. Because the ruling covered only recitation in public schools, the legality of the pledge in other circumstances had neither been addressed nor decided.

Although a petition was filed for a rehearing en banc by a panel of all the Ninth Circuit judges, it was defeated. A spirited dissent by one judge noted that both precedent and common sense compelled a contrary result in the case because reciting the pledge was a patriotic act, not religious act, a fact clear to almost everyone except the two judges who approved the majority opinion. There was some speculation that the judges voted down the rehearing because it was likely that the panel might affirm the decision. Other commentators speculated that a rehearing might have been voted down in hopes that the Supreme Court would accept the case to resolve the issue. This had not happened as of 2003, when this manuscript was being prepared.

The reaction to the *Newdow* case was swift, sharp, and predictable. Politicians of all political stripes vilified the judges without having read the opinion. However, the reaction was more transitory than the reaction to the school prayer case forty years earlier.

Whatever the ultimate fate of the *Newdow* opinion, it raises some interesting points about aspects of civic religion in the United States. Although the Court sometimes speaks of a wall of separation between church and state, it is also clear that religious references have always been and continue to be a part of public life. Government chaplains swearing oaths on Bibles and no mail delivery on Sunday are all long-standing practices and offend very few people. However, Bible reading and prayer in the public schools were also long-standing practices until the Supreme Court realized that they offended non-Christians and were a rather obvious violation of the Establishment Clause.

The *Newdow* case may be a harbinger of a more critical examination of some of these "innocuous" religious references. One needs to ask whether the current national motto "In God We Trust" is really an appropriate one in an increasingly pluralistic society. The Supreme Court has never directly considered this question. Although only a tiny minority may find the phrase offensive, the Establishment Clause was enacted to protect them as well as the majority. As Justice Kennedy wrote in the graduation prayer case, *Lee v. Weisman,* "What to most believers may seem nothing more than a reasonable request that a nonbeliever respect their [public] religious practices . . . may appear to the nonbeliever or dissenter to be an attempt to employ the machinery of the State to enforce a religious orthodoxy."

The Antievolution Statute Cases

Chapter 3 detailed two notable trials involving state antievolution statutes. In *Scopes v. Tennessee* (1925), Clarence Darrow was pitted against Williams Jennings Bryan over the constitutionality of a Tennessee statute that forbade teachers or professors from teaching about evolution. William Jennings Bryan won the case and the antievolution statute was upheld. The publicity attendant to the trial did result in a number of other southern states enacting their own antievolution statutes. One of those statutes was still on the books until it was challenged, forty-three years after *Scopes,* in *Epperson v. Arkansas.* The *Epperson* case, which reached the U.S. Supreme Court in 1968, had a far-reaching effect. The U.S. Supreme Court decision in *Epperson* was intended by the Court to send a clear message to educators and state legislators that states could not outlaw the teaching of evolution in the public schools or universities.

Although the justices in *Epperson* may have made a rule, the rule did not automatically change the beliefs of millions of Americans who believed in the literal truth of the Bible. Many of these individuals believed the Court was dead wrong on the issue. Coupled with the Supreme Court's ban on school prayer and Bible reading, many religious individuals were sincerely convinced that the Supreme Court had become antireligious. They felt that in protecting the rights of the minority the Court was trampling on the rights of the religious majority.

Court decisions typically have no self-enforcement mechanism, and some school districts may have quietly continued to omit teaching evolution in the classroom. A teacher might have done this out of personal beliefs or to avoid harassment from parents of schoolchildren or school administrators who wished that children not be exposed to the theory, which ran against many people's sincere religious beliefs. An administrator in a school district whose students include many fundamentalist Christians might have subtly suggested to a teacher that it would be less controversial for everyone to just avoid mentioning evolution altogether. The decision in *Epperson* merely provided that a state could not outlaw the teaching of evolution—it did not require that it be taught. Of course, many biology teachers believe that it would be unprofessional to omit a discussion of evolution from a modern biology course.

Although some people assume that the 1968 *Epperson* case ended the controversy over teaching evolution in the schools once and for all, the issue and controversy has persisted. Shortly after the Supreme Court's decision in *Epperson,* creationists started labeling their body of information supporting the biblical version of creation as "creation science." Biology textbooks appeared that taught creation science in place of evolution or alongside evolution as a competing theory. They noted that the fossil record contains many gaps that call the theory of evolution into question. Proponents of creation science wanted at least a "balanced treatment" of evolution and creation science in biology classes.

Of course, it is perfectly legal to teach the biblical account in addition to or as an alternative to evolution in a private school. However, after *Epperson,* it was an open question whether a school district could teach evolution and "creation science" side by side. The *Epperson* decision predated "creation science," so the matter was never before the Court in that trial. This is a good example of how the courts' decisions are restricted to the precise issues before it. The holding in *Epperson* applied only to banning the teaching of evolution and not to the teaching of creation science. That issue would have to be decided by another court case involving another set of facts and individuals. The case was not long in coming.

The Louisiana legislature passed a law called "Balanced Treatment for Creation-Science and Evolution-Science in Public School Instruction," which mandated that any school teaching evolution must also provide equal classroom time to the teaching of creation science, based on the biblical account of creation. Although applauded by fundamentalist Christian religious leaders, the law was immediately challenged as unconstitutional.

In *Edwards v. Aguillard,* the U.S. Supreme Court invalidated Louisiana's "Balanced Treatment Act," the law requiring public schools to provide equal time for the teaching of evolution and creation science. The Court found that the primary purpose for the law was to promote the teachings of Christianity. The Court noted that teachers were already free to question the theory of evolution and to provide alternatives. The statute merely mandated that they also provide the biblical explanation. The Court held that this favoritism violated the Establishment Clause of the First Amendment.

Although the courts have consistently struck down the teaching of creationism as contrary to the Constitution, proponents continue to actively lobby for its inclusion in curriculums and for the exclusion of evolution. Despite the ruling in *Aguillard,* proponents of creationism have sought novel ways to sidestep the Court's decision. For example, in one Louisiana parish (Louisiana has parishes in place of the more traditional counties) biology teachers were required to read a disclaimer that said that any discussion of evolution should not dissuade the biblical version of the creation. This disclaimer was challenged and ruled unconstitutional in the 2000 Fifth Circuit Court of Appeals case, *Freiler v. Tangipahoa Parish Board of Education.*

Public school curriculum issues draw less attention than school prayer cases, but have also created their share of controversy. Religious parents are extremely concerned about the content of school curriculums, and nonreligious parents get alarmed when a school curriculum contains religious content. No issue has generated more controversy than the teaching of evolution. Many Christians deny the validity of Darwin's theory of evolution. These parents believe in the literal truth of the biblical account of the creation, and they strongly object to the teaching of evolution in the schools. On the other hand, many parents strongly object to the teaching of the biblical account as the inappropriate teaching of religious dogma in the public schools. This is one issue where there is little middle ground. Today in the courtroom the pendulum has clearly swung in favor of evolution, but not always in the classroom.

Conservative Christians have been successful in promoting their curriculum concerns through lobbying both publishers and school boards on textbook content. Because school textbooks are sold nationally, publishers are naturally reluctant to offend a significant number of parents and school boards. Accordingly, biology textbooks contain only a limited discussion of evolution and many also contain a reference or a discussion about the biblical account of creation. Conservative Christians also lobby school boards to adopt textbooks and readers that promote traditional family values. They strongly object to readings that adopt a "relativistic" approach to problems. Instead, they prefer materials that illustrate moral values and situations that have clear right and wrong answers.

In 1999 the statewide Kansas Board of Education voted by a 6–4 majority to approve a new voluntary statewide biology curriculum that would omit evolution. A subcommittee of the board had originally developed biology standards that would have included evolution. However, board members who were evangelical Christians or who had such constituents objected to the original proposal and offered a curriculum that included what they called "intelligent design." *Intelligent design* is another phrase for creationism. Although intelligent design was jettisoned, so were evolution, natural selection, and the big bang theory. The board's vote was eventually reversed after Kansas received unwelcome and unflattering publicity nationwide. The fight over the teaching of evolution in the schools should be expected to continue in the new century.

Lynch v. Donnelly

Detailed in Chapter 3, *Lynch v. Donnelly* upheld the financing of a crèche on city-owned land in Pawtucket, Rhode Island. A divided Supreme Court found that the practice was not an endorsement of religion as long as the crèche was accompanied by other traditional holiday decorations. Supreme Court observers who read Justice Brennan's bitter dissent would not have been surprised that the Christmas decoration issue had not been laid to rest in *Lynch*. Just a few years later, the Court accepted a similar case from Pittsburgh, but this time the decorations did not fare as well. The case was *County of Allegheny v. Greater Pittsburgh ACLU* (1989). The local chapter of the American Civil Liberties Union (ACLU) brought the case alleging that a holiday display violated the Establishment Clause.

Allegheny County, Pennsylvania, maintained a Christmas display, including a crèche, in both its courthouse and its city and county office building. During the 1986–1987 holiday season, the crèche was on display on the courthouse's Grand Staircase from November 26 to January 9. It had a wooden fence on three sides and bore a plaque stating: "This Display Donated by the Holy Name Society." Sometime during the week of December 2, the county placed red and white poinsettia plants around the fence. The county also placed poinsettia plants and a small evergreen tree, decorated with a red bow, behind each of the two end posts of the fence. An angel was at the apex of the crèche display. No figures of Santa Claus or other decorations appeared on the Grand Staircase.

The county used the crèche as the setting for its annual Christmas carol program. During the 1986 season, the county invited high school choirs and other musical groups to perform during weekday lunch hours from December 3 through December 23. The county dedicated this program to world peace and to the families of prisoners of war and of persons missing in action in Southeast Asia.

The city and county building, about a block away from the county courthouse, is jointly owned by the city of Pittsburgh and Allegheny County. The city's portion of the building housed the city's principal offices, including the mayor's. The city is responsible for the building's Grant Street entrance, which has three rounded arches supported by columns. For a number of years, the city of Pittsburgh had a large Christmas tree under the middle arch outside the Grant Street entrance, decorated with lights and ornaments. In 1986 the city placed at the foot of the tree a sign bearing the mayor's name and entitled "Salute to Liberty." Beneath the title, the sign stated: "During this holiday season, the city of Pittsburgh salutes liberty. Let these festive lights remind us that we are the keepers of the flame of liberty and our legacy of freedom."

At least since 1982, the city had expanded its Grant Street holiday display to include a symbolic representation of Chanukah, the annual Jewish holiday that falls closest to Christmas Day each year. In 1986, Chanukah began at sundown on December 26.

In what still seems an amazingly long opinion (more than 100 pages) for a factually simple case, the Court split over the decorations. Justice Blackmun's opinion relied on the endorsement test used in *Lynch* in which the Court had barely approved Pawtucket's crèche. That test looked at whether the state's actions sent a message that it favored religion or a particular religion. The dissent, written by Justice Kennedy, urged the Court to use the "coercion" test, which is less likely to find an Establishment Clause violation. Interestingly, it was Justice Kennedy who penned the opinion in *Lee v. Weisman* outlawing nondenominational prayers at school graduations as violative of the Establishment Clause.

Three justices, led by Justice Brennan, thought the entire display violated the Establishment Clause. However, six justices approved Pittsburgh's menorah. Interestingly, Justices Blackmun and O'Connor approved it, using the endorsement test. They essentially reasoned that since the menorah was near the Christmas trees and the "Salute to Liberty" sign, "this was not an endorsement of religious faith but simply a recognition of cultural diversity." The other justices approved the menorah under the coercion test. Remarkably, five of the justices voted that the crèche was in violation of the Establishment Clause. This included the three justices that disapproved of the entire display along with Justices Blackmun and O'Connor. This group objected to the crèche because it was positioned alone and away from the menorah and the secular decorations—no reindeer or Santa stood nearby. In the Pawtucket display the crèche was positioned close to the Santa house and other holiday decorations. The fact that the crèche was paid for by the Catholic Church made no difference in the result, but the banner on the crèche that read "Gloria in Excelsis Deo" ("Glory to God in the Highest") was a purely religious message showing that the display was religious rather than secular. This was too much for the crèche to pass the endorsement test.

In dissent Justice Kennedy, like Chief Justice Burger in *Lynch*, defended the crèche as "traditional and noncoercive." He viewed the holiday displays as traditional elements of American "civic religion"—like the congressional and armed service chaplains swearing oaths on the Bible and the national motto "In God We Trust." Kennedy also viewed the display as inoffensive and a reasonable accommodation of the religious majority who wanted and enjoyed the annual display. In his view, if non-Christians were offended by the city's display they could merely turn their backs and look away.

The Supreme Court's two Christmas display cases settled nothing other than the fact that this is one area where there is little agreement about where to draw the lines between church and state. The High Court may not be eager to venture back into this thicket anytime soon.

Schools and Religion

Religious activities in the schools, such as the posting of the Lord's Prayer or the Ten Commandments or the singing of hymns are normally impermissible, using the same logic applied in the school prayer cases. Allowing such religious activities in state-supported schools is an impermissible endorsement of a particular religion. Christmas pageants and decorations in the public schools are also viewed with suspicion, although a few courts have recognized that both Thanksgiving and Christmas have also become secular and commercialized holidays and are no longer purely religious holidays. For example, it should be easy to conclude that singing the song "Rudolph the Rednosed Reindeer" has no religious significance whatsoever. Some might argue that any reference to Christmas is an endorsement of religion.

Along with organized prayer and Bible reading, the public schools have largely tried to avoid giving preference to any particular religions to avoid legal challenges. This has resulted in the banning of Christmas displays and music at holiday festivals. Many Americans feel that both the courts and the schools have gone too far in making schools a religion-free zone and that this infringes on the rights of religious students to express their own religious beliefs.

The 1962 Supreme Court case, *Engel v. Vitale,* also known as the "Regent's Prayer Case," which banned organized school prayer, was one of the most controversial cases the Supreme Court delivered in the twentieth century. In the following year the Court followed up by handing down its opinion in *Abington School District v. Schempp,* which banned Bible reading in public schools.

Many Americans found the Court's decisions shocking and out of step with the views of most Americans of the time. Predictably, the case ignited a firestorm of protest from many religious leaders and members of their congregations. The Supreme Court became popularly and derisively known as "that Godless Court" and groups lobbied to impeach some of its members. Although the shift in dealing with religion in the schools was radical, it was also inevitable and mirrored the larger society.

The United States has always had a Protestant majority. With the exception of John Kennedy, who was elected in 1960, every U.S. president has been white, male, and Protestant. Although the United States has always had significant minority religions, Protestantism has dominated. Students of religion in the United States have noted that the late nineteenth and early-twentieth-century's "civic religion" in the United States reflected the composition of the population and was vaguely mainline Protestant. The Protestant version of the Lord's Prayer was recited in public schools and readings from the King James Version of the Bible were common.

After World War II there seems to have been a shift in U.S. culture and a shift in the civic religion. Jews and Catholics became more accepted. Politicians no longer talked about Christian values but about Judeo-Christian values. Civic religion, though still mainstream, was no longer exclusively Protestant. With this shift, the days of reading the Protestant Bible and reciting Protestant prayers in school were numbered. It is not surprising that the most resistance to the banning of school prayer came in the South, which has the fewest non-Protestant churchgoers.

Following World War II the Supreme Court heard approximately a dozen major cases involving religion in the schools. These cases created a new body of First Amendment law that simply had not existed before. This body of law set up new operating rules about how the public schools should accommodate religion and how the government should interact with parochial schools. Although both *Engel* and *Abington* caused a sensation, they must also be viewed as links in a chain that started even before Earl Warren was appointed to the Supreme Court by President Dwight Eisenhower in 1953. One of the first of these cases was also one of the most shocking. In 1948, the Supreme Court handed down the first in a line of major cases that would change the contours of U.S. society by largely eliminating religious activities in the public schools. The case, *People of Illinois ex rel. McCollum v. Board of Education,* banned use of public school buildings for release-time religious instruction.

Vashti McCollum gained the national spotlight when she filed a lawsuit objecting to the religion classes being given in her son's school. A local group, the Council on Religious Education, was formed to provide religious instruction in the Champaign, Illinois, school system. The students were released early from class and children with parental permission attended religion classes in their own schools. Nearly all the children participated, and instruction was available for Jews, Catholics, and Protestants. Although Vashti had given her son Terry permission to attend the classes when he was in fourth grade, she grew uncomfortable with the instruction and did not give permission the next year. Although Terry was not compelled to attend, he was required to sit alone in a small anteroom outside the teacher's rest room or to sit alone in the hall. He was the subject of teasing from his fellow students and disapproval from his teachers. When the school district failed to improve the situation, Vashti McCollum sued.

The U.S. Supreme Court in *McCollum v. Board of Education* (1948) agreed with Mrs. McCollum, holding that the teaching of religion on the school grounds violated the First Amendment's Establishment Clause. Following on the footsteps of *Everson v. Board of Education* the previous year, which held that state and local governments, including the public schools, were subject to the Establishment Clause, the Court used its power of judicial review to invalidate the state law that established the release-time program. No federal or state law can be contrary to a constitutional provision. Although declaring laws contrary to the Constitution is a judicial power, it also gives the Supreme Court a vast power to control how the law is applied in a particular area. The effect of this decision was not only to outlaw Illinois's program but any existing or potential programs that suffered from the same defects.

McCollum's case really set the stage for all of the later cases that banned religious expression in the public schools. Vashti McCollum paid a personal price for her beliefs. She later wrote that she and her family were harassed all during the legal proceedings and she was called an "emissary of Satan, a Communist, and a fiend in human form."

In 1952 the Court considered another release-time case, *Zorach v. Clauson.* This time the Supreme Court upheld the release-time program taking place outside public school grounds. The release-time program was structured to allow public school students to be dismissed early to attend religion classes away from the public school grounds. Parents could give permission to the public school for their children to be released early for such classes. If permission was not granted the children were required to stay at the public school.

Earlier release-time programs, in which religion classes were taught in public school classrooms during the release-time period, were struck down in 1948 by the Supreme Court as a violation of the Establishment Clause. The Court clearly felt more comfortable with the classes being held off the school premises. That the school system assisted the programs by helping with registration and permitting the students to leave school did not seem important to the Court. In any event, any entanglements were outweighed by the general benefits of the program. Justice William O. Douglas's opinion noted that although it was clear that the First Amendment required a separation of church and state, it was equally clear that the Establishment Clause does not require "a philosophy of hostility to religion," which "respects the religious nature of our people and accommodates the public service to their spiritual needs." Three justices wrote dissenting opinions noting that there was not much to distinguish this case from the 1948 case (*McCollum*) that had disapproved of release-time programs. That in this case the children attended the classes at church rather than in the school itself seemed trivial to the dissenters.

Today release-time programs remain a feature of U.S. education. Proponents of release-time programs argue that they are a reasonable accommodation of religion that fall just short of endorsement. Opponents argue that release-time programs discriminate against both nonreligious students and students whose religions cannot provide them with a program during the release time. Those students must normally sit in "study halls" during the release-time period. Opponents argue that they are merely being warehoused so the majority of students can go to get religious instruction during the school day. These opponents argue that if students and their parents want them to get religious instruction, it should be done after school or on weekends, not during the normal school day.

The ban on school prayer also includes a ban on prayers said at graduations and sports events. A divided Supreme Court, in *Lee v. Weisman* (1992), found that an invocation at a public school graduation ceremony in Providence, Rhode Island, violated the Establishment Clause. Justice Kennedy, writing for the majority, argued that the public atmosphere created an improper coercion on students, which amounted to proselytizing. The majority felt that since the graduation ceremony was a required event, a prayer at the graduation was no more acceptable than a prayer in the classroom at the start of the school day. Justice Scalia wrote a bitter dissent accusing the majority of "laying waste" to traditional nonsectarian prayers at public events and accused the majority's use of the concept of "coercion" of being a "bulldozer of its social engineering."

Despite the ban on school prayer, states have sometimes tried to reintroduce prayer through legal means. For example, Mississippi enacted a law allowing student-initiated voluntary prayer at all assemblies, sporting events, commencement exercises, and other school-related events. The law was passed after an incident at a Mississippi high school. A high school principal had allowed a student to recite a daily prayer over the school public address system. When some parents complained about the practice, the board of education threatened to fire the principal. Many Mississippians are strongly religious and favor school prayer, and the entire episode caused a local furor, which prompted the legislature to pass the law.

The law was immediately challenged by the ACLU, and a Mississippi federal district judge upheld the section of the law allowing prayers at commencement exercises but struck down the parts of the act allowing prayer at assemblies and other school-related events (*Ingebretsen v. Jackson Public School District*). Currently, a few states still have laws in effect that allow school prayer. They may be found illegal if challenged in court.

Prayer in the public schools continues to be a contentious issue. Both federal and state courts have almost uniformly struck down compulsory and voluntary group prayers in public schools as contrary to the First Amendment's Establishment Clause, which bars the government from favoring one religion over another. Silent prayer and student-initiated prayer are not banned by these court rulings—only prayers organized by the schools themselves.

However, banning organized prayer from the schools also limits religious expression for students and teachers. Many have argued that the courts have gone too far by banning school prayer. They argue that the Establishment Clause requires only that the government be neutral toward religion by not favoring one church or religion over another. These proponents argue that by enacting an outright ban on organized school prayer, the government is being hostile rather than neutral toward religious practice. They also argue that by banning school prayer, the government has also limited the right of students and teachers to practice their religion. Those who support this view argue that the courts need to make a reasonable accommodation to those who want to express their religious practices during the day.

On the other hand, there are many who feel that allowing any kind of prayer in the schools—even a supposedly nondenominational prayer—is an overt support of religion in violation of the Establishment Clause's wall of separation between church and state. These proponents would argue that students also have the constitutional right to be free from a particular religion or free from all religion. By requiring a mandatory school prayer, the government violates the rights of students and teachers who do not wish to practice religion. They also argue that no court has ever banned a student from saying an individual prayer at school.

Moment of Silence

Individual school districts and state legislators have both seized upon the idea of allowing a moment of silence before the start of the school day as a substitute for a group prayer. At the high school level this moment is typically observed in the homeroom before classes begin. The goal is to allow students and teachers to pray silently or to meditate. The legality of such moments of silence depends on their intent—if they are really moments for prayer, then they are illegal.

For example, the Supreme Court, in *Wallace v. Jaffree* (1985), invalidated an Alabama law allowing a one-minute period of silence at the start of each school day "for meditation or voluntary prayer." A divided court (6–3) concluded that this mandated moment of silence amounted to "the State's endorsement of prayer activity" that transgressed the proper wall of separation between church and state. Merely allowing students to be excused was held insufficient to save the law. The Court did say, however, that it was possible for a moment of silence to pass muster if it was not solely for sectarian purposes. The problem with the Alabama law was that it was avowedly for prayer. Presumably, a statute that required a moment of silence for no reason would have avoided the constitutional problems. Of course, the Supreme Court has never prohibited prayer in the public schools. Students are free to pray silently or out loud. However, the school cannot conduct religious ceremonies including the recitation of prayers in the classroom.

Although organized prayer in the schools is illegal, a properly devised moment of silence will withstand a legal challenge. The key is for the law to avoid outright religious intent. For example, Georgia enacted a Moment of Quiet Reflection that allows public school teachers to begin the school day with an interval of silence. Although the practice was immediately attacked as a "silent prayer," the Georgia silent moment law was upheld by a federal court because the law establishing the moment specifically disclaimed any religious purpose. Accordingly, the federal district court held that the law did not violate the Constitution (*Bowen v. Gwinnett School District*).

Today about half the states have a law specifically authorizing a moment of silence at the start of the school day. Some of these are probably legal, whereas others may be found illegal if challenged.

Those in favor of the moment of silence argue that it is a reasonable accommodation to those students and teachers who wish to practice their religion by praying in school without offending or inconveniencing those who do not wish to participate. Those who are opposed argue that the school districts are sneaking prayer into the schools through the back door. Although less offensive than a compulsory group prayer, the mandatory moment of silence is an obvious endorsement of prayer and religion. Those who oppose the moment of silence also argue that students and teachers are free to pray silently to themselves at any time during the school day. Accordingly, the only purpose of the moment of silence is really aimed at other students who would not ordinarily think of praying, to encourage them to pray at least once during the school day.

The U.S. Supreme Court's position on a moment of silence has been neutral, but its decisions have also led to confusion in this area. The Court's position is that the constitutionality of a moment of silence depends on the wording and the intent of the state statute. If the intent of the statute is to encourage and promote prayer, then the moment of silence is unconstitutional. However, if the intent were not to actively promote prayer, then the moment of silence would pass constitutional muster. In the 1985 case, *Wallace v. Jaffree*, described earlier, which involved Alabama's moment of silence statute, the Court struck down the Alabama moment of silence because the state legislature's intent was to promote and encourage prayer in the public schools.

Other states and individual school districts have also adopted moments of silence. Because school prayer is such a contentious issue, the subject has also become a political issue. Although some elected officials oppose the moment of silence, even more seem to favor it. A number of U.S. presidents—including former President Bill Clinton—have endorsed the moment of silence concept as a reasonable accommodation for religious practice. They argue that banning even the unintrusive moment of silence shows not neutrality but an active hostility to any religious practice in the schools. However, it is not always clear if politicians adopt stands in favor of school prayer and moments of silence out of a sincere belief or merely to curry favor with voters.

Over the years, those unhappy with the First Amendment's religion clauses have proposed a number of amendments aimed at allowing prayer and other religious activities in the schools. These decisions rekindled the movement to add an amendment to the Constitution allowing school prayer. Although there was a good deal of enthusiasm for a school prayer amendment, the proposals never gained the required two-thirds vote required.

Those who support organized prayer, Bible reading, and subjects with other religious content in the schools have sought to overturn the results in these court cases by amending the U.S. Constitution. Although the Congress might be willing to pass a law authorizing organized school prayer, such a law would probably be held unconstitutional by the Supreme Court. In fact, the Court often announces in its decisions that there are areas in the law that Congress should address. The Supreme Court has not invited Congress to pass laws to interpret the meaning of the First Amendment's religion clauses, however. It is clear that the Court believes that it is the body best equipped to interpret the scope of the First Amendment protections.

In our system of government there is a long tradition that Congress cannot change the Constitution on its own initiative. Likewise, the Congress does not have the ability to overturn a specific Supreme Court decision that it dislikes or that is unpopular with their constituents. If members of Congress or citizens want the Constitution changed, they must amend the Constitution itself. For example, the Twenty-Sixth Amendment, ratified in 1971, gave eighteen-year-old citizens the right to vote.

During the late 1800s members of Congress proposed no fewer than eleven different constitutional amendments dealing with church and state and religion in the schools. Generally, these amendments attempted to reduce the power of the states in dealing with religion. Although the existence of so many proposed amendments demonstrates that they had wide support, none of the proposed amendments has ever garnered the two-thirds majority.

The most famous of these proposed amendments was the so-called Blaine Amendment, which was an early (1876) attempt to ban any state aid to church-supported schools. Although there was broad support for this amendment, it never received enough votes in Congress to be referred to the states for ratification. Interestingly, although the Blaine Amendment banned federal or state aid to church-supported schools and also banned school prayer in public schools, it specifically stated that it did not prohibit Bible reading in the schools.

In 1980, presidential candidate Ronald Reagan endorsed a school prayer amendment. Although supporters of school prayer were buoyed by his endorsement, they must have been disappointed when he seemingly lost interest in the issue once elected. During the 1980s fundamentalist and conservative Christian organizations, particularly the Moral Majority and the Christian Coalition, assumed the lead in arguing for a school prayer amendment. Although none of the proposed amendments has been successful, the enthusiasm for an amendment continues. In 1994 the Proposed Religious Equality Amendment was introduced in Congress. At least two other amendments addressing religious expression were introduced in Congress in 1995.

Democrat Bill Clinton was elected president in 1992, and a Republican Congress was elected in 1994. The Republicans, led by Representative Newt Gingrich of Georgia, fashioned a "Contract With America," a program that emphasized a smaller government and a return to traditional American values. As part of its Contract With America, Newt Gingrich and the Republican leaders of Congress promised to introduce a school prayer amendment to the Constitution. Although a number of prominent Republican Party leaders endorsed the idea, the amendment was not introduced until 1997. Written by Representative Ernest Istook of Oklahoma, the 1997 amendment not only asked for organized school prayer but also allowance for religious symbols such as crosses to be displayed in the schools and the use of tax dollars to support private religious schools. The amendment was reintroduced in 2003.

The primary resistance to proposed prayer amendments comes from two fronts. The first front is composed of individuals and groups such as Americans United for Separation of Church and State and People for the American Way, who believe that the wall of separation established by the U.S. Supreme Court in the 1960s should be maintained. These individuals and groups are entirely opposed to any change to the First Amendment protections.

Surprisingly, the second front resisting amendments comes from the religious right. Although many conservative politicians and religious leaders agree that some sort of amendment is required to dismantle the wall of separation, that is where the agreement ends. Many of these individuals and groups disagree about the focus that the amendment should take. Some think that the emphasis should be on restoring organized school prayer and daily Bible reading in the classroom, whereas others want a much less specific amendment that would address any "discrimination" against religious speech and activity.

This squabbling among those associated with the religious right has prevented these groups from forming a consensus behind any of the recently proposed religious amendments. The result has been than none of the proposed amendments has gathered significant support in Congress. For example, although numerous religiously and politically conservative groups had called for a school prayer amendment, several prominent conservative groups withheld their support from the 1994 Religious Equality Amendment because they disagreed with the wording.

The situation became worse in 1995 when there were two competing amendments introduced. Although each amendment gathered supporters, no consensus emerged that would allow either one to get a two-thirds vote in Congress. One amendment penned by Representative Ernest Istook Jr. of Oklahoma focused on the school prayer issue and would guarantee organized student-sponsored school prayer in the public schools and would also allow communities to decide if they could erect religious holiday displays including Christmas trees and crosses on Easter. The second amendment introduced in Congress by Representative Henry Hyde of Illinois had a broader focus and was aimed at prohibiting discrimination against religious speech and those individuals who want to express such views in public. Supporters of this amendment feel that the real problem is discrimination against individuals and groups because of their religious expression. The net result of the squabble was to split support in the Congress between the two amendments, which prevented either from gaining the necessary votes to succeed.

Access for Religious Groups

After the school prayer case, many schools reacted by banning all religious activities in the schools. In addition to terminating in-school release-time programs, school boards also banned student religious clubs and after-school Bible study groups. Parents complained that this amounted to discrimination against religious students who had a constitutional right to express their religious beliefs and associate with one another.

In response, Congress passed the federal Equal Access Act, which prohibits discrimination against student groups on the basis of religious, political, or philosophical views. If a public school allows "noncurriculum related groups" like clubs to use its facilities, then the school must give equal access to those facilities to religious groups. The act was controversial from the start as some asserted that allowing a religious club in the schools would violate the Establishment Clause by favoring one particular religion.

The legality of the Equal Access Act was uncertain because of potential "entanglements" of the schools with religious groups. The issue was finally resolved in *Board of Education of the Westside Community Schools v. Mergens* (1990), which upheld the constitutionality of the federal Equal Access Act, enacted to give equal access to public school facilities for religious groups and clubs.

Relying on the *Lemon* test, the Supreme Court held that a public school district must allow students access to school facilities for religious clubs. Under the Equal Access Act, public schools that receive federal aid and provide a "limited open forum" cannot deny equal access to students who wish to meet together in a religious club. The Court held that although there was some involvement of school officials in the appealed cases, this did not amount to prohibited "entanglement" with religion nor an endorsement of any particular religion. Clearly, changes of personnel on the Court over the years had made a difference. One can speculate that if this case had been brought two decades earlier, the Court would have found the entire act unconstitutional.

The Court has also ruled that the public schools can be used by nonstudent religious groups. In *Lamb's Chapel v. Center Moriches Union Free Public School District* (1993) the Supreme Court held that a school district could not deny access to school facilities to a church group that wanted to show a film on child rearing. The school district had rented space to other groups for secular activities but denied access to the religious group out of concern over promoting religion at the school. Although the film was only shown to the church group after school hours, the Court held that any benefit to the group was merely "incidental."

Proponents of equal access to public school facilities argue that religious clubs should be treated no differently than other school clubs. They argue that to do otherwise would amount to discrimination against the religious and would also infringe on their First Amendment right to free speech and freedom of association. Opponents argue that the schools cannot be used for religious clubs because this amounts to an implicit endorsement of a particular religion by the school. They also argue that this will inevitably discriminate against students who are members of minority religions, who will have no opportunity to participate in a club of their choice because there would be too few students.

Public Support for Church-Affiliated Schools

Another major conflict area involving religion and the schools is the provision of government aid for private, church-affiliated schools. The Catholic Church has operated a system of parochial schools for more than 100 years. These schools are especially common in urban areas. Many fundamentalist Christians have children enrolled in private academies or participate in the growing home-schooling movement. The Catholics started their school system to teach religion as well as academic subjects. Fundamentalist Christians, who are often disappointed with the secular approach of the public schools, desire to provide education that contains a strong moral component. Although the doctrine of the separation of church and state would seem to bar aid to nonpublic schools, state legislatures and courts have recognized a number of exceptions for very practical reasons. The courts justify these exceptions by holding that the aid goes to the schoolchildren and not to the private schools.

In 1925 the U.S. Supreme Court held in *Pierce v. Society of Sisters* that the Fourteenth Amendment protected students' rights to attend private schools. However, the high court has never held that government tax dollars should contribute to their support. In other countries, including Canada, government tax dollars are used to support parochial schools. In the United States such support is avoided because of our doctrine of the separation of church and state. The separation is mandated not only by long tradition but also by the U.S. Constitution.

A large number of parents do prefer to send their children to church-affiliated schools, and many of these parents feel that their tax dollars should be used to help support those schools. Local school systems and taxpayers also benefit because local districts save between $4,000 and $12,000 for each student who is educated outside the public school system. Accordingly, the states have tried to devise systems to aid church-supported schools, not by providing direct financial grants, but through providing textbooks, bus service, and other educational services. States legislatures argue that these services go to the children, not to the schools, and therefore do not run afoul of the Establishment Clause. Very often the courts have agreed with this argument.

For example, in *Board of Education v. Allen* (1968), the Supreme Court allowed a state program that loaned textbooks on secular topics to private and parochial school students. The divided Court upheld the practice, reasoning that the aid went to the students or their parents rather than to the schools. The Court has also approved reimbursement of the costs of state-mandated standardized tests but has disapproved of providing free teaching materials other than textbooks.

However, in *Lemon v. Kurtzman* (1971) the U.S. Supreme Court prohibited salary supplements for lay teachers in parochial schools.

Chief Justice Warren Burger wrote the majority opinion, saying that: "parochial schools involve substantial religious activity and purpose." The case also established a three-prong test to see if a law offends the Establishment Clause. All three prongs must be met:

1. The statute must have a secular purpose.
2. Its primary effect must neither advance nor inhibit religion.
3. It must avoid excessive governmental entanglement with religion.

The *Lemon* test was to be used by the Court for approximately twenty-five years and also found its way into the Religious Freedom Restoration Act, which was itself declared unconstitutional by the Court in 1997.

The Supreme Court has also held that a school district cannot provide instructional materials such as maps, magazines, tape recorders, and buses for field trips to parochial school students even though these are all used for secular rather than religious instruction. The Court held that the Establishment Clause was violated because of the "impossibility of separating the secular education function from the sectarian" (*Wollman v. Walter* [1977]).

In *Everson v. Board of Education* (1947) the Supreme Court upheld a New Jersey subsidy of bus service to parochial schools. The provision of bus service was not a direct subsidy but peripheral or incidental, similar to providing the school fire and police protection. The majority opinion focused on the fact that the aid went to the students or their parents, not directly to the school. The Court found no constitutional problem with "a general program to help parents get their children, regardless of their religion, safely and expeditiously to and from accredited schools." Accordingly, the wall of separation between church and state was not violated. In *Everson* the Supreme Court for the first time announced that the Establishment Clause of the First Amendment of the Constitution also applies to the states. Accordingly, it applies to the actions of local school districts.

Justice Black believed that the Constitution's Establishment Clause demanded an absolute wall of separation between church and state. In *Everson* he explained his conception of the Establishment Clause, echoing Jefferson's earlier view: "The first Amendment has erected a wall between church and state. That wall must be kept high and impregnable. We [the Supreme Court] could not approve the slightest breach." Surprisingly, Black's opinion held that there was no breach in the *Everson* case in which New Jersey had paid the bus fare of children riding public transit to parochial schools. Although Black would not countenance the "slightest breach" of the wall of separation, he reasoned that the reimbursement of the bus fare benefited the schoolchildren and their families rather than the parochial schools.

Special Education

Initially, the Court was hostile to state programs to provide special education to parochial school students. The Supreme Court struck down a state plan to reimburse private and parochial schools for administering standardized achievement tests. The Court was troubled by the fact that the state could not guarantee that the funds would not be used for religious purposes and that the private school teachers participated in preparing the tests (*Levitt v. Committee for Public Education and Religious Liberty* [1973]). Similarly, in *Meek v. Pittenger* (1975) the Supreme Court struck down state payment of auxiliary services such as the purchase of AV equipment at parochial schools (curiously this case involved the same law that was upheld in the 1968 *Allen* case.

The results in these cases were not predictable and were often fact-specific. For example, in *Wollman v. Walter* (1977) the Supreme Court approved a program whereby the public school employees provided speech and hearing and psychological testing services for parochial school students at their schools. The Court reasoned that such services had no "educational content" and the Court saw no danger of proselytizing. Just two years earlier in *Meek v. Pittenger* the Court had struck down a similar program in part because the services were offered in a parochial school. In *Committee for Public Education and Religious Liberty v. Regan* (1980) the Supreme Court upheld a state-funded program in which the state reimbursed private and parochial schools for the cost of administering standardized tests. The private schools exercised no control over the tests themselves, which the Court felt prevented any forbidden entanglement between church and state.

In what was the major case on this topic, the Supreme Court in *Aguilar v. Felton* (1985) struck down a program that used federal funds to pay the salaries of public school guidance counselors and teachers who were providing remedial and clinical help to disadvantaged parochial school students. The Court held that the plan created an excessive government entanglement with religion and therefore failed the *Lemon* test. In *Aguilar*'s "companion case," *School District of Grand Rapids v. Ball* (1985), the Supreme Court struck down a school district's program that allowed public school teachers to give secular classes in parochial school classrooms. The majority opinion held that the "symbolic union" of government and religion in one sectarian enterprise entangles the government with religion by implicitly endorsing the church that ran the school. Payment of the teacher's salaries was also seen as a direct subsidy to the parochial school.

In the decade following these cases the Reagan and Bush appointees to the Court adopted a more flexible stance that favored aid to church-supported schools. The Supreme Court found no Establishment Clause violation in *Zobrest v. Catalina Foothills School District* (1993), in which a California school district provided a sign language interpreter for a deaf student at a Catholic high school. The Court reasoned that there was no constitutional violation when the parochial school received only an "attenuated financial benefit" from the educational program that provided benefits neutrally without reference to the student's religious affiliation. Compare this case with the earlier case, *Wollman* (1977), in which the Court found payment for instructional materials in parochial schools to violate the Establishment Clause.

Finally, the Supreme Court in *Agostini v. Felton* (1997) overturned its 1985 holding in *Aguilar v. Felton,* which held that remedial education funded by federal aid under Title 1 could not take place in parochial school buildings. In the 1985 case, a divided Supreme Court decided that remedial education funded by federal aid under Title I of the Elementary and Secondary Education Act of 1965 and performed by public school teachers could not take place in parochial school buildings. The case held that the Establishment Clause did not prohibit public school teachers from giving remedial instruction in a parochial school. This was a major change in policy by the Supreme Court that had uniformly held for more than thirty years that public school teachers could not teach in parochial schools, even when there was no religious instruction involved.

The U.S. Supreme Court in *Board of Education of Kiryas Joel Village School District v. Grumet* struck down New York State's creation of a special public school district to provide state-funded special education services for a community of Hasidic Jews. The community of approximately 8,500, the Satmae Hasidim sect of Orthodox Jews established a private school based on the needs of their religious students including gender segregation, a special dress code, and speaking Yiddish. In order to obtain state aid to the village's handicapped children, the state legislature allowed the village to establish a separate public school district that would only deal with the problems of the village's handicapped children. All children in the village attended private parochial schools except handicapped children who attended the public school that provided services exclusively to the special needs children. The public school was staffed by secular teachers and had a purely secular curriculum. The Supreme Court held that this was a violation of the Establishment Clause. Because New York had created the school district along religious lines it violated the Constitution's requirement that government maintain its impartiality toward religion.

Proponents of state aid to children attending church-affiliated schools argue that the government should support the education of all schoolchildren, regardless of which school they select. They further argue that aid such as loaned textbooks, bus service, and special education services helps the children but not the schools. Opponents of such aid argue that the courts have merely used a technicality to dodge the real issue. Pushed to its logical conclusion, there would be no limit on aid to church schools—including the payment of staff salaries—because the ultimate beneficiaries of the education are the students. Clearly, the courts—and especially the present Supreme Court—are receptive to allowing state support of students who attend church-affiliated schools.

Vouchers

The ultimate support of church-affiliated school would be government payment of a student's tuition at private and parochial schools. The U.S. Supreme Court has held that such reimbursement—whether directly or indirectly through tax credits—is unconstitutional (*Committee v. Nyquist* [1973]; *Sloan v. Lemon* [1973]). However, the Court re-examined this issue in 2002.

In *Mueller v. Allen* (1983), a closely divided Supreme Court upheld a Minnesota law allowing parents of private and parochial school students to take a tax deduction for tuition and other educational expenses. The case is significant because the Court had struck down a similar law. What saved the Minnesota law was that the deduction was also "available" to parents of public school students. The Court conveniently sidestepped the issue that parents of public school students do not actually pay tuition and thereby would not benefit in real terms. Nevertheless, Chief Justice Rehnquist, writing for the Court, found the tax scheme to be neutral. The fact that the bulk of the benefits would go to the parents of private and parochial school students was held to be irrelevant. The majority opinion stressed the value of supporting private schools not just for those students attending the schools but also for the public in general. Rehnquist noted that the public benefited because each student educated in private school reduced the taxpayer's burden of educating the student. Furthermore, the private school system provided a benchmark for the public system as well as educational diversity.

In 1999 an Ohio state court struck down the Ohio Pilot Scholarship Program that provided vouchers of up to $2,500 to Cleveland public school students to attend private and parochial schools. The state court in *Simmons-Harris v. Goff* held that the voucher program violated the Establishment Clause because it provides direct and substantial nonneutral government aid to sectarian schools.

After the Wisconsin Supreme Court split on the issue of the validity of Milwaukee's voucher program in 1996, the case was sent back to the trial court. The trial court decided that the program was an unconstitutional violation of the church-state provisions of the Wisconsin state constitution. That decision was reversed by the Wisconsin Supreme Court, but that hardly settled the voucher issue, since the ruling was quite narrow.

Because of the change in judicial attitudes toward public support of church-affiliated schools, the issue of vouchers and government payment of private school tuition promises to remain a critical issue. The issue of religion in the schools promises to be a major political and cultural issue well into the twenty-first century. There is substantial disagreement in the country about how these issues should be treated, and this disagreement promises to keep the area a controversial one.

Because the issue is so emotionally laden, it is also an area that draws the interest of political leaders, whether out of conviction or opportunism. Because a substantial minority—or even a majority of voters—disagree with many of the current approaches to this issue, a politician who promises change can build a strong base of support. The issue of religion in the schools has the potential to become a major political issue over the next decade. Although both Presidents Ronald Reagan and George H. W. Bush supported the concept of a school prayer amendment to the Constitution, it was never at the top of their political agendas and they never leant their full support to any movement to infuse more religion into the pubic schools. Bill Clinton, a moderate Democrat, never endorsed a school prayer amendment. Clinton's education department did issue guidelines that take a moderate approach and allow some accommodation of religion in the schools while preserving the basic contours of our traditional church-state separation.

Future presidents will have the opportunity to control the future of this contentious issue. On the one hand, a future president may continue the policy of recent presidents and let the courts control the content of religion in the schools. On the other hand, a president could be forceful in his or her beliefs by proposing legislation to Congress to promote religion in the schools. If such legislation were overturned by the Supreme Court, the president could appeal to Congress and the state legislatures to support a constitutional amendment. Additionally, future presidents will have the opportunity to shape the area through their judicial appointments. There will be a number of vacancies to fill on the U.S. Supreme Court and other federal courts, and the beliefs and attitudes of these judges will play a large role in determining the law in this area.

The most important issue in the religion in the schools area appears to be the issue of vouchers. As discussed earlier in the chapter, several states have considered voucher systems that would give the parents of children attending private and church-affiliated schools a voucher that would pay part or all of the student's tuition with public tax dollars. There are obvious constitutional problems with allowing the state to pay the tuition of a student who wants to attend a church-affiliated school. Although the Supreme Court has struck down such payments in the past, those cases were decided long ago, and the present justices have been far more receptive to aid to church-supported schools. Although early attempts at establishing voucher systems have run afoul of constitutional arguments, it may be possible for a state to design a system that may get judicial approval. An examination of past court cases reveals that the states have been able to draft legislation to give a good deal of aid to church-affiliated schools by designing systems that target the aid to the students rather than to the schools.

In *Zelman v. Simmons-Harris* (2002), the U.S. Supreme Court finally accepted a major school voucher case. The majority of the justices approved the Ohio school voucher plan despite arguments that it violated the Establishment Clause. The Ohio plan gives a state-paid voucher to a family that can be used to pay tuition in a private or religious school. The Court noted that fully 82 percent of the nonpublic schools participating in the program were religiously affiliated and that 91 percent of the students using the vouchers went to those religious schools.

However, the majority ruled that the establishment argument was inapplicable. The Court upheld the program based on two findings: first, the purpose of the state's program was to provide assistance to poor children in failing school districts, and second, the program provided a true private family choice that did not have the effect of advancing religion.

Like similar controversial cases involving church and state, the *Zelman* decision probably did little to change people's opinions about school vouchers. It did embolden proponents of vouchers. In the summer of 2003 Colorado launched a pilot state-wide voucher system similar to that of Ohio, and other states were expected to follow.

Application of the President and Directors of Georgetown College (1964)

In this case discussed in Chapter 3, a judge ordered a hospital to administer blood transfusions to save the life of a patient, over the patient's religious objection. Many individuals have religious objections to blood transfusions and other lifesaving medical procedures. As the *Georgetown College* case illustrated, the state also has an interest in preserving life. In this case, the state had both a general interest in preserving life, but also an interest in preserving the patient's life because the patient was the parent of a minor child.

Although the *Georgetown College* case garnered wide attention, especially in the medical community, the decision had little value as a precedent, first, because it was decided under District of Columbia law and, second, because the case only involved the issuance of an order to the hospital.

Norwood Hospital v. Munoz (1991)

The issue in the *Georgetown College* case—compelling medical treatment over a patient's religious objections—was sure to arise again. More than twenty-five years after *Georgetown College,* a Massachusetts court was faced with a similar legal question in the *Norwood Hospital* case. Although the two cases are similar, there are also differences. In the *Georgetown College* case discussed in Chapter 3, the judge had to make a decision at the hospital, with no time for research. The Massachusetts case occurred after the event, which gave the judges time to reflect on the issues. The Massachusetts case also illustrates the fact-intensive nature of the trials in this area.

The *Norwood Hospital* case involved a competent adult who was a Jehovah's Witness and the mother of a minor child. She appealed a judgment of the probate and family court authorizing Norwood Hospital to administer blood or blood products without her consent.

The facts in the case were important to the court. Yolanda Munoz, a thirty-eight-year-old woman, lived in Dedham, Massachusetts, with her minor son, Ernesto Jr., her husband, Ernesto, and her seventy-two-year-old father-in-law. Mrs. Munoz had a history of stomach ulcers, and approximately ten years before the trial, she had surgery for a bleeding ulcer. One spring day she vomited blood and collapsed in her home. During the week before she collapsed, she had taken two aspirin every four hours to alleviate a pain in her arm. The aspirin had apparently made her ulcer bleed. Her husband, Ernesto, took her to the Norwood Hospital emergency room. Physicians at Norwood Hospital gave Mrs. Munoz medication that stopped the bleeding. She was then admitted to the hospital as an inpatient and was placed under the care of Dr. Joseph L. Perrotto. It was his medical opinion that she had a 50 percent probability of hemorrhaging again. If she started to bleed, Dr. Perrotto believed that she would in all probability die unless she received a blood transfusion. Mrs. Munoz, however, refused to consent to a blood transfusion in the event of a new hemorrhage. She and her husband were members of the Jehovah's Witnesses and believed, based on interpretations of the Bible, that the act of receiving blood or blood products precludes an individual from resurrection and everlasting life after death.

Norwood Hospital had a written policy regarding patients who refused to consent to the administration of blood or blood products. According to this policy, if a patient arrived at the hospital in need of emergency medical treatment and there was no time to investigate the patient's circumstances or competence to make decisions regarding treatment, the blood transfusion would be performed if it was necessary to save the patient's life. If the patient, in a nonemergency situation, refused to consent to a blood transfusion, and the patient was a competent adult, not pregnant, and did not have minor children, the hospital would accede to the patient's refusal. If the patient, in a nonemergency situation, refused to consent to a blood transfusion, and the patient was a minor, an incompetent adult, pregnant, or a competent adult with minor children, the hospital's policy was to go to court to settle the rights and responsibilities of the parties.

Although Mrs. Munoz was no longer in an emergency situation once her ulcer stopped bleeding, she had a minor child. Accordingly, the hospital followed its policy and sought a court order requiring blood transfusions that her attending physician believed to be reasonably necessary to save her life.

On that same day, the judge granted a temporary order authorizing the hospital to "administer transfusions of blood or blood products in the event that [the patient] hemorrhages to the extent that her life is severely threatened by loss of blood in the opinion of her attending physicians." Dr. Perrotto stated in an unchallenged affidavit to the court that if Ms. Munoz were to begin bleeding again, she would have an excellent chance of recovering if she received a blood transfusion. However, if she started to bleed and did not receive a blood transfusion, she would probably die. Although recognizing that a competent adult may refuse medical treatment, the judge stated that the physicians could administer the blood transfusions because, if they did not and Mrs. Munoz subsequently died, Ernesto Jr. would be "abandoned." The judge concluded that the state's interest in protecting the well-being of Ernesto Jr. outweighed Mrs. Munoz's right to refuse the medical treatment.

The judge knew that Mrs. Munoz's husband, Ernesto, worked sixteen hours a day, Monday through Friday, and seven hours on Saturday driving his own commercial truck. The judge also found that although her father-in-law was available to assist in caring for Ernesto Jr., his assistance would be inadequate because of his advanced age, his inability to speak English, his unemployment, his lack of a driver's license, and because he had not, in the past, played a significant role in caring for his grandson. The judge ruled that "[t]he State, as *parens patriae,* will not allow a parent to abandon a child, and so it should not allow this most ultimate of voluntary abandonment."

Mrs. Munoz's lawyer argued that as a competent adult, Mrs. Munoz had every legal right to refuse lifesaving medical treatment. The appeals court agreed that there was a long common law tradition of guaranteeing an individual's "bodily integrity," which requires them to give "informed consent" before they are subjected to any medical procedure. The fact that the procedures in question were lifesaving had no bearing on the legal issues.

Although the appeals court also noted that other courts had allowed Christian Scientists to refuse blood transfusions based on their First Amendment free exercise rights, the court felt that it could resolve the case without determining the free exercise issue at all.

The court noted that the Massachusetts courts had previously decided that declining life-sustaining medical treatment may not properly be viewed as an attempt to commit suicide. Refusing medical intervention merely allows the disease to take its natural course; if death were eventually to occur, it would be the result, primarily, of the underlying disease, and not the result of a self-inflicted injury.

The court concluded that the right of a competent individual to refuse medical treatment and to be free from nonconsensual invasion of his or her bodily integrity exists irrespective of that individual's religious beliefs. The court reasoned that the application of a rule that would allow a patient to refuse lifesaving medical treatment depending on the presence or absence of particular religious beliefs was unworkable.

Because there was no compelling evidence that Mrs. Munoz's son actually would be abandoned after her death, the state's interest in protecting the well-being of the child did not outweigh the mother's right to refuse medical treatment. Accordingly, the court concluded that the state's interest in preserving Mrs. Munoz's life did not outweigh her right to medical privacy and the right to decline lifesaving treatment. Whether or not her choice sprang from religious conviction was irrelevant to the majority.

The concurring opinion agreed with the result, but not the reasoning of the majority opinion. The concurring judge felt that the majority had approved legalized suicide. The concurring judge believed that Mrs. Munoz's right to decline medical help even at the risk of death sprang precisely from her desire to preserve her immortal soul.

Not long after the *Norwood Hospital* case, the Massachusetts courts were faced with an even more difficult case that made headlines nationwide. In *Commonwealth v. Twitchell* (1993) the court had to deal with the aftermath of the tragic death of a child. The parents, David and Ginger Twitchell, had been convicted of the crime of involuntary manslaughter in connection with the death of their two-and-one-half-year-old son, Robyn. The Twitchells were Christian Scientists who relied on faith healing, not doctors and hospitals. The question for the court was: Were the parents criminals or was their behavior excused because they sincerely believed in faith healing?

Robyn Twitchell, age two-and-one-half years, died of the consequences of peritonitis caused by the perforation of his bowel, which had been obstructed as a result of an anomaly known as Meckel's diverticulum. There was evidence that the condition could have been corrected by a surgical procedure known to have a high success rate. Robyn's parents did not bring him to a hospital.

After Robyn's death, the couple was charged and tried for the crime of involuntary manslaughter. Massachusetts, like other states, imposes a legal duty on parents to obtain adequate medical care for their children. Involuntary manslaughter involves wanton or reckless conduct that leads to death. Criminal convictions require a showing of "criminal intent." The perpetrator must have had knowledge that what they were doing was wrongful. During Robyn's five-day illness his parents retained a Christian Science practitioner, a Christian Science nurse, and at one time consulted with Nathan Talbot, who held a position in their church known as the "Committee on Publication." As a result of that consultation, David Twitchell read a church publication concerning the legal rights and obligations of Christian Scientists in Massachusetts. That publication quoted a portion of a Massachusetts statute that could be interpreted to mean that relying on faith healing was not a crime. There was also evidence that the intensity of Robyn's distress ebbed and flowed, perhaps causing his parents to believe that prayer would lead to the healing of the illness. Despite these mitigating facts, the jury found the Twitchells guilty. They appealed their convictions.

After reviewing the evidence from the trial the Massachusetts Supreme Court concluded that in the circumstances the Twitchells could have been liable for involuntary manslaughter if the jury found their conduct wanton or reckless. However, the court also concluded that special circumstances in the case could justify a jury finding that the Twitchells reasonably believed that they could rely on spiritual treatment without fear of criminal prosecution. This affirmative defense should have been asserted at the trial and presented to the jury. Because it was not, there was a substantial risk of a miscarriage of justice in this case, and, therefore, the criminal convictions were overturned and a new trial ordered.

During their trial the Twitchells had argued that the Massachusetts criminal statute contained a special provision protecting parents who rely on spiritual "treatment" rather than traditional medical care. The appeals court found that the statute did not in fact contain such a provision. The court did agree with the Twitchells that they had been denied fair warning of the criminal potential of their actions because they were officially misled by an opinion of the Massachusetts attorney general on spiritual healing.

The court thought that a reasonable person not trained in the law might fairly read the attorney general's comments and might come to the conclusion that parents who fail to provide medical services to children on the basis of religious beliefs are not subject to criminal prosecution in any circumstances.

Although the Twitchells were not aware of the attorney general's opinion, they knew of a Christian Science publication called "Legal Rights and Obligations of Christian Scientists in Massachusetts," which did rely on that attorney general's opinion. The court also noted that Nathan Talbot, who served on the Committee on Publication for the church and with whom the Twitchells spoke on the Sunday or Monday before Robyn's death, might well have given the Twitchells different advice had he known that the Twitchells might face criminal charges for failing to get Robyn traditional medical care. The court noted, "Although it has long been held that 'ignorance of the law is no defense' . . . there is substantial justification for treating as a defense the belief that conduct is not a violation of law when a defendant has reasonably relied on an official statement of the law, later determined to be wrong, contained in an official interpretation of the public official who is charged by law with the responsibility for the interpretation or enforcement of the law defining the offense."

During their trial the Twitchells were not allowed to introduce evidence about the attorney general's opinion or the relevant portion of the church's publication. The appeals court held that inclusion of this evidence would have provided them with an affirmative defense to the criminal charges. Because the evidence had not been allowed, the Twitchells did not receive a fair trial. Accordingly, the appeals court set aside the jury's verdicts, and the cases against the parents were remanded for a new trial.

Although child deaths resulting from religiously motivated medical neglect are not numerous, they are more common than one might expect. They can also lead to civil lawsuits. In 1993 a father sued his ex-wife and her Christian Scientist spouse for allowing his son to die without medical care. The eleven-year-old Minnesota boy had juvenile diabetes, which could have been treated with insulin and regulation of the boy's diet and exercise. The boy's mother and her new husband—both Christian Scientists—chose to rely instead on spiritual healing. A jury found the mother, her spouse, a Christian Science nursing home, the local "Committee on Publication," and the church itself liable for $5 million in compensatory damages (which was later reduced in amount). The jury ordered the Christian Science church to pay $9 million in "punitive" damages. Although the parties appealed the case to the U.S. Supreme Court as a violation of their freedom to practice their religion, the Court let the jury verdicts stand. A few months after the case, the Massachusetts legislature repealed the religious exemption for spiritual healing.

Although many devout Christians believe in the healing power of prayer, most also place their faith in conventional medicine. The refusal of medical care for children also extends to mandatory vaccinations. All states have laws requiring medical vaccinations of schoolchildren. In some states, like Washington, parents with religious objections can opt not to have their children vaccinated based on their own religious beliefs. This creates an obvious public health risk for everyone else. These kinds of exemptions might be challenged under the logic of the *Smith* case, discussed in Chapter 3.

Parental neglect statutes are generally aimed at parents who simply fail to provide for their children. Christian Science parents who refuse medical treatment for their children are sincerely motivated by their religious beliefs. Christian Science is based on the teachings of Mary Baker Eddy, who believed she had rediscovered primitive Christianity's lost element of healing that was employed by Jesus himself. Eddy's 1875 book, *Science and Health,* which explains how the faithful can heal themselves, remains the basis for the sect's spiritual healing. Christian Scientists believe that they are not engaged in "faith healing."

Christian Scientists and others have actively lobbied for their right to refuse medical treatment not only for themselves but also for their children. These groups were helped by the federal government. When the Department of Health, Education, and Welfare was dispensing federal child abuse grants in the 1970s, the agency denied grants to states whose laws did not stipulate that relying on faith healing was not abuse. A number of states added these exemptions to receive the grant. (The federal regulation has since been repealed.) Although all states have laws requiring parents to provide food, shelter, and medical care for their children, thirty-eight states still have laws allowing parents to reject conventional medical treatment in favor of spiritual healing or faith healing. In many states parents are required to consult a doctor if the child's condition is life threatening.

Christian Scientists and Jehovah's Witnesses are not the only Christian sects who object to conventional medical treatment. Nationwide there are a number of fundamentalist sects who believe in faith healing and refuse medical treatment for themselves and their children. These groups are also protected by state laws from prosecution for child neglect. In 1999 eleven-year-old diabetic Bo Phillips died at home in Oregon City, Oregon, not far from Portland. Bo's parents were member of a conservative Christian sect, the Followers of Christ, who refused conventional medical treatment. Although an insulin injection probably would have saved his life, his parents relied on the power of prayer. Newspaper reporters discovered that Bo was the third child who had died that year in the congregation. Public records revealed that as many as twenty-five children from the congregation may have died from lack of medical care over the preceding twenty-five years. Like the Massachusetts legislature after Twitchell, the Oregon legislature also deleted the religious exemptions from its criminal neglect statute.

Although most states now recognize that adults have a right to refuse medical treatment, cases involving alleged child neglect will continue. Refusal of medical care is not so much an issue about criminal liability as about a child's right to live versus the parent's right to practice their religion.

Employment Division v. Smith

In this 1990 case, the Supreme Court upheld denial of unemployment benefits to two individuals who had used peyote in a Native American religious ceremony. Although the case only involved two individuals, because it was a U.S. Supreme Court case, it also served as a precedent for other courts nationwide. Viewed as a "drug case," *Smith* did not break new ground. Its application would be somewhat limited because about half the states exempt the religiously inspired use of peyote from their criminal drug laws, and other state legislatures are free to change their laws to create the same type of exemption.

What was important about *Smith* was Justice Scalia's treatment of Smith's and Black's claim that their conduct should be judged under *Sherbert*'s balancing test. Justice Scalia caused a firestorm of protest from religious leaders of all faiths when he almost entirely eliminated the protections of the *Sherbert* test for the faithful.

Recall the pledge case in Chapter 3, *Minersville School District v. Gobitis* (1940), which held that Jehovah's Witnesses could be compelled to recite the pledge of allegiance in public school despite their religious objections. The Court ruled that although religious individuals have a right to freely practice their religions, they are not automatically exempt from laws of "general application" such as a law requiring all schoolchildren to recite the pledge of allegiance. Similarly, the Court had held in *Reynolds v. United States* (1879) that the Mormons could not ignore laws about polygamy merely because their church condoned the practice.

Over the years the Court rethought its position and moved to provide greater religious freedom for individuals who found that adherence to certain laws of "general application" violated their religious beliefs. In the case *Sherbert v. Verner* (1963) the Supreme Court devised a "compelled accommodations" test. Mrs. Sherbert was a member of the Seventh-Day Adventists, who, like some other groups, recognizes Saturday, not Sunday, as the Sabbath. Mrs. Sherbert refused to work on Saturday for religious reasons but was fired. She was denied unemployment benefits because she had refused suitable work "without good cause." In fact, Mrs. Sherbert had turned down jobs because the jobs required Saturday working hours.

The Supreme Court reasoned that the state had imposed a substantial burden on Mrs. Sherbert's exercise of religion. The Court declared that the state could only place such a substantial burden on her free exercise of religion if the state had some "compelling" interest. Because the state had no evidence that exempting religiously motivated refusal to take a job would either lead to fraudulent claims or an excessive number of claims, the state did not have such a compelling interest.

Accordingly, because conditioning benefits on Mrs. Sherbert's working on her Sabbath was a substantial burden on her free exercise of religion, the regulation violated the Free Exercise Clause.

The Court applied the same reasoning in *Wisconsin v. Yoder* (1972) in providing a dispensation for Amish children from attending public high schools. Wisconsin had a compulsory education law, but Amish parents refused to send children over fourteen years old to the public or private schools. Amish parents feared that their children would be exposed to harmful "worldly influences." The Court reasoned that the compulsory education law placed a substantial burden on the Amish's religious beliefs and that Wisconsin's interest in seeing all children educated was not compelling. The *Yoder* decision is notable because it carves out a special exemption for one religious group, which seems to be favoritism.

From this high-water mark in *Yoder,* the doctrine of compelled accommodations started to recede. For example, in *Jimmy Swaggart Ministries v. Board of Equalization* (1990), the Court held that a ministry was not exempt from the general duty to collect and pay sales tax on the sale of Bibles. Although there was a burden, the ministry—unlike Mrs. Sherbert or the Amish—could not show that compliance with the law would violate its religious precepts. Similarly, in 1982 the Supreme Court refused to exempt Amish employers from collecting Social Security taxes from their employees even though the Amish generally "cared for their own." It is clear that this would have amounted to favoritism to members of a particular sect. If *Yoder* had been tried in 1982, the Amish children may have been compelled to attend a school.

In *Smith* the two plaintiffs who were denied unemployment benefits for using peyote argued that they should be exempted from the state's criminal drug laws because their use was religiously inspired. Justice Scalia's majority opinion in *Smith,* however, held that the Free Exercise Clause did not exempt believers from "neutral laws of general application" such as the state criminal statutes against using controlled substances. Scalia wrote that as long as the state generally prohibits an action, the state does not have to provide a compelling reason to apply the rule to religious practices. Accordingly, although the Oregon criminal drug laws placed a substantial burden on the Native American Church, Oregon did not have to provide any compelling reason why the drug laws should apply to religiously inspired use of the illegal substance.

Scalia did leave room for accommodation of religious practice that conflicted with a general law. However, the believer would have the burden of showing that the accommodations were in concert with other constitutional protections, such as freedom of speech or association. Under *Smith*, accommodation is still available in limited circumstances, but it is no longer automatic.

Religious leaders were furious with the *Smith* decision. They recognized that without the *Sherbert* test, minority groups like the Amish would find it far harder to get accommodation from the law for their particular religious practices. Religious leaders viewed the *Smith* decisions as a dangerous precedent that retreated from the Court's earlier vigorous protection of religious practices. Accordingly, religious leaders of various persuasions petitioned Congress to overturn *Smith* legislatively. In 1993 Congress passed the Religious Freedom Restoration Act (RFRA), specifically to over turn *Smith*.

The Religious Freedom Restoration Act's stated purposes were, first, to restore the compelling interest test as set forth in *Sherbert v. Verner* and *Wisconsin v. Yoder* and to guarantee its application in all cases where free exercise of religion is substantially burdened; and, second, to provide a claim or defense to persons whose religious exercise is substantially burdened by government (2000bb). The full text of the act is found in Part 2 of this book.

The act provided a statutory right to challenge state and local laws under the Free Exercise Clause. The state would allow religion to be burdened only if a strict scrutiny test was met, as follows:

> Government shall not substantially burden a person's exercise of religion even if the burden results from a rule of general applicability, except . . . government may substantially burden a person's exercise of religion only if it demonstrates that application of the burden to the person (1) is in furtherance of a compelling government interest; and (2) is the least restrictive means of furthering that compelling governmental interest." (sec. 2000bb–1a and 1b)

Although it looked as if Congress had once again expanded protection for religious practice by using the RFRA to overturn *Smith*, it was not long before the RFRA itself was overturned by the same Court that had penned *Smith*. In 1997 in *City of Boerne v. Flores*, the U.S. Supreme Court overturned the 1993 RFRA. This effectively revived the *Smith* rule.

In *Boerne* the Archbishop of San Antonio applied for a building permit to expand St. Peter's Church located in Boerne, Texas. The Boerne City Council passed an ordinance authorizing the city's Historic Landmark Commission to prepare a preservation plan with proposed historic landmarks and districts. Under the ordinance, the commission had to preapprove construction affecting historic landmarks or buildings in a historic district. City authorities, relying on the ordinance and the designation of a historic district, denied the building permit application.

The archbishop challenged the permit denial in the U.S. District Court, relying on the RFRA as one basis for relief from the refusal to issue the permit. The district court concluded that by enacting RFRA, Congress exceeded the scope of its enforcement power under Article V of the Fourteenth Amendment. The court certified its order for interlocutory appeal, and the fifth circuit reversed, finding RFRA to be constitutional. The U.S. Supreme Court granted certiorari, and in a 6–3 decision reversed, holding the RFRA unconstitutional.

The majority opinion, citing *Marbury v. Madison,* held that the act was unconstitutional because the statute changed the substantive meaning of rights, which was incompatible with the judiciary being the final arbiter of the Constitution's meaning. The majority opinion stated that Congress had gone past enforcing the Free Exercise Clause and had attempted to alter its meaning—a meaning defined by the Court. This could have resulted in mischief: "Shifting legislative majorities could change the Constitution and effectively circumvent the difficult and detailed amendment process contained in Article V." Although senators and representatives immediately proposed a new irreversible version of the act, none has been forthcoming. Accordingly, Free Exercise cases like the zoning dispute are governed by *Smith.*

Part Two

Documents

Court Cases

Abington v. Schempp (1963)

JUSTICE CLARK delivered the opinion of the Court.

[A Pennsylvania law required that] at least ten verses from the Holy Bible shall be read, without comment, at the opening of each public school on each school day. Any child shall be excused from such Bible reading, or attending such Bible reading, upon the written request of his parent or guardian.

The Schempp family, husband and wife and two of their three children, brought suit to enjoin enforcement of the statute, contending that their rights under the Fourteenth Amendment to the Constitution of the United States are, have been, and will continue to be, violated unless this statute be declared unconstitutional as violative of these provisions of the First Amendment.

On each school day at the Abington Senior High School between 8:15 and 8:30 A.M., while the pupils are attending their home rooms or advisory sections, opening exercises are conducted pursuant to the statute. The exercises are broadcast into each room in the school building through an intercommunications system, and are conducted under the supervision of a teacher by students attending the school's radio and television workshop. Selected students from this course gather each morning in the school's workshop studio for the exercises, which include readings by one of the students of 10 verses of the Holy Bible, broadcast to each room in the building. This is followed by the recitation of the Lord's Prayer, likewise over the intercommunications system, but also by the students in the various classrooms, who are asked to stand and join in repeating the prayer in unison. The exercises are closed with the flag salute and such pertinent announcements as are of interest to the students. Participation in the opening exercises, as directed by the statute, is voluntary. The student reading the verses from the Bible may select the passages and read from any version he chooses, although the only copies furnished by the school are the King James version, copies of which were circulated to each teacher by the school district. During the period in which the exercises have been conducted, the King James, the Douay, and the Revised Standard versions of the Bible have been used, as well as the Jewish Holy Scriptures. There are no prefatory statements, no questions asked or solicited, no comments or explanations made, and no interpretations given at or during the exercises. The students and parents are advised that the student may absent himself from the classroom or, should he elect to remain, not participate in the exercises.

It appears from the record that, in schools not having an intercommunications system, the Bible reading and the recitation of the Lord's Prayer were conducted by the home-room teacher, who chose the text of the verses and read them herself or had students read them in rotation or by volunteers. This was followed by a standing recitation of the Lord's Prayer, together with the Pledge of Allegiance to the Flag by the class in unison and a closing announcement of routine school items of interest . . .

The reading of the verses, even without comment, possesses a devotional and religious character and constitutes, in effect, a religious observance. The devotional and religious nature of the morning exercises is made all the more apparent by the fact that the Bible reading is followed immediately by a recital in unison by the pupils of the Lord's Prayer. The fact that some pupils, or, theoretically, all pupils, might be excused from attendance at the exercises does not mitigate the obligatory nature of the ceremony. . . . The exercises are held in the school buildings, and perforce are conducted by and under the authority of the local school authorities, and during school sessions. Since the statute requires the reading of the "Holy Bible," a Christian document, the practice . . . which prefers the Christian religion. . . .

It is true that religion has been closely identified with our history and government. The history of man is inseparable from the history of religion. And . . . since the beginning of that history, many people have devoutly believed that "More things are wrought by prayer than this world dreams of. . . . In *Zorach v. Clauson* . . . we gave specific recognition to the proposition that "[w]e are a religious people whose institutions presuppose a Supreme Being." . . . [T]his Court has decisively settled that the First Amendment's mandate that "Congress shall make no law respecting an establishment of religion, or prohibiting the free exercise thereof" has been made wholly applicable to the States by the Fourteenth Amendment. Twenty-three years ago, in *Cantwell v. Connecticut* . . . this Court, through Mr. Justice Roberts, said: "The fundamental concept of liberty embodied in that [Fourteenth] Amendment embraces the liberties guaranteed by the First Amendment. The First Amendment declares that Congress shall make no law respecting an establishment of religion or prohibiting the free exercise thereof. The Fourteenth Amendment has rendered the legislatures of the states as incompetent as Congress to enact such laws . . . [T]his Court has rejected unequivocally the contention that the Establishment Clause forbids only governmental preference of one religion over another. Almost 20 years ago in *Everson* . . . the Court said that [n]either a state nor the Federal Government can set up a church. Neither can pass laws which aid one religion, aid all religions, or prefer one religion over another."

County of Allegheny v. Greater Pittsburgh ACLU (1989)

During the 1986–1987 holiday season, the crèche was on display on the Grand Staircase from November 26 to January 9. It had a wooden fence on three sides and bore a plaque stating: "This Display Donated by the Holy Name Society." Sometime during the week of December 2, the county placed red and white poinsettia plants around the fence. The county also placed a small evergreen tree, decorated with a red bow, behind each of the two end posts of the fence. These trees stood alongside the manger backdrop and were slightly shorter than it was. The angel thus was at the apex of the crèche display. Altogether, the crèche, the fence, the poinsettias, and the trees occupied a substantial amount of space on the Grand Staircase. No figures of Santa Claus or other decorations appeared on the Grand Staircase . . .

The county uses the crèche as the setting for its annual Christmas-carole program. During the 1986 season, the county invited high school choirs and other musical groups to perform during weekday lunch hours from December 3 through December 23. The county dedicated this program to world peace and to the families of prisoners-of-war and of persons missing in action in Southeast Asia . . .

. . . For a number of years, the city has had a large Christmas tree under the middle arch outside the Grant Street entrance. Following this practice, city employees on November 17, 1986, erected a 45-foot tree under the middle arch and decorated it with lights and ornaments. A few days later, the city placed at the foot of the tree a sign bearing the mayor's name and entitled "Salute to Liberty." Beneath the title, the sign stated: "During this holiday season, the city of Pittsburgh salutes liberty. Let these festive lights remind us that we are the keepers of the flame of liberty and our legacy of freedom." At least since 1982, the city has expanded its Grant Street holiday display to include a symbolic representation of Chanukah, an 8-day Jewish holiday that begins on the 25th day of the Jewish lunar month of Kislev. The 25th of Kislev usually occurs in December, and thus Chanukah is the annual Jewish holiday that falls closest to Christmas Day each year. In 1986, Chanukah began at sundown on December 26.

. . . Chanukah, like Christmas, is a winter holiday; according to some historians, it was associated in ancient times with the winter solstice. Just as some Americans celebrate Christmas without regard to its religious significance, some nonreligious American Jews celebrate Chanukah as an expression of ethnic identity, and "as a cultural or national event, rather than as a specifically religious event." . . . Instead of alienating the Jew from the general culture, Chanukah helps situate him as a participant in that culture. Chanukah, in short, becomes for some the Jewish Christmas. . . . Additionally, menorahs—like Chanukah itself—have a secular as well as a religious dimension. The record in this litigation contains a passing reference to the fact that menorahs "are used extensively by secular Jewish organizations to represent the Jewish people." On December 22 of the 1986 holiday season . . . the menorah was placed next to the city's 45-foot Christmas tree . . . The menorah is owned by Chabad [also known as Lubavitch], a Jewish group, but is stored, erected, and removed each year by the city.

This litigation began . . . when . . . the Greater Pittsburgh Chapter of the American Civil Liberties Union and seven local residents, filed suit against the county and the city, seeking permanently to enjoin the county from displaying the crèche in the county courthouse and the city from displaying the menorah in front of the City/County Building. Respondents claim that the displays of the crèche and the menorah each violate the Establishment Clause of the First Amendment.

In addition to agreeing with the city that the menorah's display does not violate the Establishment Clause, Chabad contends that it has a constitutional right to display the menorah in front of the City-County Building. In light of the Court's disposition of the Establishment Clause question as to the menorah, there is no need to address Chabad's contention.... the District Court denied respondents' request for a permanent injunction. Relying on, the court stated that "the crèche was but part of the holiday decoration of the stairwell and a foreground for the high school choirs which entertained each day at noon." Regarding the menorah, the court concluded that "it was but an insignificant part of another holiday display." The court also found that "the displays had a secular purpose" and "did not create an excessive entanglement of government with religion." Respondents appealed, and a divided panel of the Court of Appeals reversed ...

Precisely because of the religious diversity that is our national heritage, the Founders added to the Constitution a Bill of Rights, the very first words of which declare: "Congress shall make no law respecting an establishment of religion, or prohibiting the free exercise thereof...." Perhaps in the early days of the Republic these words were understood to protect only the diversity within Christianity, but today they are recognized as guaranteeing religious liberty and equality to "the infidel, the atheist, or the adherent of a non-Christian faith such as Islam or Judaism." ... In recent years, we have paid particularly close attention to whether the challenged governmental practice either has the purpose or effect of "endorsing" religion. We have had occasion in the past to apply Establishment Clause principles to the government's display of objects with religious significance ... we held that the display of a copy of the Ten Commandments on the walls of public classrooms violates the Establishment Clause. Closer to the facts of this litigation is *Lynch v. Donnelly*, in which we upheld [Pawtucket, Rhode Island's] inclusion of the crèche in a display, holding ... that the inclusion of the crèche did not have the impermissible effect of advancing or promoting religion.

... There is no doubt, of course, that the crèche itself is capable of communicating a religious message ... Indeed, the crèche in this lawsuit uses words, as well as the picture of the Nativity scene, to make its religious meaning unmistakably clear. "Glory to God in the Highest!" says the angel in the crèche—Glory to God because of the birth of Jesus. This praise to God in Christian terms is indisputably religious—indeed sectarian—just as it is when said in the Gospel or in a church service.

Under the Court's holding in the effect of a crèche display turns on its setting. . . . [In Pawtucket] Santa's house and his reindeer were objects of attention separate from the crèche, and had their specific visual story to tell. Similarly, whatever a "talking" wishing well may be, it obviously was a center of attention separate from the crèche. Here, in contrast, the crèche stands alone: it is the single element of the display on the Grand Staircase.

The presence of Santas or other Christmas decorations elsewhere in the county courthouse, and of the nearby gallery forum, fail to negate the endorsement effect of the crèche. The record demonstrates clearly that the crèche, with its floral frame, was its own display distinct from any other decorations or exhibitions in the building. . . . Furthermore, the crèche sits on the Grand Staircase, the "main" and "most beautiful part" of the building that is the seat of county government. No viewer could reasonably think that it occupies this location without the support and approval of the government. Thus, by permitting the "display of the crèche in this particular physical setting," . . . the county sends an unmistakable message that it supports and promotes the Christian praise to God that is the crèche's religious message.

In sum, *Lynch v. Donnelly* teaches that government may celebrate Christmas in some manner and form, but not in a way that endorses Christian doctrine. Here, Allegheny County has transgressed this line. It has chosen to celebrate Christmas in a way that has the effect of endorsing a patently Christian message: Glory to God for the birth of Jesus Christ. Under and the rest of our cases, nothing more is required to demonstrate a violation of the Establishment Clause. The display of the crèche in this context, therefore, must be permanently enjoined.

City of Boerne v. Flores (1997)

JUSTICE KENNEDY delivered the opinion of the Court.

Situated on a hill in the city of Boerne, Texas, some 28 miles northwest of San Antonio, is St. Peter Catholic Church. Built in 1923, the church's structure replicates the mission style of the region's earlier history. The church seats about 230 worshippers, a number too small for its growing parish. Some 40 to 60 parishioners cannot be accommodated at some Sunday masses. In order to meet the needs of the congregation the Archbishop of San Antonio gave permission to the parish to plan alterations to enlarge the building.

A few months later, the Boerne City Council passed an ordinance authorizing the city's Historic Landmark Commission to prepare a preservation plan with proposed historic landmarks and districts. Under the ordinance, the commission must preapprove construction affecting historic landmarks or buildings in a historic district. Soon afterwards, the Archbishop applied for a building permit so construction to enlarge the church could proceed. City authorities, relying on the ordinance and the designation of a historic district (which, they argued, included the church), denied the application. The Archbishop brought this suit challenging the permit denial in the United States District Court . . . [relying in part on the Religious Freedom Restoration Act (RFRA) which would limit the city's right to regulate the church's proposed expansion. The district court found the RFRA unconstitutional] . . . The [district] court certified its order for interlocutory appeal and the Fifth Circuit reversed, finding RFRA to be constitutional . . . We granted certiorari . . . and now reverse [and find the RFRA unconstitutional].

Congress enacted RFRA in direct response to the Court's decision in . . . *Employment Div., Dept. of Human Resources of Oregon v. Smith* . . . There we considered a Free Exercise Clause claim brought by members of the Native American Church who were denied unemployment benefits when they lost their jobs because they had used peyote. Their practice was to ingest peyote for sacramental purposes, and they challenged an Oregon statute of general applicability which made use of the drug criminal. In evaluating the claim, we declined to apply the balancing test set forth in *Sherbert v. Verner,* . . . under which we would have asked whether Oregon's prohibition substantially burdened a religious practice and, if it did, whether the burden was justified by a compelling government interest. We stated: "[G]overnment's ability to enforce generally applicable prohibitions of socially harmful conduct . . . cannot depend on measuring the effects of a governmental action on a religious objector's spiritual development. To make an individual's obligation to obey such a law contingent upon the law's coincidence with his religious beliefs, except where the State's interest is 'compelling' . . . contradicts both constitutional tradition and common sense." . . .

Four Members of the Court disagreed. They argued the law placed a substantial burden on the Native American Church members so that it could be upheld only if the law served a compelling state interest and was narrowly tailored to achieve that end. . . . These points of constitutional interpretation were debated by Members of Congress in hearings and floor debates. Many criticized the Court's reasoning, and this disagreement resulted in the passage of RFRA. . . .

The Act's stated purposes are:

"(1) to restore the compelling interest test as set forth in *Sherbert v. Verner,* and *Wisconsin v. Yoder,* and to guarantee its application in all cases where free exercise of religion is substantially burdened; and

"(2) to provide a claim or defense to persons whose religious exercise is substantially burdened by government." . . .

RFRA prohibits "[g]overnment" from "substantially burden[ing]" a person's exercise of religion even if the burden results from a rule of general applicability unless the government can demonstrate the burden "(1) is in furtherance of a compelling governmental interest; and (2) is the least restrictive means of furthering that compelling governmental interest."

Under our Constitution, the Federal Government is one of enumerated powers . . . The judicial authority to determine the constitutionality of laws, in cases and controversies, is based on the premise that the "powers of the legislature are defined and limited; and that those limits may not be mistaken, or forgotten, the Constitution is written."

Congress relied on its Fourteenth Amendment enforcement power in enacting the most far-reaching and substantial of RFRA's provisions, those which impose its requirements on the States . . . The Fourteenth Amendment provides, in relevant part:

"Section 1. . . . No State shall make or enforce any law which shall abridge the privileges or immunities of citizens of the United States; nor shall any State deprive any person of life, liberty, or property, without due process of law, nor deny to any person within its jurisdiction the equal protection of the laws.

. . .

"Section 5. The Congress shall have power to enforce, by appropriate legislation, the provisions of this article."

The parties disagree over whether RFRA is a proper exercise of Congress' § 5 power "to enforce" by "appropriate legislation" the constitutional guarantee that no State shall deprive any person of "life, liberty, or property, without due process of law" nor deny any person "equal protection of the laws."

In defense of the Act, respondent the Archbishop contends, with support from the United States, that RFRA is permissible enforcement legislation. Congress, it is said, is only protecting by legislation one of the liberties guaranteed by the Fourteenth Amendment's Due Process Clause, the free exercise of religion . . . [However] Legislation which alters the meaning of the Free Exercise Clause cannot be said to be enforcing the Clause. Congress does not enforce a constitutional right by changing what the right is. It has been given the power "to enforce," not the power to determine what constitutes a constitutional violation. Were it not so, what Congress would be enforcing would no longer be, in any meaningful sense, the "provisions of [the Fourteenth Amendment]."

While the line between measures that remedy or prevent unconstitutional actions and measures that make a substantive change in the governing law is not easy to discern, and Congress must have wide latitude in determining where it lies, the distinction exists and must be observed . . .

If Congress could define its own powers by altering the Fourteenth Amendment's meaning, no longer would the Constitution be "superior paramount law, unchangeable by ordinary means." It would be "on a level with ordinary legislative acts, and, like other acts, . . . alterable when the legislature shall please to alter it." Under this approach, it is difficult to conceive of a principle that would limit congressional power . . .

Regardless of the state of the legislative record, RFRA cannot be considered remedial, preventive legislation, if those terms are to have any meaning. RFRA is so out of proportion to a supposed remedial or preventive object that it cannot be understood as responsive to, or designed to prevent, unconstitutional behavior. It appears, instead, to attempt a substantive change in constitutional protections. . . . [The act's] Sweeping coverage ensures its intrusion at every level of government, displacing laws and prohibiting official actions of almost every description and regardless of subject matter. RFRA's restrictions apply to every agency and official of the Federal, State, and local Governments . . . Any law is subject to challenge at any time by any individual who alleges a substantial burden on his or her free exercise of religion . . . The reach and scope of RFRA distinguish it from other measures passed under Congress' enforcement power . . . the statute . . . would require searching judicial scrutiny of state law with the attendant likelihood of invalidation. This is a considerable congressional intrusion into the States' traditional prerogatives and general authority to regulate for the health and welfare of their citizens.

. . . RFRA's substantial-burden test, however, is not even a discriminatory effects or disparate-impact test. It is a reality of the modern regulatory state that numerous state laws, such as the zoning regulations at issue here, impose a substantial burden on a large class of individuals. When the exercise of religion has been burdened in an incidental way by a law of general application, it does not follow that the persons affected have been burdened any more than other citizens, let alone burdened because of their religious beliefs . . .

Our national experience teaches that the Constitution is preserved best when each part of the Government respects both the Constitution and the proper actions and determinations of the other branches. When the Court has interpreted the Constitution, it has acted within the province of the Judicial Branch, which embraces the duty to say what the law is. . . . When the political branches of the Government act against the background of a judicial interpretation of the Constitution already issued, it must be understood that in later cases and controversies the Court will treat its precedents with the respect due them under settled principles, including *stare decisis,* and contrary expectations must be disappointed. RFRA was designed to control cases and controversies, such as the one before us; but as the provisions of the federal statute here invoked are beyond congressional authority, it is this Court's precedent, not RFRA, which must control.

It is for Congress in the first instance to "determin[e] whether and what legislation is needed to secure the guarantees of the Fourteenth Amendment," and its conclusions are entitled to much deference. Congress' discretion is not unlimited, however, and the courts retain the power, as they have since *Marbury v. Madison,* to determine if Congress has exceeded its authority under the Constitution. Broad as the power of Congress is under the Enforcement Clause of the Fourteenth Amendment, RFRA contradicts vital principles necessary to maintain separation of powers and the federal balance. The judgment of the Court of Appeals sustaining the Act's constitutionality is reversed.

Engel v. Vitale (1962)

JUSTICE BLACK delivered the opinion of the Court.

The respondent Board of Education of Union Free School District No. 9, New Hyde Park, New York, acting in its official capacity under state law, directed the School District's principal to cause the following prayer to be said aloud by each class in the presence of a teacher at the beginning of each school day:

Almighty God, we acknowledge our dependence upon Thee, and we beg Thy blessings upon us, our parents, our teachers and our Country.

This daily procedure was adopted on the recommendation of the State Board of Regents, a governmental agency created by the State Constitution to which the New York Legislature has granted broad supervisory, executive, and legislative powers over the State's public school system. These state officials composed the prayer which they recommended and published as a part of their "Statement on Moral and Spiritual Training in the Schools," saying:

We believe that this Statement will be subscribed to by all men and women of good will, and we call upon all of them to aid in giving life to our program.

Shortly after the practice of reciting the Regents' prayer was adopted by the School District, the parents of ten pupils brought this action in a New York State Court insisting that use of this official prayer in the public schools was contrary to the beliefs, religions, or religious practices of both themselves and their children. Among other things, these parents challenged the constitutionality of both the state law authorizing the School District to direct the use of prayer in public schools and the School District's regulation ordering the recitation of this particular prayer on the ground that these actions of official governmental agencies violate that part of the First Amendment of the Federal Constitution which commands that "Congress shall make no law respecting an establishment of religion"—a command which was "made applicable to the State of New York by the Fourteenth Amendment of the said Constitution." The New York Court of Appeals . . .

sustained an order of the lower state courts which had upheld the power of New York to use the Regents' prayer as a part of the daily procedures of its public schools so long as the schools did not compel any pupil to join in the prayer over his or his parents' objection.

We think that, by using its public school system to encourage recitation of the Regents' prayer, the State of New York has adopted a practice wholly inconsistent with the Establishment Clause. There can, of course, be no doubt that New York's program of daily classroom invocation of God's blessings as prescribed in the Regents' prayer is a religious activity. It is a solemn avowal of divine faith and supplication for the blessings of the Almighty. The nature of such a prayer has always been religious, none of the respondents has denied this, and the trial court expressly so found . . .

The religious nature of prayer was recognized by Jefferson, and has been concurred in by theological writers, the United States Supreme Court, and State courts and administrative officials, including New York's Commissioner of Education. A committee of the New York Legislature has agreed. The Board of Regents as amicus curiae, the respondents, and intervenors all concede the religious nature of prayer, but seek to distinguish this prayer because it is based on our spiritual heritage. . . .

The petitioners contend, among other things, that the state laws requiring or permitting use of the Regents' prayer must be struck down as a violation of the Establishment Clause because that prayer was composed by governmental officials as a part of a governmental program to further religious beliefs. For this reason, petitioners argue, the State's use of the Regents' prayer in its public school system breaches the constitutional wall of separation between Church and State. We agree with that contention, since we think that the constitutional prohibition against laws respecting an establishment of religion must at least mean that, in this country, it is no part of the business of government to compose official prayers for any group of the American people to recite as a part of a religious program carried on by government. . . .

By the time of the adoption of the Constitution, our history shows that there was a widespread awareness among many Americans of the dangers of a union of Church and State. These people knew, some of them from bitter personal experience, that one of the greatest dangers to the freedom of the individual to worship in his own way lay in the

Government's placing its official stamp of approval upon one particular kind of prayer or one particular form of religious services . . .

There can be no doubt that New York's state prayer program officially establishes the religious beliefs embodied in the Regents' prayer. The respondents' argument to the contrary, which is largely based upon the contention that the Regents' prayer is "nondenominational" and the fact that the program, as modified and approved by state courts, does not require all pupils to recite the prayer, but permits those who wish to do so to remain silent or be excused from the room, ignores the essential nature of the program's constitutional defects. Neither the fact that the prayer may be denominationally neutral nor the fact that its observance on the part of the students is voluntary can serve to free it from the limitations of the Establishment Clause, as it might from the Free Exercise Clause, of the First Amendment, both of which are operative against the States by virtue of the Fourteenth Amendment. Although these two clauses may, in certain instances, overlap, they forbid two quite different kinds of governmental encroachment upon religious freedom. The Establishment Clause, unlike the Free Exercise Clause, does not depend upon any showing of direct governmental compulsion and is violated by the enactment of laws which establish an official religion whether those laws operate directly to coerce nonobserving individuals or not. This is not to say, of course, that laws officially prescribing a particular form of religious worship do not involve coercion of such individuals. When the power, prestige and financial support of government is placed behind a particular religious belief, the indirect coercive pressure upon religious minorities to conform to the prevailing officially approved religion is plain. But the purposes underlying the Establishment Clause go much further than that.

Its first and most immediate purpose rested on the belief that a union of government and religion tends to destroy government and to degrade religion. The history of governmentally established religion, both in England and in this country, showed that whenever government had allied itself with one particular form of religion, the inevitable result had been that it had incurred the hatred, disrespect and even contempt of those who held contrary beliefs. That same history showed that many people had lost their respect for any religion that had relied upon the support of government to spread its faith.

The Establishment Clause thus stands as an expression of principle on the part of the Founders of our Constitution that religion is too personal, too sacred, too holy, to permit its "unhallowed perversion" by a civil magistrate. Another purpose of the Establishment Clause rested upon an awareness of the historical fact that governmentally established religions and religious persecutions go hand in hand. The Founders knew that, only a few years after the Book of Common Prayer became the only accepted form of religious services in the established Church of England, an Act of Uniformity was passed to compel all Englishmen to attend those services and to make it a criminal offense to conduct or attend religious gatherings of any other kind—a law which was consistently flouted by dissenting religious groups in England and which contributed to widespread persecutions of people like John Bunyan who persisted in holding "unlawful [religious] meetings . . . to the great disturbance and distraction of the good subjects of this kingdom. . . ." And they knew that similar persecutions had received the sanction of law in several of the colonies in this country soon after the establishment of official religions in those colonies. It was in large part to get completely away from this sort of systematic religious persecution that the Founders brought into being our Nation, our Constitution, and our Bill of Rights, with its prohibition against any governmental establishment of religion.

The New York laws officially prescribing the Regents' prayer are inconsistent both with the purposes of the Establishment Clause and with the Establishment Clause itself. The judgment of the Court of Appeals of New York is reversed, and the cause remanded for further proceedings not inconsistent with this opinion. Reversed and remanded.

Epperson v. Arkansas (1968)

JUSTICE FORTAS delivered the opinion of the Court.

This appeal challenges the constitutionality of the 'anti-evolution' statute which the State of Arkansas adopted in 1928 to prohibit the teaching in its public schools and universities of the theory that man evolved from other species of life. The statute was a product of the upsurge of 'fundamentalist' religious fervor of the twenties. The Arkansas statute was an adaptation of the famous Tennessee 'monkey law,' which that State adopted in 1925. The constitutionality of the Tennessee law was upheld by the Tennessee Supreme Court in the celebrated *Scopes* case in 1925.

The Arkansas law makes it unlawful for a teacher in any state-supported school or university 'to teach the theory or doctrine that mankind ascended or descended from a lower order of animals,' or 'to adopt or use in any such institution a textbook that teaches' this theory. Violation is a misdemeanor and subjects the violator to dismissal from his position.

The present case concerns the teaching of biology in a high school in Little Rock. The Chancery Court . . . held that the statute violated the Fourteenth Amendment to the United States Constitution. The court noted that this Amendment encompasses the prohibitions upon state interference with freedom of speech and thought which are contained in the First Amendment. On appeal, the Supreme Court of Arkansas reversed. Its two-sentence opinion is set forth in the margin. It sustained the statute as an exercise of the State's power to specify the curriculum in public schools. It did not address itself to the competing constitutional considerations.

. . . the law must be stricken because of its conflict with the constitutional prohibition of state laws respecting an establishment of religion or prohibiting the free exercise thereof. The overriding fact is that Arkansas' law selects from the body of knowledge a particular segment which it proscribes for the sole reason that it is deemed to conflict with a particular religious doctrine; that is, with a particular interpretation of the Book of Genesis by a particular religious group.

Government in our democracy, state and national, must be neutral in matters of religious theory, doctrine, and practice. It may not be hostile to any religion or to the advocacy of no religion; and it may not aid, foster, or promote one religion or religious theory against another or even against the militant opposite. The First Amendment mandates governmental neutrality between religion and religion, and between religion and nonreligion.

. . . There is and can be no doubt that the First Amendment does not permit the State to require that teaching and learning must be tailored to the principles or prohibitions of any religious sect or dogma. In *Everson v. Board of Education,* this Court, in upholding a state law to provide free bus service to school children, including those attending parochial schools, said: 'Neither (a State nor the Federal Government) can pass laws which aid one religion, aid all religions, or prefer one religion over another.' . . .

At the following Term of Court, in *People of State of Ill. ex rel. McCollum v. Board of Education,* . . . the Court held that Illinois could not release pupils from class to attend classes of instruction in the school buildings in the religion of their choice. This, it said, would involve the State in using tax-supported property for religious purposes, thereby breaching the 'wall of separation' which, according to Jefferson, the First Amendment was intended to erect between church and state. . . . While study of religions and of the Bible from a literary and historic viewpoint, presented objectively as part of a secular program of education, need not collide with the First Amendment's prohibition, the State may not adopt programs or practices in its public schools or colleges which 'aid or oppose' any religion. . . . This prohibition is absolute. It forbids alike the preference of a religious doctrine or the prohibition of theory which is deemed antagonistic to a particular dogma. . . .

These precedents inevitably determine the result in the present case. The State's undoubted right to prescribe the curriculum for its public schools does not carry with it the right to prohibit, on pain of criminal penalty, the teaching of a scientific theory or doctrine where that prohibition is based upon reasons that violate the First Amendment. . . .

In the present case, there can be no doubt that Arkansas has sought to prevent its teachers from discussing the theory of evolution because it is contrary to the belief of some that the Book of Genesis must be the exclusive source of doctrine as to the origin of man. No suggestion has been made that Arkansas' law may be justified by considerations of state policy other than the religious views of some of its citizens. It is clear that fundamentalist sectarian conviction was and is the law's reason for existence. Its antecedent, Tennessee's 'monkey law,' candidly stated its purpose: to make it unlawful 'to teach any theory that denies the story of the Divine Creation of man as taught in the Bible, and to teach instead that man has descended from a lower order of animals.' Perhaps the sensational publicity attendant upon the Scopes trial induced Arkansas to adopt less explicit language. It eliminated Tennessee's reference to 'the story of the Divine Creation of man' as taught in the Bible, but there is no doubt that the motivation for the law was the same: to suppress the teaching of a theory which, it was thought, 'denied' the divine creation of man.

Arkansas' law cannot be defended as an act of religious neutrality. Arkansas did not seek to excise from the curricula of its schools and universities all discussion of the origin of man. The law's effort was confined to an attempt to blot out a particular theory because of its supposed conflict with the Biblical account, literally read. Plainly, the law is contrary to the mandate of the First, and in violation of the Fourteenth, Amendment to the Constitution.

The judgment of the Supreme Court of Arkansas is reversed.

Application of the President and Directors of Georgetown College (1964)

J. SKELLY WRIGHT, Circuit Judge.

Attorneys for Georgetown Hospital applied for an emergency writ at 4:00 P.M., September 17, 1963, seeking relief from the action of the United States District Court for the District of Columbia denying the hospital's application for permission to administer blood transfusions to an emergency patient. The application recited that 'Mrs. Jesse E. Jones is presently a patient at Georgetown University Hospital,' 'she is in extremis,' according to the attending physician 'blood transfusions are necessary immediately in order to save her life,' and 'consent to the administration thereof can be obtained neither from the patient nor her husband.' The patient and her husband based their refusal on their religious beliefs as Jehovah's Witnesses. The order sought provided that the attending physicians 'may' administer such transfusions to Mrs. Jones as might be 'necessary to save her life.' After the proceedings detailed in Part IV of this opinion, I signed the order at 5:20 P.M. Initially, it may be well to put this matter into fuller legal context, including 'the nature of the controversy, the relation and interests of the parties, and the relief sought in the instant case. The application was in the nature of a petition in equity to the United States District Court for the District of Columbia, a court of general jurisdiction. Though not fully articulated therein, the application sought a decree in the nature of an injunction and declaratory judgment to determine the legal rights and liabilities between the hospital and its agents on the one hand, and Mrs. Jones and her husband on the other. Mrs. Jones subsequently appeared in the cause, in this court, as respondent to the application. The treatment proposed by the hospital in its application was not a single transfusion, but a series of transfusions. The hospital doctors sought a court determination before undertaking either this course of action or some alternative. The temporary order issued was more limited than the order proposed in the original application, in that the phrase 'to save her life' was added, thus limiting the transfusions in both time and number. Such a temporary order to preserve the life of the patient was necessary if the cause were not to be mooted by the death of the patient.

At any time during the series of transfusions which followed, the cause could have been brought on for hearing by motion before the motions division of this court, and the order either vacated, continued, or superseded by an order of a more permanent nature, such as an interlocutory injunction. Neither the patient, her husband, nor the hospital, however, undertook further proceedings in this court or in the District Court during the succeeding days while blood was being administered to the patient.

Mrs. Jones was brought to the hospital by her husband for emergency care, having lost two thirds of her body's blood supply from a ruptured ulcer. She had no personal physician, and relied solely on the hospital staff. She was a total hospital responsibility. It appeared that the patient, age 25, mother of a seven-month-old child, and her husband were both Jehovah's Witnesses, the teachings of which sect, according to their interpretation, prohibited the injection of blood into the body. When death without blood became imminent, the hospital sought the advice of counsel, who applied to the District Court in the name of the hospital for permission to administer blood. Judge Tamm of the District Court denied the application, and counsel immediately applied to me, as a member of the Court of Appeals, for an appropriate writ.

I called the hospital by telephone and spoke with Dr. Westura, Chief Medical Resident, who confirmed the representations made by counsel. I thereupon proceeded with counsel to the hospital, where I spoke to Mr. Jones, the husband of the patient. He advised me that, on religious grounds, he would not approve a blood transfusion for his wife. He said, however, that if the court ordered the transfusion, the responsibility was not his. I advised Mr. Jones to obtain counsel immediately. He thereupon went to the telephone and returned in 10 or 15 minutes to advise that he had taken the matter up with his church and that he had decided that he did not want counsel.

I asked permission of Mr. Jones to see his wife. This he readily granted. Prior to going into the patient's room, I again conferred with Dr. Westura and several other doctors assigned to the case. All confirmed that the patient would die without blood and that there was a better than 50 per cent chance of saving her life with it. Unanimously they strongly recommended it. I then went inside the patient's room.

Her appearance confirmed the urgency which had been represented to me. I tried to communicate with her, advising her again as to what the doctors had said. The only audible reply I could hear was 'Against my will.' It was obvious that the woman was not in a mental condition to make a decision. I was reluctant to press her because of the seriousness of her condition and because I felt that to suggest repeatedly the imminence of death without blood might place a strain on her religious convictions. I asked her whether she would oppose the blood transfusion if the court allowed it. She indicated, as best I could make out, that it would not then be her responsibility.

I returned to the doctors' room where some 10 to 12 doctors were congregated, along with the husband and counsel for the hospital. The President of Georgetown University, Father Bunn, appeared and pleaded with Mr. Jones to authorize the hospital to save his wife's life with a blood transfusion. Mr. Jones replied that the Scriptures say that we should not drink blood, and consequently his religion prohibited transfusions. The doctors explained to Mr. Jones that a blood transfusion is totally different from drinking blood in that the blood physically goes into a different part and through a different process in the body. Mr. Jones was unmoved. I thereupon signed the order allowing the hospital to administer such transfusions as the doctors should determine were necessary to save her life

This opinion is being written solely in connection with the emergency order authorizing the blood transfusions 'to save her life.' It should be made clear that no attempt is being made here to determine the merits of the underlying controversy. Actually, the issue on the merits is *res nova*. Because of the demonstrated imminence of death from loss of blood, signing the order was necessary to maintain the status quo and prevent the issue respecting the rights of the parties in the premises from becoming moot before full consideration was possible. But maintaining the status quo is not the only consideration in determining whether an emergency writ should issue. The likelihood of eventual success on appeal is of primary importance, and thus must be here considered.

Before proceeding with this inquiry, it may be useful to state what this case does not involve. This case does not involve a person who, for religious or other reasons, has refused to seek medical attention. It does not involve a disputed medical judgment or a dangerous or crippling operation. Nor does it involve the delicate question of saving the newborn in preference to the mother. Mrs. Jones sought medical attention and placed on the hospital the legal responsibility for her proper care. In its dilemma, not of its own making, the hospital sought judicial direction.

It has been firmly established that the courts can order compulsory medical treatment of children for any serious illness or injury . . . and that adults, sick or well, can be required to submit to compulsory treatment or prophylaxis, at least for contagious diseases. And there are no religious exemptions from these orders. Of course, there is here no sick child or contagious disease. However, the sick child cases may provide persuasive analogies because Mrs. Jones was in extremis and hardly compos mentis at the time in question; she was as little able competently to decide for herself as any child would be. Under the circumstances, it may well be the duty of a court of general jurisdiction, such as the United States District Court for the District of Columbia, to assume the responsibility of guardianship for her, as for a child, at least to the extent of authorizing treatment to save her life. And if, as shown above, a parent has no power to forbid the saving of his child's life, a fortiori the husband of the patient here had no right to order the doctors to treat his wife in a way so that she would die.

The child cases point up another consideration. The patient, 25 years old, was the mother of a seven-month-old child. The state, as *parens patriae,* will not allow a parent to abandon a child, and so it should not allow this most ultimate of voluntary abandonments. The patient had a responsibility to the community to care for her infant. Thus the people had an interest in preserving the life of this mother.

Apart from the child cases, a second range of factors may be considered. It is suggested that an individual's liberty to control himself and his life extends even to the liberty to end his life. Thus, 'in those states where attempted suicide has been made lawful by statute (or the lack of one), the refusal of necessary medical aid (to one's self), whether equal to or less than attempted suicide, must be conceded to be lawful.' . . . And, conversely, it would follow that where attempted suicide is illegal by the common law or by statute, a person may not be allowed to refuse necessary medical assistance when death is likely to ensue without it. Only quibbles about the distinction between misfeasance and nonfeasance, or the specific intent necessary to be guilty of attempted suicide, could be raised against this latter conclusion.

If self-homicide is a crime, there is no exception to the law's command for those who believe the crime to be divinely ordained. The

Mormon cases in the Supreme Court establish that there is no religious exception to criminal laws, and state obiter the very example that a religiously inspired suicide attempt would be within the law's authority to prevent. . . . But whether attempted suicide is a crime is in doubt in some jurisdictions, including the District of Columbia.

The Gordian knot of this suicide question may be cut by the simple fact that Mrs. Jones did not want to die. Her voluntary presence in the hospital as a patient seeking medical help testified to this. Death, to Mrs. Jones, was not a religiously commanded goal, but an unwanted side effect of a religious scruple. There is no question here of interfering with one whose religious convictions counsel his death, like the Buddhist monks who set themselves afire. Nor are we faced with the question of whether the state should intervene to reweigh the relative values of life and death, after the individual has weighed them for himself and found life wanting. Mrs. Jones wanted to live.

A third set of considerations involved the position of the doctors and the hospital. Mrs. Jones was their responsibility to treat. The hospital doctors had the choice of administering the proper treatment or letting Mrs. Jones die in the hospital bed, thus exposing themselves, and the hospital, to the risk of civil and criminal liability in either case. It is not certain that Mrs. Jones had any authority to put the hospital and its doctors to this impossible choice. The normal principle that an adult patient directs her doctors is based on notions of commercial contract which may have less relevance to life-or-death emergencies. It is not clear just where a patient would derive her authority to command her doctor to treat her under limitations which would produce death. The patient's counsel suggests that this authority is part of constitutionally protected liberty. But neither the principle that life and liberty are inalienable rights, nor the principle of liberty of religion, provides an easy answer to the question whether the state can prevent martyrdom. Moreover, Mrs. Jones had no wish to be a martyr. And her religion merely prevented her consent to a transfusion. If the law undertook the responsibility of authorizing the transfusion without her consent, no problem would be raised with respect to her religious practice. Thus, the effect of the order was to preserve for Mrs. Jones the life she wanted without sacrifice of her religious beliefs.

The final, and compelling, reason for granting the emergency writ was that a life hung in the balance. There was no time for research and reflection. Death could have mooted the cause in a matter of minutes, if action were not taken to preserve the status quo. To refuse to act, only to find later that the law required action, was a risk I was unwilling to accept. I determined to act on the side of life.

Lee v. Weisman (1992)

JUSTICE KENNEDY delivered the opinion of the Court.

School principals in the public school system of the city of Providence, Rhode Island, are permitted to invite members of the clergy to offer invocation and benediction prayers as part of the formal graduation ceremonies for middle schools and for high schools. The question before us is whether including clerical members who offer prayers as part of the official school graduation ceremony is consistent with the Religion Clauses of the First Amendment, provisions the Fourteenth Amendment makes applicable with full force to the States and their school districts.

Deborah Weisman graduated from Nathan Bishop Middle School, a public school in Providence, at a formal ceremony in June 1989. She was about 14 years old. For many years it has been the policy of the Providence School Committee and the Superintendent of Schools to permit principals to invite members of the clergy to give invocations and benedictions at middle school and high school graduations. Many, but not all, of the principals elected to include prayers as part of the graduation ceremonies. Acting for himself and his daughter, Deborah's father, Daniel Weisman, objected to any prayers at Deborah's middle school graduation, but to no avail. The school principal, petitioner Robert E. Lee, invited a rabbi to deliver prayers at the graduation exercises for Deborah's class. Rabbi Leslie Gutterman, of the Temple Beth El in Providence, accepted.

It has been the custom of Providence school officials to provide invited clergy with a pamphlet entitled "Guidelines for Civic Occasions," prepared by the National Conference of Christians and Jews. The Guidelines recommend that public prayers at nonsectarian civic ceremonies be composed with "inclusiveness and sensitivity," though they acknowledge that "[p]rayer of any kind may be inappropriate on some civic occasions." . . . The principal gave Rabbi Gutterman the pamphlet before the graduation and advised him the invocation and benediction should be nonsectarian.

Rabbi Gutterman's prayers were as follows:

INVOCATION
"God of the Free, Hope of the Brave:
"For the legacy of America where diversity is celebrated and the rights of minorities are protected, we thank You. May these young men and women grow up to enrich it.
"For the liberty of America, we thank You. May these new graduates grow up to guard it.
"For the political process of America in which all its citizens may participate, for its court system where all may seek justice we thank You. May those we honor this morning always turn to it in trust.
"For the destiny of America we thank You. May the graduates of Nathan Bishop Middle School so live that they might help to share it.
"May our aspirations for our country and for these young people, who are our hope for the future, be richly fulfilled.
      AMEN"

BENEDICTION
"O God, we are grateful to You for having endowed us with the capacity for learning which we have celebrated on this joyous commencement.
"Happy families give thanks for seeing their children achieve an important milestone. Send Your blessings upon the teachers and administrators who helped prepare them.
"The graduates now need strength and guidance for the future, help them to understand that we are not complete with academic knowledge alone. We must each strive to fulfill what You require of us all: To do justly, to love mercy, to walk humbly.
"We give thanks to You, Lord, for keeping us alive, sustaining us and allowing us to reach this special, happy occasion.
      AMEN"

Deborah [Weisman] and her family attended the graduation, where the prayers were recited. In July 1989, Daniel Weisman filed an amended complaint seeking a permanent injunction barring petitioners, various officials of the Providence public schools, from inviting the clergy to deliver invocations and benedictions at future graduations. . . .

The District Court [granted an injunction]... based on its reading of our precedents.... The court determined that the practice of including invocations and benedictions, even so-called nonsectarian ones, in public school graduations creates an identification of governmental power with religious practice, endorses religion, and violates the Establishment Clause.... On appeal, the United States Court of Appeals for the First Circuit affirmed.... We grant certiorari, and now affirm.

The principle that government may accommodate the free exercise of religion does not supersede the fundamental limitations imposed by the Establishment Clause. It is beyond dispute that, at a minimum, the Constitution guarantees that government may not coerce anyone to support or participate in religion or its exercise, or otherwise act in a way which "establishes a [state] religion or religious faith, or tends to do so." ... The State's involvement in the school prayers challenged today violates these central principles....

Divisiveness, of course, can attend any state decision respecting religions, and neither its existence nor its potential necessarily invalidates the State's attempts to accommodate religion in all cases. The potential for divisiveness is of particular relevance here though, because it centers around an overt religious exercise in a secondary school environment where, as we discuss below, subtle coercive pressures exist and where the student had no real alternative which would have allowed her to avoid the fact or appearance of participation ...

The degree of school involvement here made it clear that the graduation prayers bore the imprint of the State and thus put school-age children who objected in an untenable position. We turn our attention now to consider the position of the students, both those who desired the prayer and she who did not ...

We need not look beyond the circumstances of this case to see the phenomenon at work. The undeniable fact is that the school district's supervision and control of a high school graduation ceremony places public pressure, as well as peer pressure, on attending students to stand as a group or, at least, maintain respectful silence during the invocation and benediction. This pressure, though subtle and indirect, can be as real as any overt compulsion. Of course, in our culture standing or remaining silent can signify adherence to a view or simple respect for the views of others. And no doubt some persons who have no desire to join a prayer have little objection to standing as a sign of respect for those who do. But for the dissenter of high school age, who has a reasonable perception that she is being forced by the State to pray in a manner her conscience will not allow, the injury is no less real. There can be no doubt that for many, if not most, of the students at the graduation, the act of standing or remaining silent was an expression of participation in the rabbi's prayer. That was the very point of the religious exercise. It is of little comfort to a dissenter, then, to be told that for her the act of standing or remaining in silence signifies mere respect, rather than participation. What matters is that, given our social conventions, a reasonable dissenter in this milieu could believe that the group exercise signified her own participation or approval of it . . .

We do not hold that every state action implicating religion is invalid if one or a few citizens find it offensive. People may take offense at all manner of religious as well as nonreligious messages, but offense alone does not in every case show a violation. We know too that sometimes to endure social isolation or even anger may be the price of conscience or nonconformity. But, by any reading of our cases, the conformity required of the student in this case was too high an exaction to withstand the test of the Establishment Clause. The prayer exercises in this case are especially improper because the State has in every practical sense compelled attendance and participation in an explicit religious exercise at an event of singular importance to every student, one the objecting student had no real alternative to avoid.

Our jurisprudence in this area is of necessity one of line-drawing, of determining at what point a dissenter's rights of religious freedom are infringed by the State.

The First Amendment does not prohibit practices which by any realistic measure create none of the dangers which it is designed to prevent and which do not so directly or substantially involve the state in religious exercises or in the favoring of religion as to have meaningful and practical impact. It is of course true that great consequences can grow from small beginnings, but the measure of constitutional adjudication is the ability and willingness to distinguish between real threat and mere shadow. . . .

Lynch v. Donnelly (1984)

CHIEF JUSTICE BURGER delivered the opinion of the Court.

We granted certiorari to decide whether the Establishment Clause of the First Amendment prohibits a municipality from including a crèche, or Nativity scene, in its annual Christmas display.

Each year, in cooperation with the downtown retail merchants' association, the City of Pawtucket, Rhode Island, erects a Christmas display as part of its observance of the Christmas holiday season. The display is situated in a park owned by a nonprofit organization and located in the heart of the shopping district. The display is essentially like those to be found in hundreds of towns or cities across the Nation—often on public grounds—during the Christmas season. The Pawtucket display comprises many of the figures and decorations traditionally associated with Christmas, including, among other things, a Santa Claus house, reindeer pulling Santa's sleigh, candy-striped poles, a Christmas tree, carolers, cutout figures representing such characters as a clown, an elephant, and a teddy bear, hundreds of colored lights, a large banner that reads "SEASONS GREETINGS," and the crèche at issue here. All components of this display are owned by the City.

The crèche, which has been included in the display for 40 or more years, consists of the traditional figures, including the Infant Jesus, Mary and Joseph, angels, shepherds, kings, and animals, all ranging in height from 5" to 5'. In 1973, when the present crèche was acquired, it cost the City $1365; it now is valued at $200. The erection and dismantling of the crèche costs the City about $20 per year; nominal expenses are incurred in lighting the crèche. No money has been expended on its maintenance for the past 10 years.

Respondents, Pawtucket residents and individual members of the Rhode Island affiliate of the American Civil Liberties Union, and the affiliate itself, brought this action in the United States District Court for Rhode Island, challenging the City's inclusion of the crèche in the annual display. The District Court held that the City's inclusion of the crèche in the display violates the Establishment Clause, . . . The District Court found that, by including the crèche in the Christmas display, the City has "tried to endorse and promulgate religious beliefs," . . . and that "erection of the crèche has the real and substantial effect of affiliating the City with the Christian beliefs that the crèche represents." . . . This "appearance of official sponsorship," it believed, "confers more than a remote and incidental benefit on Christianity." . . . Last, although the court acknowledged the absence of administrative entanglement, it found that excessive entanglement has been fostered as a result of the political divisiveness of including the crèche in the celebration. . . . The City was permanently enjoined from including the crèche in the display. A divided panel of the Court of Appeals for the First Circuit affirmed . . . and we reverse.

This Court has explained that the purpose of the Establishment and Free Exercise Clauses of the First Amendment is "to prevent, as far as possible, the intrusion of either [the church or the state] into the precincts of the other." At the same time, however, the Court has recognized that "total separation is not possible in an absolute sense. Some relationship between government and religious organizations is inevitable." In every Establishment Clause case, we must reconcile the inescapable tension between the objective of preventing unnecessary intrusion of either the church or the state upon the other, and the reality that, as the Court has so often noted, total separation of the two is not possible.

The Court has sometimes described the Religion Clauses as erecting a "wall" between church and state, ... The concept of a "wall" of separation is a useful figure of speech probably deriving from views of Thomas Jefferson. The metaphor has served as a reminder that the Establishment Clause forbids an established church or anything approaching it. But the metaphor itself is not a wholly accurate description of the practical aspects of the relationship that in fact exists between church and state.

No significant segment of our society and no institution within it can exist in a vacuum or in total or absolute isolation from all the other parts, much less from government. "It has never been thought either possible or desirable to enforce a regime of total separation. . . . " . . . Nor does the Constitution require complete separation of church and state; it affirmatively mandates accommodation, not merely tolerance, of all religions, and forbids hostility toward any. . . . Anything less would require the "callous indifference" we have said was never intended by the Establishment Clause. . . . Indeed, we have observed, such hostility would bring us into "war with our national tradition as embodied in the First Amendment's guaranty of the free exercise of religion."

. . .

Executive Orders and other official announcements of Presidents and of the Congress have proclaimed both Christmas and Thanksgiving National Holidays in religious terms. And, by Acts of Congress, it has long been the practice that federal employees are released from duties on these National Holidays, while being paid from the same public revenues . . . Other examples of reference to our religious heritage are found in the statutorily prescribed national motto "In God We Trust," . . . which Congress and the President mandated for our currency, . . . and in the language "One nation under God," as part of the Pledge of Allegiance to the American flag . . . Art galleries supported by public revenues display religious paintings . . . The very chamber in which oral arguments on this case were heard is decorated with a notable and permanent—not seasonal—symbol of religion: Moses with Ten Commandments . . . This history may help explain why the Court consistently has declined to take a rigid, absolutist view of the Establishment Clause.

In the line-drawing process we have often found it useful to inquire whether the challenged law or conduct has a secular purpose, whether its principal or primary effect is to advance or inhibit religion, and whether it creates an excessive entanglement of government with religion. . . . In this case, the focus of our inquiry must be on the crèche in the context of the Christmas season. The District Court inferred from the religious nature of the crèche that the City has no secular purpose for the display . . . The display is sponsored by the City to celebrate the Holiday and to depict the origins of that Holiday. These are legitimate secular purposes. . . . We are satisfied that the City has a secular purpose for including the crèche, that the City has not impermissibly advanced religion, and that including the crèche does not create excessive entanglement between religion and government.

. . . The display engenders a friendly community spirit of good will in keeping with the season. The crèche may well have special meaning to those whose faith includes the celebration of religious masses, but none who sense the origins of the Christmas celebration would fail to be aware of its religious implications. That the display brings people into the central city, and serves commercial interests and benefits merchants and their employees, does not, as the dissent points out, determine the character of the display . . .

We hold that, notwithstanding the religious significance of the crèche, the City of Pawtucket has not violated the Establishment Clause of the First Amendment.

Justice BRENNAN, dissenting.

. . . In my view, Pawtucket's maintenance and display at public expense of a symbol as distinctively sectarian as a crèche simply cannot be squared with our prior cases. And it is plainly contrary to the purposes and values of the Establishment Clause to pretend, as the Court does, that the otherwise secular setting of Pawtucket's nativity scene dilutes in some fashion the crèche's singular religiosity, or that the City's annual display reflects nothing more than an "acknowledgment" of our shared national heritage. Neither the character of the Christmas holiday itself, nor our heritage of religious expression supports this result. . . . That the crèche retained this religious character for the people and municipal government of Pawtucket is suggested by the Mayor's testimony at trial in which he stated that for him, as well as others in the City, the effort to eliminate the nativity scene from Pawtucket's Christmas celebration "is a step towards establishing another religion, non-religion that it may be." Plainly, the City and its leaders understood that the inclusion of the crèche in its display would serve the wholly religious purpose of "keep[ing] 'Christ in Christmas.'"

Finally, and most importantly, even in the context of Pawtucket's seasonal celebration, the crèche retains a specifically Christian religious meaning. I refuse to accept the notion implicit in today's decision that non-Christians would find that the religious content of the crèche is eliminated by the fact that it appears as part of the City's otherwise secular celebration of the Christmas holiday . . .

The inclusion of a crèche in Pawtucket's otherwise secular celebration of Christmas clearly violates these principles. Unlike such secular figures as Santa Claus, reindeer and carolers, a nativity scene represents far more than a mere "traditional" symbol of Christmas. The essence of the crèche's symbolic purpose and effect is to prompt the observer to experience a sense of simple awe and wonder appropriate to the contemplation of one of the central elements of Christian dogma—that God sent His son into the world to be a Messiah. Contrary to the Court's suggestion, the crèche is far from a mere representation of a "particular historic religious event." It is, instead, best understood as a mystical re-creation of an event that lies at the heart of Christian faith. To suggest, as the Court does, that such a symbol is merely "traditional" and therefore no different from Santa's house or reindeer is not only offensive to those for whom the crèche has profound significance, but insulting to those who insist for religious or personal reasons that the story of Christ is in no sense a part of "history" nor an unavoidable element of our national "heritage."

Minersville School District v. Gobitis (1940)

JUSTICE FRANKFURTER delivered the opinion of the Court.

Lillian Gobitis, aged twelve, and her brother William, aged ten, were expelled from the public schools of Minersville, Pennsylvania, for refusing to salute the national flag as part of a daily school exercise. The local Board of Education required both teachers and pupils to participate in this ceremony. The ceremony is a familiar one. The right hand is placed on the breast and the following pledge recited in unison: 'I pledge allegiance to my flag, and to the Republic for which it stands; one nation indivisible, with liberty and justice for all.' While the words are spoken, teachers and pupils extend their right hands in salute to the flag. The Gobitis family are affiliated with 'Jehovah's Witnesses,' for whom the Bible as the Word of God is the supreme authority. The children had been brought up conscientiously to believe that such a gesture of respect for the flag was forbidden by command of scripture.

We must decide whether the requirement of participation in such a ceremony, exacted from a child who refuses upon sincere religious grounds, infringes without due process of law the liberty guaranteed by the Fourteenth Amendment. Centuries of strife over the erection of particular dogmas as exclusive or all-comprehending faiths led to the inclusion of a guarantee for religious freedom in the Bill of Rights. The First Amendment, and the Fourteenth through its absorption of the First, sought to guard against repetition of those bitter religious struggles by prohibiting the establishment of a state religion and by securing to every sect the free exercise of its faith. So pervasive is the acceptance of this precious right that its scope is brought into question, as here, only when the conscience of individuals collides with the felt necessities of society.

Certainly the affirmative pursuit of one's convictions about the ultimate mystery of the universe and man's relation to it is placed beyond the reach of law. Government may not interfere with organized or individual expression of belief or disbelief. Propagation of belief—or even of disbelief in the supernatural—is protected, whether in church or chapel, mosque or synagogue, tabernacle or meetinghouse. Likewise the Constitution assures generous immunity to the individual from imposition of penalties for offending, in the course of his own religious activities, the religious views of others, be they a minority or those who are dominant in government. . . .

But the manifold character of man's relations may bring his conception of religious duty into conflict with the secular interests of his fellow-men. When does the constitutional guarantee compel exemption from doing what society thinks necessary for the promotion of some great common end, or from a penalty for conduct which appears dangerous to the general good? To state the problem is to recall the truth that no single principle can answer all of life's complexities. The right to freedom of religious belief, however dissident and however obnoxious to the cherished beliefs of others—even of a majority—is itself the denial of an absolute. But to affirm that the freedom to follow conscience has itself no limits in the life of a society would deny that very plurality of principles which, as a matter of history, underlies protection of religious toleration. . . . Our present task then, as so often the case with courts, is to reconcile two rights in order to prevent either from destroying the other. But, because in safeguarding conscience we are dealing with interests so subtle and so dear, every possible leeway should be given to the claims of religious faith.

. . . The religious liberty which the Constitution protects has never excluded legislation of general scope not directed against doctrinal loyalties of particular sects. Judicial nullification of legislation cannot be justified by attributing to the framers of the Bill of Rights views for which there is no historic warrant. Conscientious scruples have not, in the course of the long struggle for religious toleration, relieved the individual from obedience to a general law not aimed at the promotion or restriction of religious beliefs. The mere possession of religious convictions which contradict the relevant concerns of a political society does not relieve the citizen from the discharge of political responsibilities. The necessity for this adjustment has again and again been recognized. . . .

The question remains whether school children, like the Gobitis children, must be excused from conduct required of all the other children in the promotion of national cohesion. We are dealing with an interest inferior to none in the hierarchy of legal values. National unity is the basis of national security. To deny the legislature the right to select appropriate means for its attainment presents a totally different order of problem from that of the propriety of subordinating the possible ugliness of littered streets to the free expression of opinion through distribution of handbills. . . .

The ultimate foundation of a free society is the binding tie of cohesive sentiment. Such a sentiment is fostered by all those agencies of the mind and spirit which may serve to gather up the traditions of a people, transmit them from generation to generation, and thereby create that continuity of a treasured common life which constitutes a civilization. 'We live by symbols.' The flag is the symbol of our national unity, transcending all internal differences, however large, within the framework of the Constitution. This Court has had occasion to say that ' . . . the flag is the symbol of the nation's power,—the emblem of freedom in its truest, best sense. . . . it signifies government resting on the consent of the governed; liberty regulated by law; the protection of the weak against the strong; security against the exercise of arbitrary power; and absolute safety for free institutions against foreign aggression.' . . .

The wisdom of training children in patriotic impulses by those compulsions which necessarily pervade so much of the educational process is not for our independent judgment. Even were we convinced of the folly of such a measure, such belief would be no proof of its unconstitutionality. For ourselves, we might be tempted to say that the deepest patriotism is best engendered by giving unfettered scope to the most crotchety beliefs. Perhaps it is best, even from the standpoint of those interests which ordinances like the one under review seek to promote, to give to the least popular sect leave from conformities like those here in issue. But the court-room is not the arena for debating issues of educational policy. It is not our province to choose among competing considerations in the subtle process of securing effective loyalty to the traditional ideals of democracy, while respecting at the same time individual idiosyncrasies among a people so diversified in racial origins and religious allegiances. So to hold would in effect make us the school board for the country. That authority has not been given to this Court, nor should we assume it.

We are dealing here with the formative period in the development of citizenship. Great diversity of psychological and ethical opinion exists among us concerning the best way to train children for their place in society. Because of these differences and because of reluctance to permit a single, iron-cast system of education to be imposed upon a nation compounded of so many strains, we have held that, even though public education is one of our most cherished democratic institutions, the Bill of Rights bars a state from compelling all children to attend the public schools. . . . But it is a very different thing for this Court to exercise censorship over the conviction of legislatures that a particular program or exercise will best promote in the minds of children who attend the common schools an attachment to the institutions of their country.

What the school authorities are really asserting is the right to awaken in the child's mind considerations as to the significance of the flag contrary to those implanted by the parent. . . . That the flag salute is an allowable portion of a school program for those who do not invoke conscientious scruples is surely not debatable. But for us to insist that, though the ceremony may be required, exceptional immunity must be given to dissidents, is to maintain that there is no basis for a legislative judgment that such an exemption might introduce elements of difficulty into the school discipline, might cast doubts in the minds of the other children which would themselves weaken the effect of the exercise. . . .

Judicial review, itself a limitation on popular government, is a fundamental part of our constitutional scheme. But to the legislature no less than to courts is committed the guardianship of deeply-cherished liberties.

To fight out the wise use of legislative authority in the forum of public opinion and before legislative assemblies rather than to transfer such a contest to the judicial arena, serves to vindicate the self-confidence of a free people.

Reversed.

McCollum v. Board of Education (1948)

. . . . Vashti McCollum [was] a resident and taxpayer of Champaign and a parent whose child was then enrolled in the Champaign public schools. Illinois has a compulsory education law which, with exceptions, requires parents to send their children, aged seven to sixteen, to its tax-supported public schools, where the children are to remain in attendance during the hours when the schools are regularly in session. Parents who violate this law commit a misdemeanor punishable by fine unless the children attend private or parochial schools which meet educational standards fixed by the State.

. . . In 1940, interested members of the Jewish, Roman Catholic, and a few of the Protestant faiths formed a voluntary association called the Champaign Council on Religious Education. They obtained permission from the Board of Education to offer classes in religious instruction to public school pupils in grades four to nine, inclusive. Classes were made up of pupils whose parents signed printed cards requesting that their children be permitted to attend; they were held weekly, thirty minutes for the lower grades, forty-five minutes for the higher. The council employed the religious teachers at no expense to the school authorities, but the instructors were subject to the approval and supervision of the superintendent of schools. The classes were taught in three separate religious groups by Protestant teachers, Catholic priests, and a Jewish rabbi. . . . Classes were conducted in the regular classrooms of the school building. Students who did not choose to take the religious instruction were not released from public school duties; they were required to leave their classrooms and go to some other place in the school building for pursuit of their secular studies. On the other hand, students who were released from secular study for the religious instructions were required to be present at the religious classes. Reports of their presence or absence were to be made to their secular teachers.

The foregoing facts . . . show the use of tax supported property for religious instruction and the close cooperation between the school authorities and the religious council in promoting religious education. The operation of the State's compulsory education system thus assists and is integrated with the program of religious instruction carried on by separate religious sects. Pupils compelled by law to go to school for secular education are released in part from their legal duty upon the condition that they attend the religious classes. This is beyond all question a utilization of the tax-established and tax-supported public school system to aid religious groups to spread their faith. And it falls squarely under the ban of the First Amendment (made applicable to the States by the Fourteenth) . . . counsel for the respondents challenge those views as dicta, and urge that we reconsider and repudiate them. They argue that, historically, the First Amendment was intended to forbid only government preference of one religion over another, not an impartial governmental assistance of all religions. In addition, they ask that we distinguish or overrule our holding in the *Everson* case that the Fourteenth Amendment made the "establishment of religion" clause of the First Amendment applicable as a prohibition against the States. After giving full consideration to the arguments presented, we are unable to accept either of these contentions.

To hold that a state cannot, consistently with the First and Fourteenth Amendments, utilize its public school system to aid any or all religious faiths or sects in the dissemination of their doctrines and ideals does not, as counsel urge, manifest a governmental hostility to religion or religious teachings. A manifestation of such hostility would be at war with our national tradition as embodied in the First Amendment's guaranty of the free exercise of religion. For the First Amendment rests upon the premise that both religion and government can best work to achieve their lofty aims if each is left free from the other within its respective sphere. Or, as we said in the *Everson* case, the First Amendment has erected a wall between Church and State which must be kept high and impregnable.

Here not only are the State's tax-supported public school buildings used for the dissemination of religious doctrines. The State also affords sectarian groups an invaluable aid in that it helps to provide pupils for their religious classes through use of the State's compulsory public school machinery. This is not separation of Church and State.

The cause is reversed and remanded to the State Supreme Court for proceedings not inconsistent with this opinion.

Reversed and remanded.

Newdow v. U.S. Congress (9th Circuit 2002)

Newdow is an atheist whose daughter attends public elementary school in the Elk Grove Unified School District ("EGUSD") in California. In accordance with state law and a school district rule, EGUSD teachers begin each school day by leading their students in a recitation of the Pledge of Allegiance ("the Pledge"). The California Education Code requires that public schools begin each school day with "appropriate patriotic exercises" and that "[t]he giving of the Pledge of Allegiance to the Flag of the United States of America shall satisfy" this requirement. Cal. Educ. Code § 52720 (1989) (hereinafter "California statute"). To implement the California statute, the school district that Newdow's daughter attends has promulgated a policy that states, in pertinent part: "Each elementary school class [shall] recite the pledge of allegiance to the flag once each day."

The classmates of Newdow's daughter in the EGUSD are led by their teacher in reciting the Pledge codified in federal law. On June 22, 1942, Congress first codified the Pledge as "I pledge allegiance to the flag of the United States of America and to the Republic for which it stands, one Nation indivisible, with liberty and justice for all." . . . On June 14, 1954, Congress [voted] to add the words "under God" after the word "Nation." . . . The Pledge is currently codified as "I pledge allegiance to the Flag of the United States of America, and to the Republic for which it stands, one nation under God, indivisible, with liberty and justice for all." 4 U.S.C. § 4 (1998) (Title 36 was revised and recodified by Pub.L. No. 105–225, § 2(a), 112 Stat. 1494 (1998). Section 172 was abolished, and the Pledge is now found in Title 4.)

Newdow does not allege that his daughter's teacher or school district requires his daughter to participate in reciting the Pledge. [FN3] Rather, he claims that his daughter is injured when she is compelled to "watch and listen as her state-employed teacher in her state-run school leads her classmates in a ritual proclaiming that there is a God, and that our's [sic] is 'one nation under God.'"

Newdow's complaint in the district court challenged the constitutionality, under the First Amendment, of the 1954 Act, the California statute, and the school district's policy requiring teachers to lead willing students in recitation of the Pledge. He sought declaratory and injunctive relief, but did not seek damages.

. . . . Although the district court lacks jurisdiction over the President and the Congress, the question of the constitutionality of the 1954 Act remains before us. While the court correctly dismissed the claim against those parties, it survives against [the State of California and the school district]. . . .

The Establishment Clause of the First Amendment states that "Congress shall make no law respecting an establishment of religion," U.S. Const. amend. I, a provision that "the Fourteenth Amendment makes applicable with full force to the States and their school districts." . . . Over the last three decades, the Supreme Court has used three interrelated tests to analyze alleged violations of the Establishment Clause in the realm of public education: . . . We are free to apply any or all of the three tests, and to invalidate any measure that fails any one of them. . . . The magistrate judge found that "the ceremonial reference to God in the pledge does not convey endorsement of particular religious beliefs." Supreme Court precedent does not support that conclusion.

In the context of the Pledge, the statement that the United States is a nation "under God" is an endorsement of religion. It is a profession of a religious belief, namely, a belief in monotheism. The recitation that ours is a nation "under God" is not a mere acknowledgment that many Americans believe in a deity. Nor is it merely descriptive of the undeniable historical significance of religion in the founding of the Republic. Rather, the phrase "one nation under God" in the context of the Pledge is normative. To recite the Pledge is not to describe the United States; instead, it is to swear allegiance to the values for which the flag stands: unity, indivisibility, liberty, justice, and—since 1954—monotheism. The text of the official Pledge, codified in federal law, impermissibly takes a position with respect to the purely religious question of the existence and identity of God. A profession that we are a nation "under God" is identical, for Establishment Clause purposes, to a profession that we are a nation "under Jesus," a nation "under Vishnu," a nation "under Zeus," or a nation "under no god," because none of these professions can be neutral with respect to religion. "[T]he government must pursue a course of complete neutrality toward religion." . . . Furthermore, the school district's practice of teacher-led recitation of the Pledge aims to inculcate in students a respect for the ideals set forth in the Pledge, and thus amounts to state endorsement of these ideals. Although students cannot be forced to participate in recitation of the Pledge, the school district is nonetheless conveying a message of state endorsement of a religious belief when it requires public school teachers to recite, and lead the recitation of, the current form of the Pledge.

The Supreme Court recognized the normative and ideological nature of the Pledge in *Barnette*. . . . There, the Court held unconstitutional a school district's wartime policy of punishing students who refused to recite the Pledge and salute the flag . . . The Court noted that the school district was compelling the students "to declare a belief," . . . and "requir[ing] the individual to communicate by word and sign his acceptance of the political ideas [the flag] . . . bespeaks," . . . "[T]he compulsory flag salute and pledge requires affirmation of a belief and an attitude of mind." *Id.* The Court emphasized that the political concepts articulated in the Pledge were idealistic, not descriptive: " '[L]iberty and justice for all,' if it must be accepted as descriptive of the present order rather than an ideal, might to some seem an overstatement." . . . The Court concluded that: "If there is any fixed star in our constitutional constellation, it is that no official, high or petty, can prescribe what shall be orthodox in politics, nationalism, religion, or other matters of opinion or force citizens to confess by word or act their faith therein." [*Barnette*, discussed in Chapter 4 of this book, was decided before "under God" was added, and thus the Court's discussion was limited to the political ideals contained in the pledge.]

The Pledge, as currently codified, is an impermissible government endorsement of religion because it sends a message to unbelievers "that they are outsiders, not full members of the political community, and an accompanying message to adherents that they are insiders, favored members of the political community." . . .

Similarly, the policy and the Act fail the coercion test. Just as in *Lee*, the policy and the Act place students in the untenable position of choosing between participating in an exercise with religious content or protesting. As the Court observed with respect to the graduation prayer in that case: "What to most believers may seem nothing more than a reasonable request that the nonbeliever respect their religious practices, in a school context may appear to the nonbeliever or dissenter to be an attempt to employ the machinery of the State to enforce a religious orthodoxy." . . .

Although the defendants argue that the religious content of "one nation under God" is minimal, to an atheist or a believer in certain non-Judeo-Christian religions or philosophies, it may reasonably appear to be an attempt to enforce a "religious orthodoxy" of monotheism, and is therefore impermissible. The coercive effect of this policy is particularly pronounced in the school setting given the age and impressionability of schoolchildren, and their understanding that they are required to adhere to the norms set by their school, their teacher and their fellow students. Furthermore, under *Lee*, the fact that students are not required to participate is no basis for distinguishing *Barnette* from the case at bar because, even without a recitation requirement for each child, the mere fact that a pupil is required to listen every day to the statement "one nation under God" has a coercive effect. The coercive effect of the Act is apparent from its context and legislative history, which indicate that the Act was designed to result in the daily recitation of the words "under God" in school classrooms. President Eisenhower, during the Act's signing ceremony, stated: "From this day forward, the millions of our school children will daily proclaim in every city and town, every village and rural schoolhouse, the dedication of our Nation and our people to the Almighty." 100 Cong. Rec. 8618 (1954) (statement of Sen. Ferguson incorporating signing statement of President Eisenhower). Therefore, the policy and the Act fail the coercion test.

Finally we turn to the *Lemon* test, the first prong of which asks if the challenged policy has a secular purpose. Historically, the primary purpose of the 1954 Act was to advance religion, in conflict with the first prong of the *Lemon* test. The federal defendants "do not dispute that the words 'under God' were intended" "to recognize a Supreme Being," at a time when the government was publicly inveighing against atheistic communism. Nonetheless, the federal defendants argue that the Pledge must be considered as a whole when assessing whether it has a secular purpose. They claim that the Pledge has the secular purpose of "solemnizing public occasions, expressing confidence in the future, and encouraging the recognition of what is worthy of appreciation in society." . . .

The flaw in defendants' argument is that it looks at the text of the Pledge "as a whole," and glosses over the 1954 Act. The problem with this approach is apparent when one considers the Court's analysis in *Wallace*. There, the Court struck down Alabama's statute mandating a moment of silence for "meditation or voluntary prayer" not because the final version "as a whole" lacked a primary secular purpose, but because the state legislature had amended the statute specifically and solely to add the words "or voluntary prayer." . . .

By analogy to *Wallace*, we apply the purpose prong of the *Lemon* test to the amendment that added the words "under God" to the Pledge, not to the Pledge in its final version. As was the case with the amendment to the Alabama statute in *Wallace*, the legislative history of the 1954 Act reveals that the Act's *sole* purpose was to advance religion, in order to differentiate the United States from nations under communist rule. "[T]he First Amendment requires that a statute must be invalidated if it is entirely motivated by a purpose to advance religion." . . . As the legislative history of the 1954 Act sets forth:

At this moment of our history the principles underlying our American Government and the American way of life are under attack by a system whose philosophy is at direct odds with our own. Our American Government is founded on the concept of the individuality and the dignity of the human being. Underlying this concept is the belief that the human person is important because he was created by God and endowed by Him with certain inalienable rights which no civil authority may usurp. The inclusion of God in our pledge therefore would further acknowledge the dependence of our people and our Government upon the moral directions of the Creator. At the same time it would serve to deny the atheistic and materialistic concepts of communism with its attendant subservience of the individual.

. . .

This language reveals that the purpose of the 1954 Act was to take a position on the question of theism, namely, to support the existence and moral authority of God, while "deny[ing] . . . atheistic and materialistic concepts." *Id.* Such a purpose runs counter to the Establishment Clause, which prohibits the government's endorsement or advancement not only of one particular religion at the expense of other religions, but also of religion at the expense of atheism.

[T]he Court has unambiguously concluded that the individual freedom of conscience protected by the First Amendment embraces the right to select any religious faith or none at all. This conclusion derives support not only from the interest in respecting the individual's freedom of conscience, but also from the conviction that religious beliefs worthy of respect are the product of a free and voluntary choice by the faithful, and from recognition of the fact that the political interest in forestalling intolerance extends beyond intolerance among Christian sects—or even intolerance among "religions"—to encompass intolerance of the disbeliever and the uncertain.

In language that attempts to prevent future constitutional challenges, the sponsors of the 1954 Act expressly disclaimed a religious purpose. "This is not an act establishing a religion. . . . A distinction must be made between the existence of a religion as an institution and a belief in the sovereignty of God. The phrase 'under God' recognizes only the guidance of God in our national affairs." . . . This alleged distinction is irrelevant for constitutional purposes . . . the second *Lemon* prong asks "whether the challenged government action is sufficiently likely to be perceived by adherents of the controlling denominations as an endorsement, and by the nonadherents as a disapproval, of their individual religious choices." . . . Given the age and impressionability of schoolchildren, as discussed above, particularly within the confined environment of the classroom, the policy is highly likely to convey an impermissible message of endorsement to some and disapproval to others of their beliefs regarding the existence of a monotheistic God. Therefore the policy fails the effects prong of *Lemon,* and fails the *Lemon* test. In sum, both the policy and the Act fail the *Lemon* test as well as the endorsement and coercion tests. . . .

In conclusion, we hold that (1) the 1954 Act adding the words "under God" to the Pledge, and (2) EGUSD's policy and practice of teacher-led recitation of the Pledge, with the added words included, violate the Establishment Clause. The judgment of dismissal is vacated with respect to these two claims, and the cause is remanded for further proceedings consistent with our holding. Plaintiff is to recover costs on this appeal.

Norwood Hospital v. Munoz (Mass. 1991)

In this case, a competent adult, who is a Jehovah's Witness and a mother of a minor child, appeals from a judgment of the Probate and Family Court authorizing Norwood Hospital to administer blood or blood products without her consent.

. . .

Yolanda Munoz, a thirty-eight year old woman, lives in Dedham with her husband, Ernesto Munoz, and their minor son, Ernesto, Jr. Ernesto's father, who is over seventy-five years old, also lives in the same household. Ms. Munoz has a history of stomach ulcers. Approximately ten years ago, she underwent surgery for a bleeding ulcer. On April 11, 1989, Ms. Munoz vomited blood and collapsed in her home. During the week before she collapsed, Ms. Munoz had taken two aspirin every four hours to alleviate a pain in her arm. The aspirin apparently made her ulcer bleed. Ernesto took his wife to the Norwood Hospital emergency room. Physicians at Norwood Hospital gave Ms. Munoz medication which stopped the bleeding. Ms. Munoz was then admitted to the hospital as an inpatient. . . . Ms. Munoz was placed under the care of Dr. Joseph L. Perrotto. It was his medical opinion that the patient had a 50% probability of hemorrhaging again. If Ms. Munoz started to bleed, Dr. Perrotto believed that she would in all probability die unless she received a blood transfusion. Ms. Munoz, however, refused to consent to a blood transfusion in the event of a new hemorrhage.

Ms. Munoz and her husband were baptized as Jehovah's Witnesses over sixteen years ago. They are both members of the Jamaica Plain Kingdom Hall of Jehovah's Witnesses. Ms. Munoz attends three religious meetings every week. A principal tenet of the Jehovah's Witnesses religion is a belief, based on interpretations of the Bible, that the act of receiving blood or blood products precludes an individual resurrection and everlasting life after death.

Norwood Hospital has a written policy regarding patients who refuse to consent to the administration of blood or blood products. According to this policy, if the patient arrives at the hospital in need of emergency medical treatment and there is no time to investigate the patient's circumstances or competence to make decisions regarding treatment, the blood transfusion will be performed if necessary to save the patient's life. If the patient, in a nonemergency situation, refuses to consent to a blood transfusion, and the patient is a competent adult, not pregnant, and does not have minor children, the hospital will accede to the patient's refusal. If the patient, in a non-emergency situation, refuses to consent to a blood transfusion, and the patient is a minor, an incompetent adult, pregnant, or a competent adult with minor children, the hospital's policy is to seek judicial determination of the rights and responsibilities of the parties. The patient in this case, while no longer in an emergency situation once her ulcer stopped bleeding, has a minor child.

The hospital sought a court order . . . [to require] blood transfusions which her attending physician believed to be reasonably necessary to save her life. On that same day, the judge granted a temporary restraining order authorizing the hospital to "administer transfusions of blood or blood products in the event that [the patient] hemorrhages to the extent that her life is severely threatened by loss of blood in the opinion of her attending physicians. . . . Dr. Perrotto stated in an unchallenged affidavit that, if Ms. Munoz were to begin bleeding again, she would have an excellent chance of recovering if she received a blood transfusion. If she started to bleed, however, and did not receive a blood transfusion, she would probably die . . .

While recognizing that a competent adult may usually refuse medical treatment, the judge stated that the hospital could administer the blood transfusions because, if they did not and Ms. Munoz subsequently died, Ernesto, Jr., [her son] would be "abandoned." The judge concluded that the State's interest in protecting the well-being of Ernesto, Jr., outweighed Ms. Munoz's right to refuse the medical treatment. In order further to understand the judge's reasoning, we need to discuss his factual findings in more detail. Ernesto works sixteen hours a day Monday through Friday and seven hours on Saturday driving his own commercial truck. . . . The judge also found that, while Ernesto's father was available to assist in caring for Ernesto, Jr., his assistance would be inadequate because of his advanced age, his inability to speak English, his unemployment, his lack of a driver's license, and because he had not, in the past, played a significant role in caring for his grandson. . . . The judge ruled that "[t]he State, as parens patriae, will not allow a parent to abandon a child, and so it should not allow this most ultimate of voluntary abandonments."

On appeal Ms. Munoz argues that the judge erred because she has a right, as a competent adult, to refuse life-saving medical treatment, and the State's interests do not override that right. We agree.

The general rule is that courts ordinarily will not decide moot questions. There are, however, exceptions to the general rule. We have answered moot questions "where the issue was one of public importance, where it was fully argued on both sides, where the question was certain, or at least very likely, to arise again in similar factual circumstances, and especially where appellate review could not be obtained before the recurring question would again be moot."

The instant case meets all the exceptions to the general rule. Whether a competent individual may refuse medical treatment is unquestionably an issue of public importance. In this case, the issue has been fully argued by both sides and is capable of repetition while evading review ... Cases such as this one often arise in emergency situations; patients, physicians, and trial judges must make difficult decisions in very limited periods of time. By the time the cases reach the appellate courts, the issue is usually moot because the patients have either died or left the hospital without the need for further medical treatment. Due to the importance of the issue, and because of its proclivity to repeat itself while evading review, we proceed to address the merits.

This court has recognized the right of a competent individual to refuse medical treatment. We have declared that individuals have a common law right to determine for themselves whether to allow a physical invasion of their bodies.... The right to bodily integrity has been developed further through the doctrine of informed consent, which ... [recognizes that a] physician has the duty to disclose to a competent adult "sufficient information to enable the patient to make an informed judgment whether to give or withhold consent to a medical or surgical procedure." It is for the individual to decide whether a particular medical treatment is in the individual's best interests.... The fact that the treatment involves life-saving procedures does not undermine Ms. Munoz's rights to bodily integrity and privacy, except to the extent that the right must then be balanced against the State's interests.

... [I]n addition to her rights to bodily integrity and privacy, she has a right secured by the free exercise clause of the First Amendment to the United States Constitution to object to the administration of blood or blood products because to consent to the blood transfusions would violate one of the principal tenets of her Jehovah's Witnesses faith. Some courts have recognized a free exercise right on the part of

Jehovah's Witnesses to refuse blood transfusions. . . . We do not think it is necessary, however, to decide whether Ms. Munoz has a free exercise right to refuse the administration of blood or blood products, since we have already held that she has a common law and constitutional privacy right to refuse a blood transfusion. Also, we need not decide whether a patient's right is strengthened because the objection to the medical treatment is based on religious principles.

[From the concurring opinion]

. . . The right to refuse medical treatment in life-threatening situations is not absolute. . . . We have recognized four countervailing interests: (1) the preservation of life; (2) the prevention of suicide; (3) the maintenance of the ethical integrity of the medical profession; and (4) the protection of innocent third parties. . . . The State has an interest in preserving life, especially in a case such as the present one where the patient's affliction is curable. The State's interest in preserving life has "two separate but related concerns: an interest in preserving the life of the particular patient, and an interest in preserving the sanctity of all life." . . . As to the former, the State's concern is weakened when the decision maker (the individual who refuses to consent to the treatment) is also the patient "because the life that the state is seeking to protect in such a situation is the life of the same person who has competently decided to forgo the medical intervention; it is not some other actual or potential life that cannot adequately protect itself." In cases where a competent adult refuses medical treatment for herself, the State's interest in preserving the particular patient's life will not override the individual's decision.

The second concept within the State's interest in the preservation of life is the more abstract notion of protecting the sanctity of life. In determining whether this concept applies, we must keep in mind that the right to privacy is an "expression of the sanctity of individual free choice and self-determination as fundamental constituents of life. The value of life as so perceived is lessened not by a decision to refuse treatment, but by the failure to allow a competent human being the right of choice." . . . "The duty of the State to preserve life must encompass a recognition of an individual's right to avoid circumstances in which the individual [herself] would feel that efforts to sustain life demean or degrade [her] humanity."

In this case, the patient, a fully competent adult, determined for herself that she could not consent to the administration of blood or blood products because to do so would violate a sacred religious belief. The patient decided that she would rather risk death than accept the blood transfusion. We can assume that, for this patient, death without receiving a blood transfusion is preferable to life after receiving the transfusion. The quality and integrity of this patient's life after a blood transfusion would be diminished in her view. Therefore, we conclude that the State's interest in protecting the sanctity of life must give way to the patient's decision to forgo treatment. . . . The State has an interest in maintaining the ethical integrity of the medical profession by giving hospitals and their staffs a full opportunity to assist those in their care. . . . [However] We have recognized that medical ethics do not require that a patient's life be preserved in all circumstances. . . . In the circumstances of this case, the State's interest in maintaining the ethical integrity of the profession does not outweigh the patient's right to refuse blood transfusions.

The patient had the right to refuse to consent to the blood transfusion even though she would have in all probability died if she had started to hemorrhage. The State's interests in preserving the patient's life, in maintaining the ethical integrity of the profession, and in protecting the well-being of the patient's child, did not override the patient's right to refuse life-saving medical treatment. Accordingly, the judgment is reversed and a new judgment declaring the rights of the parties, consistent with this opinion, is to be entered in the Probate Court. So ordered.

Employment Division v. Smith (1990)

JUSTICE SCALIA delivered the opinion of the Court.

This case requires us to decide whether the Free Exercise Clause of the First Amendment permits the State of Oregon to include religiously inspired peyote use within the reach of its general criminal prohibition on use of that drug, and thus permits the State to deny unemployment benefits to persons dismissed from their jobs because of such religiously inspired use.

Oregon law prohibits the knowing or intentional possession of a "controlled substance" unless the substance has been prescribed by a medical practitioner. . . . The law defines "controlled substance" as a drug classified in Schedules I through V of the Federal Controlled Substances Act, Schedule I contains the drug peyote, a hallucinogen derived from the plant *Lophophora williamsii Lemaire*. . . .

Alfred Smith and Galen Black ... were fired from their jobs with a private drug rehabilitation organization because they ingested peyote for sacramental purposes at a ceremony of the Native American Church, of which both are members. When respondents applied to [the] Employment Division ... for unemployment compensation, they were determined to be ineligible for benefits because they had been discharged for work-related "misconduct." The Oregon Court of Appeals reversed that determination, holding that the denial of benefits violated respondents' free exercise rights under the First Amendment. ... the Oregon Supreme Court, [hearing an appeal] reasoned, however, that the criminality of respondents' peyote use was irrelevant to resolution of their constitutional claim—since the [criminal] "misconduct" ... was inadequate to justify the burden that disqualification imposed on respondents' religious practice ... [On remand from the U.S. Supreme Court, the Oregon Supreme Court held that although religiously inspired use of peyote was illegal under the Oregon statute, the prohibition was invalid under the Free Exercise Clause.]

... The "exercise of religion" often involves not only belief and profession but the performance of (or abstention from) physical acts: assembling with others for a worship service, participating in sacramental use of bread and wine, proselytizing, abstaining from certain foods or certain modes of transportation. It would be true, we think (though no case of ours has involved the point), that a State would be "prohibiting the free exercise [of religion]" if it sought to ban such acts or abstentions only when they are engaged in for religious reasons, or only because of the religious belief that they display. It would doubtless be unconstitutional, for example, to ban the casting of "statues that are to be used for worship purposes," or to prohibit bowing down before a golden calf.

Respondents in the present case, however, seek to carry the meaning of "prohibiting the free exercise [of religion]" one large step further. They contend that their religious motivation for using peyote places them beyond the reach of a criminal law that is not specifically directed at their religious practice, and that is concededly constitutional as applied to those who use the drug for other reasons. They assert, in other words, that "prohibiting the free exercise [of religion]" includes requiring any individual to observe a generally applicable law that requires (or forbids) the performance of an act that his religious belief forbids (or requires). As a textual matter, we do not think the words must be given that meaning.

... We have never held that an individual's religious beliefs excuse him from compliance with an otherwise valid law prohibiting conduct that the State is free to regulate. On the contrary, the record of more than a century of our free exercise jurisprudence contradicts that proposition. As described succinctly by Justice Frankfurter in *Minersville School Dist. Bd. of Ed. v. Gobitis* [requiring schoolchildren to recite the pledge of allegiance despite their religious objections]. "Conscientious scruples have not, in the course of the long struggle for religious toleration, relieved the individual from obedience to a general law not aimed at the promotion or restriction of religious beliefs. The mere possession of religious convictions which contradict the relevant concerns of a political society does not relieve the citizen from the discharge of political responsibilities (footnote omitted)." We first had occasion to assert that principle in *Reynolds v. United States* (1879), where we rejected the claim that criminal laws against polygamy could not be constitutionally applied to those whose religion commanded the practice. "Laws," we said, "are made for the government of actions, and while they cannot interfere with mere religious belief and opinions, they may with practices.... Can a man excuse his practices to the contrary because of his religious belief? To permit this would be to make the professed doctrines of religious belief superior to the law of the land, and in effect to permit every citizen to become a law unto himself." ...

Subsequent decisions have consistently held that the right of free exercise does not relieve an individual of the obligation to comply with a "valid and neutral law of general applicability on the ground that the law proscribes (or prescribes) conduct that his religion prescribes (or proscribes)." ...

The only decisions in which we have held that the First Amendment bars application of a neutral, generally applicable law to religiously motivated action have involved not the Free Exercise Clause alone, but the Free Exercise Clause in conjunction with other constitutional protections, such as freedom of speech and of the press.... The present case does not present such a hybrid situation, but a free exercise claim unconnected with any communicative activity or parental right. Respondents urge us to hold, quite simply, that when otherwise prohibitable conduct is accompanied by religious convictions, not only the convictions but the conduct itself must be free from governmental regulation. We have never held that, and decline to do so now. There being no contention that Oregon's drug law represents an attempt to regulate religious beliefs, the communication of religious beliefs, or the raising of one's children in those beliefs, the rule to which we have adhered ever since *Reynolds* plainly controls. "Our cases do not at their farthest reach support the proposition that a stance of conscientious opposition relieves an objector from any colliding duty fixed by a democratic government."

[Smith and Black] argue that even though exemption from generally applicable criminal laws need not automatically be extended to religiously motivated actors, at least the claim for a religious exemption must be evaluated under the balancing test set forth in *Sherbert v. Verner*. . . . Under the Sherbert test, governmental actions that substantially burden a religious practice must be justified by a compelling governmental interest. . . . In *Lyng v. Northwest Indian Cemetery Protective Assn* (1988), we declined to apply Sherbert analysis to the Government's logging and road construction activities on lands used for religious purposes by several Native American Tribes, even though it was undisputed that the activities "could have devastating effects on traditional Indian religious practices," . . . Even if we were inclined to breathe into Sherbert some life beyond the unemployment compensation field, we would not apply it to require exemptions from a generally applicable criminal law . . .

The "compelling government interest" requirement seems benign, because it is familiar from other fields. But using it as the standard that must be met before the government may accord different treatment on the basis of race . . . or before the government may regulate the content of speech, is not remotely comparable to using it for the purpose asserted here. What it produces in those other fields—equality of treatment and an unrestricted flow of contending speech—are constitutional norms; what it would produce here—a private right to ignore generally applicable laws—is a constitutional anomaly.

Nor is it possible to limit the impact of respondents' proposal by requiring a "compelling state interest" only when the conduct prohibited is "central" to the individual's religion. . . . What principle of law or logic can be brought to bear to contradict a believer's assertion that a particular act is "central" to his personal faith? . . .

. . . if "compelling interest" really means what it says (and watering it down here would subvert its rigor in the other fields where it is applied), many laws will not meet the test. Any society adopting such a system would be courting anarchy, but that danger increases in direct proportion to the society's diversity of religious beliefs, and its determination to coerce or suppress none of them. . . . The rule respondents favor would open the prospect of constitutionally required religious exemptions from civic obligations of almost every conceivable kind—ranging from compulsory military service to [health and safety regulations, manslaughter, and child neglect laws, compulsory vaccination laws, drug laws, and traffic laws, social welfare legislation such as minimum wage laws, child labor laws, animal cruelty laws, environmental protection laws, and laws providing for equality of opportunity for the races]. The First Amendment's protection of religious liberty does not require this.

Values that are protected against government interference through enshrinement in the Bill of Rights are not thereby banished from the political process. . . . It is therefore not surprising that a number of States have made an exception to their drug laws for sacramental peyote use. . . . But to say that a nondiscriminatory religious-practice exemption is permitted, or even that it is desirable, is not to say that it is constitutionally required, and that the appropriate occasions for its creation can be discerned by the courts.

Because [Smith and Black's] ingestion of peyote was prohibited under Oregon law, and because that prohibition is constitutional, Oregon may, consistent with the Free Exercise Clause, deny respondents unemployment compensation when their dismissal results from use of the drug. The decision of the Oregon Supreme Court is accordingly reversed.

Commonwealth v. Twitchell (S.Ct. Mass. 1993)

David and Ginger Twitchell appeal from their convictions of involuntary manslaughter in connection with the April 8, 1986, death of their two and one-half year old son Robyn. Robyn died of the consequences of peritonitis caused by the perforation of his bowel which had been obstructed as a result of an anomaly known as Meckel's diverticulum. There was evidence that the condition could be corrected by surgery with a high success rate.

The defendants are practicing Christian Scientists who grew up in Christian Science families. They believe in healing by spiritual treatment. . . . During Robyn's five-day illness . . . they retained a Christian

Science practitioner, a Christian Science nurse, and at one time consulted with Nathan Talbot, who held a position in the church known as the "Committee on Publication." As a result of that consultation, David Twitchell read a church publication concerning the legal rights and obligations of Christian Scientists in Massachusetts. That publication quoted a portion of [the Massachusetts statute] . . . which, at least in the context of the crimes described in that section, accepted remedial treatment by spiritual means alone as satisfying any parental obligation not to neglect a child or to provide a child with physical care. . . .

We need not recite in detail the circumstances of Robyn's illness. The jury would have been warranted in concluding that Robyn was in considerable distress and that, in the absence of their belief in and reliance on spiritual treatment, the parents of a child in his condition would normally have sought medical treatment in sufficient time to save that child's life. There was also evidence that the intensity of Robyn's distress ebbed and flowed, perhaps causing his parents to believe that prayer would lead to the healing of the illness. On the other hand, the jury would have been warranted in finding that the Twitchells were wanton or reckless in failing to provide medical care for Robyn, if parents have a legal duty to provide a child with medical care in such circumstances and if the spiritual treatment provision of [the statute] did not protect them from manslaughter liability.

We shall conclude that parents have a duty to seek medical attention for a child in Robyn's circumstances, the violation of which, if their conduct was wanton or reckless, could support a conviction of involuntary manslaughter and that the spiritual healing provision in . . . [the statute] did not bar a prosecution for manslaughter in these circumstances. We further conclude, however, that special circumstances in this case would justify a jury's finding that the Twitchells reasonably believed that they could rely on spiritual treatment without fear of criminal prosecution. This affirmative defense should have been asserted and presented to the jury. Because it was not, there is a substantial risk of a miscarriage of justice in this case, and, therefore, the judgments must be reversed. . . .

The defendants argue that the spiritual treatment provision in . . . [the statute] bars any involuntary manslaughter charge against a parent who relies, as they did, on spiritual treatment and who does not seek medical attention for his or her child, even if the parent's failure to seek such care would otherwise be wanton or reckless conduct. We disagree.

. . . [The statute] provides no complete protection to a parent against a charge of involuntary manslaughter that is based on the parent's wanton or reckless failure to provide medical services to a child. . . . An involuntary manslaughter verdict does not require proof of willfulness. . . . Thus, by its terms, the spiritual treatment provision in . . . [the statute] does not apply to involuntary manslaughter.

The defendants argue that the failure to extend the protection of the spiritual treatment provision to them in this case would be a denial of due process of law because they lacked "fair warning" that their use of spiritual treatment could form the basis for a prosecution for manslaughter. Fair warning is part of the due process doctrine of vagueness, which "requires that a penal statute define the criminal offense with sufficient definiteness that ordinary people can understand what conduct is prohibited and in a manner that does not encourage arbitrary and discriminatory enforcement." . . . The defendants here argue that they have been denied fair warning . . . because they were officially misled by an opinion of the Attorney General of the Commonwealth . . .

A reasonable person not trained in the law might fairly read the Attorney General's comments as being a negative answer to the general question whether in any circumstances such parents may be prosecuted. It is true that the answer comes to focus on negligent failures of parents, and we know that wanton or reckless failures are different. But an answer that says that children may receive needed services "notwithstanding the inability to prosecute parents in such cases," and issues no caveat concerning homicide charges, invites a conclusion that parents who fail to provide medical services to children on the basis of religious beliefs are not subject to criminal prosecution in any circumstances.

Although the Twitchells were not aware of the Attorney General's opinion, they knew of a Christian Science publication called "Legal Rights and Obligations of Christian Scientists in Massachusetts." . . . It is obvious that the Christian Science Church's publication on the legal rights and obligations of Christian Scientists in Massachusetts relied on the Attorney General's 1975 opinion. That opinion was arguably misleading because of what it did not say concerning criminal liability for manslaughter. If the Attorney General had issued a caveat concerning manslaughter liability, the publication (which, based on such portions of it as appear in the record, is balanced and fair) would have referred to it in all reasonable likelihood. Nathan Talbot, who served as the Committee on Publication for the church and with whom the Twitchells spoke on the Sunday or Monday before Robyn's death, might well have given the Twitchells different advice.

Although it has long been held that "ignorance of the law is no defense" . . . there is substantial justification for treating as a defense the belief that conduct is not a violation of law when a defendant has reasonably relied on an official statement of the law, later determined to be wrong, contained in an official interpretation of the public official who is charged by law with the responsibility for the interpretation or enforcement of the law defining the offense. . . .

There is special merit to such a rule if religious beliefs are involved and if the defendant was attempting to comply with the law while adhering, as far as possible, to his religious beliefs and practices. The Twitchells were entitled to present such an affirmative defense to the jury . . . (sufficient when received indirectly). In the resolution of these factual questions, the relevant portion of the Attorney General's opinion and the relevant portion of the church's publication will be admissible. The jury should also be advised of the terms of the spiritual treatment provision of [the statute].

. . . . For these reasons, the judgments must be reversed, the verdicts must be set aside, and the cases remanded for a new trial, if the district attorney concludes that such a prosecution is necessary in the interests of justice.

So ordered.

Historical Documents

Virginia Bill for Religious Freedom (1779)

SECTION I. Well aware that the opinions and belief of men depend not on their own will, but follow involuntarily the evidence proposed to their minds; that Almighty God hath created the mind free, and manifested his supreme will that free it shall remain by making it altogether insusceptible of restraint; that all attempts to influence it by temporal punishments, or burdens, or by civil incapacitations, tend only to beget habits of hypocrisy and meanness, and are a departure from the plan of the holy author of our religion, who being lord both of body and mind, yet chose not to propagate it by coercions on either, as was in his Almighty power to do, but to extend it by its influence on reason alone; that the impious presumption of legislators and rulers, civil as well as ecclesiastical, who, being themselves but fallible and uninspired men, have assumed dominion over the faith of others, setting up their own opinions and modes of thinking as the only true and infallible, and as such endeavoring to impose them on others, hath established and maintained false religions over the greatest part of the world and through all time: That to compel a man to furnish contributions of money for the propagation of opinions which he disbelieves and abhors, is sinful and tyrannical; that even the forcing him to support this or that teacher of his own religious persuasion, is depriving him of the comfortable liberty of giving his contributions to the particular pastor whose morals he would make his pattern, and whose powers he feels most persuasive to righteousness; and is withdrawing from the ministry those temporary rewards, which proceeding from an approbation of their personal conduct, are an additional incitement to earnest and unremitting labours for the instruction of mankind; that our civil rights have no dependance on our religious opinions, any more than our opinions in physics or geometry; that therefore the proscribing any citizen as unworthy the public confidence by laying upon him an incapacity of being called to offices of trust and emolument, unless he profess or renounce this or that religious opinion, is depriving him injuriously of those privileges and advantages to which, in common with his fellow citizens, he has a natural right; that it tends also to corrupt the principles of that very religion it is meant to encourage, by bribing, with a monopoly of worldly honours and emoluments, those who will externally profess and conform to it; that though indeed these are criminal who do not withstand such temptation, yet neither are those innocent who lay the bait in their way; that the opinions of men are not the object of civil government, nor under its jurisdiction; that to suffer the civil magistrate to intrude his powers into the field of opinion and to restrain the profession or propagation of principles on supposition of their ill tendency is a dangerous fallacy, which at once destroys all religious liberty, because he being of course judge of that tendency will make his opinions the rule of judgment, and approve or condemn the sentiments of others only as they shall square with or differ from his own; that it is time enough for the rightful purposes of civil government for its officers to interfere when principles break out into overt acts against peace and good order; and finally, that truth is great and will prevail if left to herself; that she is the proper and sufficient antagonist to error, and has nothing to fear from the conflict unless by human interposition disarmed of her natural weapons, free argument and debate; errors ceasing to be dangerous when it is permitted freely to contradict them.

SECT. II. WE the General Assembly of Virginia do enact that no man shall be compelled to frequent or support any religious worship, place, or ministry whatsoever, nor shall be enforced, restrained, molested, or burthened in his body or goods, nor shall otherwise suffer, on account of his religious opinions or belief; but that all men shall be free to profess, and by argument to maintain, their opinions in matters of religion, and that the same shall in no wise diminish, enlarge, or affect their civil capacities.

SECT. III. AND though we well know that this Assembly, elected by the people for the ordinary purposes of legislation only, have no power to restrain the acts of succeeding Assemblies, constituted with powers equal to our own, and that therefore to declare this act irrevocable would be of no effect in law; yet we are free to declare, and do declare, that the rights hereby asserted are of the natural rights of mankind, and that if any act shall be hereafter passed to repeal the present or to narrow its operation, such act will be an infringement of natural right.

James Madison's *Memorial and Remonstrance*

To the Honorable the General Assembly of the Commonwealth of Virginia

Memorial and Remonstrance

We the subscribers, citizens of the said Commonwealth, having taken into serious consideration, a Bill printed by order of the last Session of General Assembly, entitled "A Bill establishing a provision for Teachers of the Christian Religion," and conceiving that the same if finally armed with the sanctions of a law, will be a dangerous abuse of power, are bound as faithful members of a free State to remonstrate against it, and to declare the reasons by which we are determined. We remonstrate against the said Bill,

1. Because we hold it for a fundamental and undeniable truth, "that religion or the duty which we owe to our Creator and the manner of discharging it, can be directed only by reason and conviction, not by force or violence." The Religion then of every man must be left to the conviction and conscience of every man; and it is the right of every man to exercise it as these may dictate.

This right is in its nature an unalienable right. It is unalienable, because the opinions of men, depending only on the evidence contemplated by their own minds cannot follow the dictates of other men: It is unalienable also, because what is here a right towards men, is a duty towards the Creator.

It is the duty of every man to render to the Creator such homage and such only as he believes to be acceptable to him. This duty is precedent, both in order of time and in degree of obligation, to the claims of Civil Society. Before any man can be considered as a member of Civil Society, he must be considered as a subject of the Governor of the Universe: And if a member of Civil Society, do it with a saving of his allegiance to the Universal Sovereign.

We maintain therefore that in matters of Religion, no man's right is abridged by the institution of Civil Society and that Religion is wholly exempt from its cognizance. True it is, that no other rule exists, by which any question which may divide a Society, can be ultimately determined, but the will of the majority; but it is also true that the majority may trespass on the rights of the minority.

2. Because Religion be exempt from the authority of the Society at large, still less can it be subject to that of the Legislative Body. The latter are but the creatures and vicegerents of the former. Their jurisdiction is both derivative and limited: it is limited with regard to the co-ordinate departments, more necessarily is it limited with regard to the constituents.

The preservation of a free Government requires not merely, that the metes and bounds which separate each department of power be invariably maintained; but more especially that neither of them be suffered to overleap the great Barrier which defends the rights of the people. The Rulers who are guilty of such an encroachment, exceed the commission from which they derive their authority, and are Tyrants. The People who submit to it are governed by laws made neither by themselves nor by an authority derived from them, and are slaves.

3. Because it is proper to take alarm at the first experiment on our liberties. We hold this prudent jealousy to be the first duty of Citizens, and one of the noblest characteristics of the late Revolution. The free men of America did not wait till usurped power had strengthened itself by exercise, and entangled the question in precedents. They saw all the consequences in the principle, and they avoided the consequences by denying the principle. We revere this lesson too much soon to forget it.

Who does not see that the same authority which can establish Christianity, in exclusion of all other Religions, may establish with the same ease any particular sect of Christians, in exclusion of all other Sects? That the same authority which can force a citizen to contribute three pence only of his property for the support of any one establishment, may force him to conform to any other establishment in all cases whatsoever?

4. Because the Bill violates the equality which ought to be the basis of every law, and which is more indispensable, in proportion as the validity or expediency of any law is more liable to be impeached. If "all men are by nature equally free and independent," all men are to be considered as entering into Society on equal conditions; as relinquishing no more, and therefore retaining no less, one than another, of their natural rights.

Above all they are to be considered as retaining an "equal title to the free exercise of Religion according to the dictates of Conscience." Whilst we assert for ourselves a freedom to embrace, to profess and to observe the Religion which we believe to be of divine origin, we cannot deny an equal freedom to those whose minds have not yet yielded to the evidence which has convinced us.

If this freedom be abused, it is an offence against God, not against man: To God, therefore, not to man, must an account of it be rendered. As the Bill violates equality by subjecting some to peculiar burdens, so it violates the same principle, by granting to others peculiar exemptions. Are the Quakers and Menonists the only sects who think a compulsive support of their Religions unnecessary and unwarrantable? Can their piety alone be entrusted with the care of public worship? Ought their Religions to be endowed above all others with extraordinary privileges by which proselytes may be enticed from all others?

We think too favorably of the justice and good sense of these denominations to believe that they either covet pre-eminences over their fellow citizens or that they will be seduced by them from the common opposition to the measure.

5. Because the Bill implies either that the Civil Magistrate is a competent Judge of Religious Truth; or that he may employ Religion as an engine of Civil policy. The first is an arrogant pretension falsified by the contradictory opinions of Rulers in all ages, and throughout the world: the second an unhallowed perversion of the means of salvation.

6. Because the establishment proposed by the Bill is not requisite for the support of the Christian Religion. To say that it is, is a contradiction to the Christian Religion itself, for every page of it disavows a dependence on the powers of this world: it is a contradiction to fact; for it is known that this Religion both existed and flourished, not only without the support of human laws, but in spite of every opposition from them, and not only during the period of miraculous aid, but long after it had been left to its own evidence and the ordinary care of Providence.

Nay, it is a contradiction in terms; for a Religion not invented by human policy, must have pre-existed and been supported, before it was established by human policy. It is moreover to weaken in those who profess this Religion a pious confidence in its innate excellence and the patronage of its Author; and to foster in those who still reject it, a suspicion that its friends are too conscious of its fallacies to trust it to its own merits.

7. Because experience witnesseth that ecclesiastical establishments, instead of maintaining the purity and efficacy of Religion, have had a contrary operation.

During almost fifteen centuries has the legal establishment of Christianity been on trial. What have been its fruits? More or less in all places, pride and indolence in the Clergy, ignorance and servility in the laity, in both, superstition, bigotry and persecution. Enquire of the Teachers of Christianity for the ages in which it appeared in its greatest luster; those of every sect, point to the ages prior to its incorporation with Civil policy.

Propose a restoration of this primitive State in which its Teachers depended on the voluntary rewards of their flocks, many of them predict its downfall. On which Side ought their testimony to have greatest weight, when for or when against their interest?

8. Because the establishment in question is not necessary for the support of Civil Government. If it be urged as necessary for the support of Civil Government only as it is a means of supporting Religion, and it be not necessary for the latter purpose, it cannot be necessary for the former. If Religion be not within the cognizance of Civil Government how can its legal establishment be necessary to Civil Government? What influence in fact have ecclesiastical establishments had on Civil Society?

In some instances they have been seen to erect a spiritual tyranny on the ruins of the Civil authority; in many instances they have been seen upholding the thrones of political tyranny: in no instance have they been seen the guardians of the liberties of the people. Rulers who wished to subvert the public liberty, may have found an established Clergy convenient auxiliaries.

A just Government instituted to secure and perpetuate it needs them not. Such a Government will be best supported by protecting every Citizen in the enjoyment of his Religion with the same equal hand which protects his person and his property; by neither invading the equal rights of any Sect, nor suffering any Sect to invade those of another.

9. Because the proposed establishment is a departure from the generous policy, which, offering an Asylum to the persecuted and oppressed of every Nation and Religion, promised a luster to our country, and an accession to the number of its citizens. What a melancholy mark is the Bill of sudden degeneracy? Instead of holding forth an Asylum to the persecuted, it is itself a signal of persecution.

It degrades from the equal rank of Citizens all those who see opinions in Religion do not bend to those of the Legislative authority. Distant as it may be in its present form from the Inquisition, it differs from it only in degree. The one is the first step, the other the last in the career of intolerance. The magnanimous sufferer under this cruel scourge in foreign Regions, must view the Bill as a Beacon on our Coast, warning him to seek some other haven, where liberty and philanthropy in their due extent, may offer a more certain repose from his Troubles.

10. Because it will have a like tendency to banish our Citizens. The allurements presented by other situations are every day thinning their number. To superadd a fresh motive to emigration by revoking the liberty which they now enjoy, would be the same species of folly which has dishonored and depopulated flourishing kingdoms.

11. Because it will destroy that moderation and harmony which the forbearance of our laws to intermeddle with Religion has produced among its several sects. Torrents of blood have been split in the old world, by vain attempts of the secular arm, to extinguish Religious discord, by proscribing all difference in Religious opinion. Time has at length revealed the true remedy. Every relaxation of narrow and rigorous policy, wherever it has been tried, has been found to assuage the disease.

The American Theater has exhibited proofs that equal and complete liberty, if it does not wholly eradicate it, sufficiently destroys its malignant influence on the health and prosperity of the State. If with the salutary effects of this system under our own eyes, we begin to contract the bounds of Religious freedom, we know no name that will too severely reproach our folly. At least let warning be taken at the first fruits of the threatened innovation.

The very appearance of the Bill has transformed "that Christian forbearance, love and charity," which of late mutually prevailed, into animosities and jealousies, which may not soon be appeased. What mischiefs may not be dreaded, should this enemy to the public quiet be armed with the force of a law?

12. Because the policy of the Bill is adverse to the diffusion of the light of Christianity. The first wish of those who enjoy this precious gift ought to be that it may be imparted to the whole race of mankind. Compare the number of those who have as yet received it with the number still remaining under the dominion of false Religions; and how small is the former! Does the policy of the Bill tend to lessen the disproportion?

No; it at once discourages those who are strangers to the light of revelation from coming into the Region of it; and countenances by example the nations who continue in darkness, in shutting out those who might convey it to them. Instead of Leveling as far as possible, every obstacle to the victorious progress of Truth, the Bill with an ignoble and unchristian timidity would circumscribe it with a wall of defense against the encroachments of error.

13. Because attempts to enforce by legal sanctions, acts obnoxious to so great a proportion of Citizens, tend to enervate the laws in general, and to slacken the bands of Society. If it be difficult to execute any law which is not generally deemed necessary or salutary, what must be the case, where it is deemed invalid and dangerous? And what may be the effect of so striking an example of impotency in the Government, on its general authority?

14. Because a measure of such singular magnitude and delicacy ought not to be imposed, without the clearest evidence that it is called for by a majority of citizens, and no satisfactory method is yet proposed by which the voice of the majority in this case may be determined, or its influence secured.

The people of the respective counties are indeed requested to signify their opinion respecting the adoption of the Bill to the next Session of Assembly. But the representatives or of the Counties will be that of the people. Our hope is that neither of the former will, after due consideration, espouse the dangerous principle of the Bill. Should the event disappoint us, it will still leave us in full confidence, that a fair appeal to the latter will reverse the sentence against our liberties.

15. Because finally, "the equal right of every citizen to the free exercise of his Religion according to the dictates of conscience" is held by the same tenure with all our other rights.

If we recur to its origin, it is equally the gift of nature; if we weigh its importance, it cannot be less dear to us; if we consult the "Declaration of those rights which pertain to the good people of Virginia, as the basis and foundation of Government," it is enumerated with equal solemnity, or rather studied emphasis.

Either then, we must say, that the Will of the Legislature is the only measure of their authority; and that in the plenitude of this authority, they may sweep away all our fundamental rights; or, that they are bound to leave this particular right untouched and sacred:

Either we must say, that they may control the freedom of the press, may abolish the Trial by Jury, may swallow up the Executive and Judiciary Powers of the State; nay that they may despoil us of our very right of suffrage, and erect themselves into an independent and hereditary Assembly or, we must say, that they have no authority to enact into the law the Bill under consideration.

Conclusion:

We the Subscribers say, that the General Assembly of this Commonwealth have no such authority: And that no effort may be omitted on our part against so dangerous an usurpation, we oppose to it, this remonstrance; earnestly praying, as we are in duty bound, that the Supreme Lawgiver of the Universe, by illuminating those to whom it is addressed, may on the one hand, turn their Councils from every act which would affront his holy prerogative, or violate the trust committed to them: and on the other, guide them into every measure which may be worthy of his [blessing, may be bound to their own praise, and may establish more firmly the liberties, the prosperity and the happiness of the Commonwealth.

Religious Freedom Restoration Act

Enacted 1993. Declared unconstitutional by the Supreme Court in June 1997.

Title: To protect the free exercise of religion.

Be it enacted by the Senate and House of Representatives of the United States of America in Congress assembled,

Section 1. Short Title.

This Act may be cited as the 'Religious Freedom Restoration Act of 1993'.

Sec. 2. Congressional Findings and Declaration of Purposes.

(a) Findings: The Congress finds that—

(1) the framers of the Constitution, recognizing free exercise of religion as an unalienable right, secured its protection in the First Amendment to the Constitution;

(2) laws 'neutral' toward religion may burden religious exercise as surely as laws intended to interfere with religious exercise;

(3) governments should not substantially burden religious exercise without compelling justification;

(4) in Employment Division v. Smith, 494 U.S. 872 (1990) the Supreme Court virtually eliminated the requirement that the government justify burdens on religious exercise imposed by laws neutral toward religion; and

(5) the compelling interest test as set forth in prior Federal court rulings is a workable test for striking sensible balances between religious liberty and competing prior governmental interests.

(b) Purposes: The purposes of this Act are—

(1) to restore the compelling interest test as set forth in Sherbert v. Verner, 374 U.S. 398 (1963) and Wisconsin v. Yoder, 406 U.S. 205 (1972) and to guarantee its application in all cases where free exercise of religion is substantially burdened; and

(2) to provide a claim or defense to persons whose religious exercise is substantially burdened by government.

Sec. 3. Free Exercise of Religion Protected.

(a) In General: Government shall not substantially burden a person's exercise of religion even if the burden results from a rule of general applicability, except as provided in subsection (b).

(b) Exception: Government may substantially burden a person's exercise of religion only if it demonstrates that application of the burden to the person—

(1) is in furtherance of a compelling governmental interest; and

(2) is the least restrictive means of furthering that compelling governmental interest.

(c) Judicial Relief: A person whose religious exercise has been burdened in violation of this section may assert that violation as a claim or defense in a judicial proceeding and obtain appropriate relief against a government. Standing to assert a claim or defense under this section shall be governed by the general rules of standing under article III of the Constitution.

Sec. 4. Attorneys Fees.

(a) Judicial Proceedings: Section 722 of the Revised Statutes (42 U.S.C. 1988) is amended by inserting 'the Religious Freedom Restoration Act of 1993,' before 'or title VI of the Civil Rights Act of 1964'.

(b) Administrative Proceedings: Section 504(b)(1)(C) of title 5, United States Code, is amended—

(1) by striking 'and' at the end of clause (ii);

(2) by striking the semicolon at the end of clause (iii) and inserting ', and'; and

(3) by inserting '(iv) the Religious Freedom Restoration Act of 1993'; after clause (iii).

Sec. 5. Definitions.

As used in this Act—

(1) the term 'government' includes a branch, department, agency, instrumentality, and official (or other person acting under color of law) of the United States, a State, or a subdivision of a State;

(2) the term 'State' includes the District of Columbia, the Commonwealth of Puerto Rico, and each territory and possession of the United States;

(3) the term 'demonstrates' means meets the burdens of going forward with the evidence and of persuasion; and

(4) the term 'exercise of religion' means the exercise of religion under the First Amendment to the Constitution.

Sec. 6. Applicability.

(a) In General.—This Act applies to all Federal and State law, and the implementation of that law, whether statutory or otherwise, and whether adopted before or after the enactment of this Act.

(b) Rule of Construction.—Federal statutory law adopted after the date of the enactment of this Act is subject to this Act unless such law explicitly excludes such application by reference to this Act.

(c) Religious Belief Unaffected.—Nothing in this Act shall be construed to authorize any government to burden any religious belief.

Sec. 7. Establishment Clause Unaffected.

Nothing in this Act shall be construed to affect, interpret, or in any way address that portion of the First Amendment prohibiting laws respecting the establishment of religion (referred to in this section as the 'Establishment Clause'). Granting government funding, benefits, or exemptions, to the extent permissible under the Establishment Clause, shall not constitute a violation of this Act. As used in this section, the term 'granting,' used with respect to government funding, benefits, or exemptions, does not include the denial of government funding, benefits, or exemptions.

Religious Land Use and Institutionalized Persons Act

An act to protect religious liberty, and for other purposes.

Be it enacted by the Senate and House of Representatives of the United States of America in Congress assembled,

Section 1. Short Title. This Act may be cited as the 'Religious Land Use and Institutionalized Persons Act of 2000'.

Sec. 2. Protection of Land Use as Religious Exercise.

(a) Substantial Burdens—

(1) General Rule—No government shall impose or implement a land use regulation in a manner that imposes a substantial burden on the religious exercise of a person, including a religious assembly or institution, unless the government demonstrates that imposition of the burden on that person, assembly, or institution—

(A) is in furtherance of a compelling governmental interest; and

(B) is the least restrictive means of furthering that compelling governmental interest.

(2) Scope of Application—This subsection applies in any case in which—

(A) the substantial burden is imposed in a program or activity that receives Federal financial assistance, even if the burden results from a rule of general applicability;

(B) the substantial burden affects, or removal of that substantial burden would affect, commerce with foreign nations, among the several States, or with Indian tribes, even if the burden results from a rule of general applicability; or

(C) the substantial burden is imposed in the implementation of a land use regulation or system of land use regulations, under which a government makes, or has in place formal or informal procedures or practices that permit the government to make individualized assessments of the proposed uses or the property involved.

(b) Discrimination and Exclusion—

(1) Equal Terms—No government shall impose or implement a land use regulation in a manner that treats a religious assembly or institution on less than equal terms with a nonreligious assembly or institution.

(2) Nondiscrimination—No government shall impose or implement a land use regulation that discriminates against any assembly or institution on the basis of religion or religious denomination.

(3) Exclusions and Limits—No government shall impose or implement a land use regulation that—

(A) totally excludes religious assemblies from a jurisdiction; or

(B) unreasonably limits religious assemblies, institutions, or structures within a jurisdiction.

Sec. 3. Protection of Religious Exercise of Institutionalized Persons.

(a) General Rule—No government shall impose a substantial burden on the religious exercise of a person residing in or confined to an institution, as defined in section 2 of the Civil Rights of Institutionalized Persons Act (42 U.S.C.1997), even if the burden results from a rule of general applicability, unless the government demonstrates that imposition of the burden on that person—

(1) is in furtherance of a compelling governmental interest; and

(2) is the least restrictive means of furthering that compelling governmental interest.

(b) Scope of Application—This section applies in any case in which—

(1) the substantial burden is imposed in a program or activity that receives Federal financial assistance; or

(2) the substantial burden affects, or removal of that substantial burden would affect, commerce with foreign nations, among the several States, or with Indian tribes.

Sec. 4. Judicial Relief.

(a) Cause of Action—A person may assert a violation of this Act as a claim or defense in a judicial proceeding and obtain appropriate relief against a government. Standing to assert a claim or defense under this section shall be governed by the general rules of standing under article III of the Constitution.

(b) Burden of Persuasion—If a plaintiff produces prima facie evidence to support a claim alleging a violation of the Free Exercise Clause or a violation of section 2, the government shall bear the burden of persuasion on any element of the claim, except that the plaintiff shall bear the burden of persuasion on whether the law (including a regulation) or government practice that is challenged by the claim substantially burdens the plaintiff's exercise of religion.

(c) Full Faith and Credit—Adjudication of a claim of a violation of section 2 in a non-Federal forum shall not be entitled to full faith and credit in a Federal court unless the claimant had a full and fair adjudication of that claim in the non-Federal forum.

(d) Attorneys' Fees—Section 722(b) of the Revised Statutes (42 U.S.C. 1988(b)) is amended—

(1) by inserting 'the Religious Land Use and Institutionalized Persons Act of 2000,' after 'Religious Freedom Restoration Act of 1993,'; and

(2) by striking the comma that follows a comma.

(e) Prisoners—Nothing in this Act shall be construed to amend or repeal the Prison Litigation Reform Act of 1995 (including provisions of law amended by that Act).

(f) Authority of United States to Enforce This Act—The United States may bring an action for injunctive or declaratory relief to enforce compliance with this Act. Nothing in this subsection shall be construed to deny, impair, or otherwise affect any right or authority of the Attorney General, the United States, or any agency, officer, or employee of the United States, acting under any law other than this subsection, to institute or intervene in any proceeding.

(g) Limitation—If the only jurisdictional basis for applying a provision of this Act is a claim that a substantial burden by a government on religious exercise affects, or that removal of that substantial burden would affect, commerce with foreign nations, among the several States, or with Indian tribes, the provision shall not apply if the government demonstrates that all substantial burdens on, or the removal of all substantial burdens from, similar religious exercise throughout the Nation would not lead in the aggregate to a substantial effect on commerce with foreign nations, among the several States, or with Indian tribes.

Sec. 5. Rules of Construction.

(a) Religious Belief Unaffected—Nothing in this Act shall be construed to authorize any government to burden any religious belief.

(b) Religious Exercise Not Regulated—Nothing in this Act shall create any basis for restricting or burdening religious exercise or for claims against a religious organization including any religiously affiliated school or university, not acting under color of law.

(c) Claims to Funding Unaffected—Nothing in this Act shall create or preclude a right of any religious organization to receive funding or other assistance from a government, or of any person to receive government funding for a religious activity, but this Act may require a government to incur expenses in its own operations to avoid imposing a substantial burden on religious exercise.

(d) Other Authority to Impose Conditions on Funding Unaffected—Nothing in this Act shall—

(1) authorize a government to regulate or affect, directly or indirectly, the activities or policies of a person other than a government as a condition of receiving funding or other assistance; or

(2) restrict any authority that may exist under other law to so regulate or affect, except as provided in this Act.

(e) Governmental Discretion in Alleviating Burdens on Religious Exercise—A government may avoid the preemptive force of any provision of this Act by changing the policy or practice that results in a substantial burden on religious exercise, by retaining the policy or practice and exempting the substantially burdened religious exercise, by providing exemptions from the policy or practice for applications that substantially burden religious exercise, or by any other means that eliminates the substantial burden.

(f) Effect on Other Law—With respect to a claim brought under this Act, proof that a substantial burden on a person's religious exercise affects, or removal of that burden would affect, commerce with foreign nations, among the several States, or with Indian tribes, shall not establish any inference or presumption that Congress intends that any religious exercise is, or is not, subject to any law other than this Act.

(g) Broad Construction—This Act shall be construed in favor of a broad protection of religious exercise, to the maximum extent permitted by the terms of this Act and the Constitution.

(h) No Preemption or Repeal—Nothing in this Act shall be construed to preempt State law, or repeal Federal law, that is equally as protective of religious exercise as, or more protective of religious exercise than, this Act.

(i) Severability—If any provision of this Act or of an amendment made by this Act, or any application of such provision to any person or circumstance, is held to be unconstitutional, the remainder of this Act, the amendments made by this Act, and the application of the provision to any other person or circumstance shall not be affected.

Sec. 6. Establishment Clause Unaffected.

Nothing in this Act shall be construed to affect, interpret, or in any way address that portion of the first amendment to the Constitution prohibiting laws respecting an establishment of religion (referred to in this section as the 'Establishment Clause'). Granting government funding, benefits, or exemptions, to the extent permissible under the Establishment Clause, shall not constitute a violation of this Act. In this section, the term 'granting,' used with respect to government funding, benefits, or exemptions, does not include the denial of government funding, benefits, or exemptions.

Sec. 7. Amendments to Religious Freedom Restoration Act.

(a) Definitions—Section 5 of the Religious Freedom Restoration Act of 1993 (42 U.S.C. 2000bb–2) is amended—

(1) in paragraph (1), by striking 'a State, or a subdivision of a State' and inserting 'or of a covered entity';

(2) in paragraph (2), by striking 'term' and all that follows through 'includes' and inserting "term 'covered entity' means"; and

(3) in paragraph (4), by striking all after 'means' and inserting 'religious exercise, as defined in section 8 of the Religious Land Use and Institutionalized Persons Act of 2000.'

(b) Conforming Amendment—Section 6(a) of the Religious Freedom Restoration Act of 1993 (42 U.S.C. 2000bb–3(a)) is amended by striking 'and State.'

Sec. 8. Definitions.

In this Act:

(1) Claimant—The term 'claimant' means a person raising a claim or defense under this Act.

(2) Demonstrates—The term 'demonstrates' means meets the burdens of going forward with the evidence and of persuasion.

(3) Free Exercise Clause—The term 'Free Exercise Clause' means that portion of the first amendment to the Constitution that proscribes laws prohibiting the free exercise of religion.

(4) Government—The term 'government'—

(A) means—

(i) a State, county, municipality, or other governmental entity created under the authority of a State;

(ii) any branch, department, agency, instrumentality, or official of an entity listed in clause (i); and

(iii) any other person acting under color of State law; and

(B) for the purposes of sections 4(b) and 5, includes the United States, a branch, department, agency, instrumentality, or official of the United States, and any other person acting under color of Federal law.

(5) Land Use Regulation—The term 'land use regulation' means a zoning or landmarking law, or the application of such a law, that limits or restricts a claimant's use or development of land (including a structure affixed to land), if the claimant has an ownership, leasehold, easement, servitude, or other property interest in the regulated land or a contract or option to acquire such an interest.

(6) Program or Activity—The term 'program or activity' means all of the operations of any entity as described in paragraph (1) or (2) of section 606 of the Civil Rights Act of 1964 (42 U.S.C. 2000d–4a).

(7) Religious Exercise—

(A) In General—The term 'religious exercise' includes any exercise of religion, whether or not compelled by, or central to, a system of religious belief.

(B) Rule—The use, building, or conversion of real property for the purpose of religious exercise shall be considered to be religious exercise of the person or entity that uses or intends to use the property for that purpose.

Arkansas Antievolution Statute

[During the first half of the twentieth century several states enacted laws banning the teaching of evolution in both public schools and universities. Religious individuals and groups object to the teaching of evolution because it runs counter to the literal explanation in the Bible. The famous "Scopes Monkey Trial" upheld Tennessee's antievolution statute in 1925. One by one these laws were challenged and declared invalid and an impermissible intrusion of religion in the schools. In 1967 the Arkansas Supreme Court upheld the following statute. The U.S. Supreme Court, however, overruled the Arkansas court and ruled the statute unconstitutional in *Epperson v. Arkansas* (1968).]

Arkansas Statutes Annotated 1947, paragraphs 80–1627, 80–1628

80–1627.—Doctrine of ascent or descent of man from lower order of animals prohibited.—It shall be unlawful for any teacher or other instructor in any University, College, Normal, Public School, or other institution of the State, which is supported in whole or in part from public funds derived by State and local taxation to teach the theory or doctrine that mankind ascended or descended from a lower order of animals and also shall it be unlawful for any teacher, textbook commission, or other authority exercising the power to select textbooks for above mentioned educational institutions to adopt or use in any such institutions a textbook that teaches the doctrine or theory that mankind descended or ascended from a lower order of animals.

80–1628.—Teaching doctrine or adopting textbooks mentioning doctrine—Penalties—Positions to be vacated.—Any teacher or other instructor or textbook commissioner who is found guilty of violation of this act by teaching the theory or doctrine mentioned in section 1 hereof, or by using, or adopting any such textbooks in any such educational institution shall be guilty of a misdemeanor and upon conviction shall be fined not exceeding five hundred dollars [$500.00]; and upon conviction shall vacate the position thus held in any educational institutions of the character above mentioned or any commission of which he may be a member.

Summary of the Williamsburg Charter (1988)

[Charter signed by a pluralistic group of Americans celebrating Freedom of Religion as guaranteed by the First Amendment]

Summary of Principles

"Congress shall make no law respecting an establishment of religion, or prohibiting the free exercise thereof . . ."

The Religious Liberty clauses of the First Amendment to the Constitution are a momentous decision, the most important political decision for religious liberty and public justice in history. Two hundred years after their enactment they stand out boldly in a century made dark by state repression and sectarian conflict. Yet the ignorance and contention now surrounding the clauses are a reminder that their advocacy and defense is a task for each succeeding generation.

We acknowledge our deep and continuing differences over religious beliefs, political policies and constitutional interpretations. But together we celebrate the genius of the Religious Liberty clauses, and affirm the following truths to be among the first principles that are in the shared interest of all Americans:

1. Religious liberty, or freedom of conscience, is a precious, fundamental and inalienable right. A society is only as just and free as it is respectful of this right for its smallest minorities and least popular communities.

2. Religious liberty is founded on the inviolable dignity of the person. It is not based on science or social usefulness and is not dependent on the shifting moods of majorities and governments.

3. Religious liberty is our nation's "first liberty," which undergirds all other rights and freedoms secured by the Bill of Rights.

4. The two Religious Liberty clauses address distinct concerns, but together they serve the same end—religious liberty, or freedom of conscience, for citizens of all faiths or none.

5. The No Establishment clause separates Church from State but not religion from politics or public life. It prevents the confusion of religion and government which has been a leading source of repression and coercion throughout history.

6. The Free Exercise clause guarantees the right to reach, hold, exercise or change beliefs freely. It allows all citizens who so desire to shape their lives, whether private or public, on the basis of personal and communal beliefs.

7. The Religious Liberty clauses are both a protection of individual liberty and a provision for ordering the relationship of religion and public life. They allow us to live with our deepest differences and enable diversity to be a source of national strength.

8. Conflict and debate are vital to democracy. Yet if controversies about religion and politics are to reflect the highest wisdom of the First Amendment and advance the best interests of the disputants and the nation, then *how* we debate, and not only what we debate, is critical.

9. One of America's continuing needs is to develop, out of our differences, a common vision for the common good. Today that common vision must embrace a shared understanding of the place of religion in public life and of the guiding principles by which people with deep religious differences can contend robustly but civilly with each other.

10. Central to the notion of the common good, and of greater importance each day because of the increase of pluralism, is the recognition that religious liberty is a universal right joined to a universal duty to respect the right. Rights are best guarded and responsibilities best

exercised when each person and group guards for all others those rights they wish guarded for themselves.

We are firmly persuaded that these principles require a fresh consideration, and that the reaffirmation of religious liberty is crucial to sustain a free people that would remain free. We therefore commit ourselves to speak, write, and act according to this vision and these principles. We urge our fellow citizens to do the same, now and in generations to come.

[reprinted in Sherrow, *Separation of Church and State*]

Proposed Constitutional Amendments

Over the years, those unhappy with the First Amendment's religion clauses have proposed a number of amendments aimed at either increasing or decreasing the role of religion in the schools. These efforts continue today.

Why An Amendment Is Being Sought

The First Amendment provides in part that: "Congress shall make no law respecting the establishment of religion, or prohibiting the free exercise thereof." The first half of the sentence is referred to as the "establishment clause" and the second half as the "free exercise clause." The U.S. Supreme Court has interpreted the establishment clause as banning organized school prayer and bible-reading in the public schools. The Court has also banned the display of the Ten Commandments and crosses on school property and the teaching of "creation science" alongside evolution in biology classes.

Those who support organized prayer, Bible reading, and subjects with other religious content in the schools have sought to overturn the results in these cases by amending the U.S. Constitution. Although the Congress might be willing to pass a law authorizing organized school prayer, such a law would probably be held unconstitutional by the Supreme Court. In fact, the Supreme Court often announces in its decisions that there are areas in the law that Congress should address. The Supreme Court has not invited Congress to pass laws to interpret the meaning of the religion clauses however. It is clear that the Court feels that the Court itself is best-equipped to interpret the scope of the First Amendment protections.

In our system of government there is a long tradition that Congress cannot change the Constitution on its own initiative. Congress does not have the ability to overturn a specific Supreme Court decision which it dislikes or which is unpopular with their constituents. If members of Congress or citizens want the Constitution changed they need to amend the Constitution itself. For example, the twenty-sixth amendment, ratified in 1971 gave 18 year olds the right to vote.

Procedure for Amending the U.S. Constitution

Article V of the U.S. Constitution provides two mechanisms to make additions to the Constitution. The first method is the one usually employed. An Amendment may be proposed in Congress, and if two-thirds of the members of both the House and Representatives and the Senate approve, the proposed amendment must then be ratified by the legislatures of three-quarters of the states.

There is a second method mentioned in the Constitution.

A constitutional convention to add amendments can be convened at the request of the legislatures of two-thirds of the states. Proposed amendments can be ratified by a three-fourths vote of the convention. To date, no amendments have ever been added by a constitutional convention because none has ever been held. There is uncertainty about both the composition of such a convention and its operation so it is unlikely to be an option.

History of Amendments

In fact, only twenty-seven amendments have been made to the original 1789 document—a very small number considering the fact that the Constitution has been in effect for more than two hundred years and the country has obviously experienced many changes in that time.

During the late 1800s Congressmen proposed no fewer than eleven different constitutional amendments dealing with church and state and religion in the schools. Generally, these amendments attempted to reduce the power of the states in dealing with religion. Although the existence of so many proposed amendments demonstrates that they had wide support, none of the proposed amendments has ever garnered the two-thirds majority.

The most famous of these proposed amendments was the so-called Blaine Amendment (reproduced in full below) which was an early

(1876) attempt to ban any state aid to church-supported schools. Although there was broad support for this amendment it never received enough votes in Congress to be referred to the states for ratification. Interestingly, although the Blaine Amendment banned federal or state aid to church-supported schools and also banned school prayer in public schools, it specifically stated that it did not prohibit Bible reading in the schools.

Proposed Blaine Amendment (1876)

Although the amendment passed the House of Representatives, it failed to receive the needed two-thirds vote in the Senate and was never forwarded to the states for ratification.

No state shall make any law respecting the establishment of religion or prohibiting the free exercise thereof; and no religious test shall ever be required as a qualification to any office or public trust under any state. No public property, and no public revenue of, nor any loan of credit by or under the authority of the United States or any state, territory, District, or municipal corporation, shall be appropriated to, or used for, the support of any school, educational, or other institution, under the control of any religious or anti-religious sect, organization, or denomination, or wherein the particular creed or tenets of any religious or anti-religious sect, organization, or denomination, or wherein the particular creed or tenets of any religious sect, organization, or denomination be taught. And no such particular creed or tenets shall be read or taught in any school or institution supported in whole or in part by such revenue or loan of credit; and no such appropriation or loan of credit shall be made to any religious or anti-religious sect, organization or denomination, or to promote its interests or tenets. This article shall not be construed to prohibit the reading of the Bible in any school or institution; and it shall not have the effect to impair rights of property already invested . . .

Proposed Prayer Amendment (1992)

Nothing in this Constitution shall be construed to prohibit individual or group prayer in public schools or other public institutions. No person shall be required by the United States or by any State to participate in prayer. Neither the United States nor any State shall compose the words of any prayer to be said in public schools.

Proposed Religious Equality Amendment (1994)

Section 1
Neither the United States nor any State shall abridge the freedom of any person or group, including students in public schools, to engage in prayer or other religious expression in circumstances in which expression of a nonreligious character would be permitted; nor deny benefits to or otherwise discriminate against any person or group on account of the religious character of their speech, ideas, motivations, or identity.

Section 2
Nothing in the Constitution shall be construed to forbid the United States or any State to give public or ceremonial acknowledgement to the religious heritage, beliefs, or traditions of its people.

Section 3
The exercise, by the people, of any freedoms under the First Amendment or under this Amendment shall not constitute an establishment of religion.

Proposed Religious Freedom Amendment (1997)

To secure the people's right to acknowledge God according to the dictates of conscience: The people's right to pray and to recognize their religious beliefs, heritage, or traditions on public property, including schools, shall not be infringed. The government shall not require any person to join in prayer or other religious activity, initiate or designate school prayers, discriminate against religion, or deny equal access to a benefit on account of religion."

Key People, Laws, and Concepts

Abington v. Schempp (1963)

Supreme Court outlaws both Bible reading and recitation of the Lord's Prayer in public schools as a violation of the Establishment Clause.

Affirmed

In the practice of the appellate courts, the decree or order is declared valid and will stand as rendered in the lower court.

Agnostic

Person who is skeptical about the existence or nonexistence of God. Immanual Kant, among other notables, was an agnostic. An agnostic might argue that it is impossible to logically conclude that God either exists or doesn't exist because of lack of reliable evidence. An agnostic might also argue that it is likewise impossible to know the ultimate origin of the universe. An "agnostic" should not be confused with an "atheist"—a person who denies the existence of God. This also contrasts with a "deist," who rejects the conception of a supreme being as the ruler and inspiration of man but still believes that there was a creator of the universe.

Aguilar v. Felton (1985)

Supreme Court holds that use of federal funds to pay salaries of public employees teaching in parochial schools violates the Establishment Clause.

American Civil Liberties Union (ACLU)

Often derided by conservatives as a "liberal," "radical," or even "communist" organization, the ACLU is in fact much harder to label. Because of its "absolutist" support of First Amendment rights, including the right to free speech, the ACLU often supports unpopular minority views. In some cases these may seem "against" religion while other cases may seem to back supporters of religion. For example, the ACLU has supported the right of the American Nazi Party to conduct demonstrations.

American Coalition for Traditional Values

Founded in 1983 by conservative religious leaders such as Jerry Falwell, James Dobson, Jimmy Swaggart, and others, the organization was headed from the start by Tim LaHaye, one of the nation's foremost conservative critics and a well-known author. The group's stated aims are to reestablish traditional moral values, and the group supports a return of religion in the public schools. The Washington, D.C.,–based organization has been a vocal proponent of a constitutional amendment to allow prayer in public schools.

Americans United for Separation of Church and State

Nationally prominent organization that supports the separation of church and state in public life. Currently headed by the Reverend Barry W. Lynn, the group should not be considered antireligious, however. Americans United, together with the ACLU and several "conservative" religious groups (with whom Americans United often disagrees), helped enact the Religious Freedom Restoration Act, which sought to limit the extent to which governments could limit an individual's religious expression.

Amicus Curiae

"Friend of the court." When a legal case is appealed from a trial court to an appeals court, the judges do not hear witnesses but rely on trial transcripts and "briefs" submitted by the parties to the lawsuit. A brief is a written document making arguments and providing legal support for a party's position. In important cases other persons or entities may file "friends of the court" briefs (amicus curiae briefs) urging the court to decide a case one way or another.

Answer

The formal written statement by a defendant responding to a civil complaint and setting forth the grounds for defense.

Anti-Defamation League of B'nai B'rith

The ADL was founded in 1913 "to stop the defamation of the Jewish people [and] to secure justice and fair treatment for all citizens alike." The ADL investigates and fights various hate groups including the Ku Klux Klan and the American Nazis. The group is a vocal proponent of separation of church and state to protect minority rights.

Appeal

A request made after a trial, asking another court (usually the court of appeals) to decide whether the trial was conducted properly. To make such a request is "to appeal" or "to take an appeal." One who appeals is called the appellant.

Appellate

About appeals; an appellate court has the power to review the judgment of another lower court or tribunal.

Atheist (Atheism)

An atheist is a person who denies the existence of God or the existence of God's works on earth. This contrasts somewhat from a "freethinker," who believes only what appears rational, and may have lost faith. An "atheist" should not be confused with an "agnostic," who merely is skeptical about the existence or nonexistence of God.

Balanced Curriculum (Balanced Treatment)

This term is used by religious educators to describe a school curriculum that presents both evolution and divine creation ("creationism") as equally plausible explanations of human origin. Only a few states have enacted laws requiring "balanced curriculums" while others have rejected such measures. Louisiana's balanced curriculum law was declared invalid by the U.S. Supreme Court in *Edwards, Governor of Louisiana v. Aguillard* (1987).

Bill of Rights

First ten amendments to the U.S. Constitution. As originally drafted the U.S. Constitution contained no list of individual rights and protections of citizens. Although the drafters argued that such protections were implicit in the document, a considerable number of prominent persons announced that they would not support ratification without such an explicit enumeration of guaranteed rights, freedoms, and protections. James Madison and other members of the Constitutional Convention debated on various amendments, many of which concerned religious freedoms. These debates culminated in the familiar first ten amendments popularly known as the Bill of Rights. Once ratified by the original states, they became part of the new Constitution in 1791. The Bill of Rights was originally interpreted to apply only to actions of the federal government, not to actions of state and local governments. Since about 1960, the courts have uniformly held that the Fourteenth Amendment applies the Bill of Rights to state and local governments as well.

Black, Hugo L. (1886–1971)

A one-time small-town Ku Klux Klan member, Hugo L. Black rose to serve on the U.S. Supreme Court and came to write one of the most enduring court opinions protecting the rights of separation of church and state. Black was appointed to the Supreme Court in 1937 by Franklin Roosevelt and served with distinction until 1971. The nomination was highly controversial because it was revealed that Black had at one time been a member of the Ku Klux Klan. However, he surprised many of his critics by becoming a strong supporter of both civil rights and freedom of religion once appointed to the Court. Black enjoyed a long tenure on the Court and was an important member of the famous "Warren Court" that handed down many liberal opinions during the 1950s and early 1960s. Black is perhaps remembered best because he wrote many of the era's important decisions, most notably, *Gideon v. Wainwright,* which requires counsel in criminal cases, and *Engel v. Vitale* (1962), which banned public school prayer. The highly controversial school prayer case thrust both the Court and Black into the limelight. He was vilified in many quarters, especially by many Christians who sincerely believed that the Court, and Black in particular, had gone far beyond the intent of the nations' founders and were attempting to make a "godless" country.

Blaine Amendment

Proposed but never enacted constitutional amendment that would have specifically extended the Establishment Clause and Free Exercise Clause of the First Amendment to the states. First proposed by James G. Blaine of Maine, who later ran unsuccessfully for president, the amendment would have also prohibited any government aid to parochial schools. Although the amendment was brought before a number of Congresses in the late 1800s, it was never enacted. However, the U.S. Supreme Court ultimately extended these amendments to the states.

Board of Education v. Allen (1968)

Supreme Court allows distribution of textbooks to parochial school children. The Court found the aid went to the students, not the schools.

Board of Education v. Mergens (1990)

The Supreme Court holds that under the Equal Access Act of 1994, a school district that provides a "limited open forum" for a variety of student clubs may not exclude a religious study group.

Brennan, William J., Jr. (1906–1997)

Appointed to the U.S. Supreme Court by President Eisenhower, Brennan proved to be a strong advocate of civil rights and freedom of religion during his term on the Court from 1956 to 1990. A member of the famous "Warren Court," Brennan later became the leader of the Supreme Court's liberal minority after 1970, and his ability to build consensus positions preserved and even extended the liberal decisions of the Court, even after the appointment of a number of avowed "conservatives." Brennan was a staunch upholder of separation of church and state, and in later years found himself more often in the minority.

Brief

A written statement submitted by the lawyer for each side in a case that explains to the judges why they should decide the case or a particular part of a case in favor of that lawyer's client. When a legal case is appealed from a trial court to an appeals court, the judges do not hear witnesses or evaluate evidence, but rely on trial transcripts and "briefs" submitted by the parties to the lawsuit. A brief is a written document making arguments and providing legal support for a party's position. A brief may be anywhere from a dozen to a hundred pages in length.

Bryan, William Jennings (1860–1925)

Bryan was an unsuccessful Democratic presidential candidate in 1896, 1902, and 1908. A renowned orator, Bryan gained a national reputation and the Democratic nomination in 1896 after making his famous "Cross of Gold Speech" aimed at the gold standard. Bryan was also a fundamentalist who believed in the literal truth of the biblical account of creation. After his retirement from politics he often delivered lectures on the religious circuit. He was staunchly opposed to the teaching of evolution in the schools. Today Bryan is best remembered for his defense of Tennessee's antievolution law in the famous 1925 "Monkey Trial."

Burger, Warren (1907–1995)

Chief justice U.S. Supreme Court, 1969–1986. Burger was appointed as a judge of the U.S. Court of Appeals for the District of Columbia, and was nominated by President Richard Nixon to be chief justice of the Supreme Court on the retirement of Earl Warren. Unlike Warren, Burger was known as a strict constructionist and the "Burger Court" proved more conservative than the Warren Court that preceded it.

However, by today's standards the Court was judicially active during Burger's reign as chief justice and the Court delivered several controversial opinions, especially in the area of religion and the schools. The chief justice has responsibility for assigning the writing of opinions. Although known as a conservative, Burger himself wrote one of the most controversial opinions in the area. For example, Burger penned the famous opinion in *Lemon v. Kurtzman* (1971), which made a strong statement by the Court that any entanglement between church and state would not be tolerated in the schools. In *Lemon*, Burger, writing for the Court, held that state salary supplements or aid for secular instruction in parochial schools offended both the Establishment Clause and the Free Exercise Clause. He also wrote the majority opinion in *Wisconsin v. Yoder* (1972), an 8–1 decision in which the Court upheld the right of Amish parents to withhold their children from public school despite the state of Wisconsin's compulsory schooling law.

Cantwell v. Connecticut (1940)

Supreme Court reverses a state conviction of Jehovah's Witnesses who were peacefully proselytizing on a public street.

Certiorari

The U.S. Supreme Court hears appeals from federal courts and from state supreme courts. However, appeal to the Court is not automatic. One or both parties must petition the Court for a writ of certiorari, which orders the litigants to appear before the Court to argue the case. Of the thousands of writs submitted annually, the Court accepts fewer than one hundred cases that it deems most important.

Chief Judge

The judge who has primary responsibility for the administration of a court but also decides cases; chief judges are determined by seniority.

Chief Justice

The chief judge of the U.S. Supreme Court. The president has the power to appoint the chief justice, but once appointed the chief justice, like other federal judges, serves for life.

Christian Advocates Serving Evangelism (CASE)

A public interest law firm based in Virginia Beach, Virginia, and headed by Jay Sekulow, CASE is dedicated to expanding the opportunities for religious expression in many areas of public life. Notably, CASE was successful in the case, *Board of Education of the Westside Community Schools v. Mergens,* in which the Supreme Court held that voluntary student Bible clubs on school premises do not offend the Establishment Clause.

Christian Coalition

Formed by evangelist Pat Robertson in 1989 as a Christian political advocacy group, the Christian Coalition soon gained enough membership to become a national political force with the ability to influence both political opinion and legislation. Under the able direction of Ralph Reed, the organization grew rapidly, enlisting a million members (two million according to their own count). The group lends its support to candidates who support traditional family values as defined by the group, including more religion in the public schools. The group distributes "congressional scorecards" to both the press and its membership rating candidates' positions on the issues.

City of Boerne v. Flores (1997)

Supreme Court overturns the 1993 Religious Freedom Restoration Act in a case involving a church's zoning dispute with a city. Court holds that religious belief does not grant automatic exemption from general laws.

Common Law

The legal system that originated in England and is now in use in the United States. It is based on judicial decisions rather than legislative action.

Compelling Interest Test

A test formulated by the U.S. Supreme Court in applying the Free Exercise Clause of the First Amendment to actual cases. The test is used to determine if a particular law is in violation of the First Amendment's protection of the free exercise of religion. Under the test, a law interfering with the person's free exercise of religion can only be applied against that person if the state demonstrated that the law furthers a compelling government interest that cannot be met by a less restrictive means. For example, a state law that required all school-age children to attend secular public school and would not allow schooling in religious schools would be judged under the compelling interest test.

Compulsory

Required. The courts have recognized that "compulsion" does not have to be overt or direct, but may also be subtle and indirect. For example, a verbalized school prayer may be labeled "voluntary." The teacher may inform students at the beginning of the school year that the class will all rise and say a prayer at the beginning of the school day. However, any child who wishes to refrain may rise and remain silent or may remain seated and not participate. The courts recognize that although the child is not being compelled to recite the prayer, the recitation of the prayer led by the teacher in the classroom amounted to subtle and indirect pressure. Abstaining students might be exposed to ridicule or ostracism because they did not share the religious beliefs of the majority of the class. Accordingly, the courts would find such a prayer "compulsory" even though other options are available.

Compulsory Education Laws

Law requiring children under a certain age to attend school. These laws have caused a controversy with parents who wish to prevent their children from attending public school because they object to the secular atmosphere of public schools or because they prefer a school that also teaches religious principles. In 1925, in *Pierce v. Society of Sisters,* the U.S. Supreme Court struck down an Oregon compulsory education law that required all students to attend public school. The case held that parents have a right to send their children to a nonpublic school. In 1972 in *Wisconsin v. Yoder,* the Supreme Court held that because of their religious beliefs Amish students were not compelled to attend school.

Concurring Opinion

When more than one judge hears a case, one or more judges on the panel may agree with the result but not the logic contained in the majority opinion. This judge may write a concurring opinion explaining why he or she agrees with the decision but offering an alternate explanation for the result in the case. If there are a number of judges who agree with the concurring opinion they may "join" or adopt the concurrence. Alternately they may write their own concurring opinions.

Conscientious Objector

A person who objects to military service or other government action on religious or moral grounds. The United States, like other nations, has long exempted conscientious objectors from combat duty in the armed forces. During wars, when most young men are conscripted into the armed forces by the draft, conscientious objectors were permitted to avoid military service entirely or to work in noncombat positions such as the medical corps. Only those opposed to war on religious grounds are exempt from service; stating moral objections is insufficient. Similarly, an objector must be opposed to war in general, not just the particular war.

Counsel

Legal advice; a term used to refer to lawyers in a case.

Counterclaim

A claim that a defendant makes against a plaintiff.

County of Allegheny v. Greater Pittsburgh ACLU (1989)

A case trying to follow the Court's *Lynch v. Donnelly* decision regarding civic holiday displays. The Court approves Pittsburgh's menorah but rejects its crèche as an entanglement with religion.

Court

Government entity authorized to resolve legal disputes. Judges sometimes use "court" to refer to themselves in the third person, as in "the court has read the briefs."

Creation Science ("Scientific Creationism")

After the U.S. Supreme Court prohibited states from banning the teaching of evolution in *Epperson v. Arkansas* (1968), creationists started labeling their body of information supporting the biblical version of creation as "creation science." By so doing, the creationists—including those that founded the Creation Science Research Center and the Institute of Creation Research, both in California—hoped to establish a scientific underpinning for the biblical account of human origins. Creation science's adherents have enjoyed some limited success in getting a couple of states to incorporate their theories in school textbooks. However, laws requiring the teaching of creation science alongside evolution in Arkansas and Louisiana were declared unconstitutional by federal courts in 1981 and 1982, respectively.

Creationism

Belief that the biblical account of the creation in the Book of Genesis is the one correct explanation of human origin. Some Christians, such as Pope John Paul, have surmised that the account in Genesis can be reconciled with the theory of evolution because the account is metaphorical rather than literal. Other Christians—including most fundamentalist Christians—believe that the account in the Bible is literally true. This of course is contrary to and irreconcilable with the theory of evolution on which much of modern science is based. Creationists who accept the biblical account literally also dispute the age of the Earth, alleging that the Earth is less ancient than scientists allege.

Damages

Money paid by defendants to successful plaintiffs in civil cases to compensate the plaintiffs for their injuries.

Darrow, Clarence (1857–1938)

Noted criminal attorney, who defended John Scopes in the famous Monkey Trial. Darrow was perhaps the best-known trial attorney of his day, defending mobsters, and businessmen, but also Eugene Debs, the socialist labor leader. Darrow volunteered to help the ACLU defend John Scopes, a Tennessee teacher who agreed to challenge the state's law prohibiting the teaching of the theory of evolution. The trial gained international attention pitting Darrow against William Jennings Bryan, who railed against Darwin and his theory.

Default Judgment

A judgment rendered because of the defendant's failure to answer or appear.

Defendant

In a civil suit, the person complained against; in a criminal case, the person accused of the crime.

Dicta

Language in a judicial opinion that is not directly relevant to deciding the case. The language amounts to the judge's observation about the state of the law. Because the language is not necessary to decide the case, the language has no value as a precedent.

Dismissed Time. *See* Release Time

Dissent

When more than one judge hears a case, one or more judges may not agree with the opinion of the majority. The dissenter may simply state his or her dissent but more likely will write a dissenting opinion explaining why he or she disagrees with the logic and result of the majority opinion. If more than one judge dissents they may all "join" or adopt one dissenting opinion or they may pen their own dissenting opinions.

Docket

A log containing brief entries of court proceedings. The cases that will be heard by a court are called its "docket." When a case is on the Supreme Court's docket it will be heard during the Court's next term.

Douglas, William O. (1898–1980)

Serving as an associate justice of the U.S. Supreme Court from 1939–1975, Douglas holds the record for longevity on the high court. Although perhaps best remembered for his reputation as a supporter of the environment, Douglas was also a Bill of Rights expert and penned many notable opinions involving religion in the schools. His lasting legacy is in the area of civil liberties, especially those guaranteed by the First Amendment. His book, *A Living Bill of Rights* (1961), deals with civil liberties. Although known as a "liberal," Douglas was a vocal supporter of religious rights. His views seem very close to those held by Justice Black, who was the staunchest supporter of absolute separation of church and state. Although Douglas had voted with the majority in *Everson v. Board of Education* (1947) to allow governments to pay for bus transportation for parochial school children, two decades later in *Board of Education v. Allen* (1968) he voted against taxpayer financial support for their textbooks. He distinguished the cases because while he viewed bus transportation as neutral, allowing the parochial schools to select books to be paid for with tax dollars was too much of an entanglement under the First Amendment. Douglas was also the lone dissenter in *Wisconsin v. Yoder*, which allowed Old Order Amish believers to avoid high school on religious grounds. Douglas dissented on the grounds that the majority's focus was on the parents' rights to withhold education but that the proper focus should be on the children's right to obtain an education. However, he thought the action of withholding children from school was beyond the bounds of the Free Exercise Clause of the First Amendment.

Due Process

The Due Process Clause of the Fifth Amendment of the U.S. Constitution guarantees that no person shall "be deprived of life, liberty, or property without due process of law." Procedural due process guarantees that before depriving anyone of liberty or property the government must provide them with a fair procedure including notice and a hearing before a neutral fact finder. The Fourteenth Amendment to the Constitution also contains a Due Process Clause that states: "Nor shall any State deprive any person of life, liberty, or property, without due process of law." The Equal Protection Clause of the Fourteenth

Amendment has been interpreted by the U.S. Supreme Court to apply to the entire Bill of Rights to the states. This requires that the First Amendment's Establishment Clause and Free Exercise Clause apply to state and local governments.

Employment Division v. Smith (1990)

The Supreme Court holds that the state of Oregon may lawfully deny unemployment benefits to individuals who were discharged from their jobs for using peyote, a controlled substance, even though the peyote was part of a traditional Native American religious ceremony. The case led to enactment of the Religious Freedom Restoration Act.

En Banc

"In the bench" or "full bench." Refers to court sessions with the entire membership of a court participating rather than the usual quorum. U.S. courts of appeals usually sit in panels of three judges, but may expand to a larger number in certain cases. They are then said to be sitting en banc.

Engel v. Vitale (1962)

Also known as the Regents' School Prayer case. New York State had written a nondenominational prayer to be recited each morning in public school. The Court held that state sponsorship of prayer was unconstitutional even though those who wished not to participate could remain silent.

Epperson v. Arkansas (1968)

The Supreme Court, in a unanimous decision, struck down an Arkansas statute that prohibited the teaching of evolution. Despite this clear mandate, the teaching of evolution remains controversial in the public schools in many states.

Equal Access Act of 1984

Federal law prohibiting discrimination against student groups based on religious, political, or philosophical grounds.

Equal Protection

The Equal Protection Clause of the Fourteenth Amendment of the U.S. Constitution provides that "No state shall . . . deny to any person within its jurisdiction the equal protection of the laws." The Equal Protection Clause has been interpreted by the U.S. Supreme Court to apply the entire Bill of Rights to the states. This requires that the First Amendment's Establishment Clause and Free Exercise Clause apply to state and local governments.

Established Church

An established church is—in effect—an "official" church, which is government-endorsed; the Anglican church in England—the Church of England—being one example. When there is an established church, there is no clear-cut line between the secular and the religious. In the United States six of the original thirteen colonies— Connecticut, Georgia, Maryland, Massachusetts, New Hampshire, and South Carolina—had established churches. In these colonies the government used tax revenues to give direct financial support to the established church. Although the established church was government-endorsed, each of these colonies also allowed a certain amount of toleration for other sects. The Establishment Clause of the First Amendment, which provides that the federal government shall make no laws "respecting the establishment of religion," prohibits the federal government from creating an established church.

Establishment Clause

The Establishment Clause of the First Amendment provides that the federal government shall make no laws "respecting the establishment of religion." Although the Establishment Clause originally applied only to the federal government, the courts have held that it also applies to states and local governments. Over the years the language has been understood not only to prohibit the federal government from sponsoring a church but also against enacting laws that favor one church over another. For example, the clause has been interpreted to prohibit government support for religious schools, including the payment of salaries of teachers in religious schools even though they teach nonreligious subjects. Although paying a teacher's salary has little to do with establishing an official national church, the courts have held that such financial "entanglements" are prohibited by the Establishment Clause. Some have suggested that while the Free Exercise Clause guarantees "freedom of religion," the Establishment Clause guarantees "freedom from religion."

Evangelical

An evangelical Christian is one who has an intense personal relationship with Jesus. Evangelical Christians typically have a "born again" experience in which they have an emotional, personal experience with Jesus that reignites their religious experience. Spreading the word of God through evangelism is an important aspect of this movement. There is no specific religion or group that uses this name; the term is applied to particular individuals or churches. Evangelicals typically are conservative Christians who may believe in the literal truth of biblical scripture and that Christian values and beliefs need to be extended not only to other individuals but also to institutions like the public schools.

Everson v. Board of Education (1947)

Supreme Court holds that public school districts may reimburse parents for transportation expenses of sending their children to public or parochial school.

Evidence

Information presented in testimony or in documents that is used to persuade the fact finder (judge or jury) to decide the case for one side or the other.

Evolution

Scientific theory that all life, including plants, animals, and humans, have evolved from simpler organisms. In contrast to the biblical depiction of creation in Genesis, the theory proposes that life on earth began as a protoplasmic mass from which life forms evolved, becoming increasingly more complex over the eons. Also known as "descent with modification," the origins of the theory can be traced to the Frenchman Jean Lamarck as early as 1801. Evolution theory gained credibility by the mid-1800s based on the works of both Alfred Russell Wallace and Charles Darwin, who independently focused on the operation of natural selection in evolution. In his *Origin of Species*, Darwin posited that natural selection, based on adaptability, determined the ultimate success and survival of both individual organisms and species. Species evolve and originate as individual adaptive traits are passed on to offspring. Modern evolutionary theory is bolstered by the study of genetics and DNA, which provides scientific verification of the observations of Darwin and others. Evolution is disputed by "creationists" who believe that life on earth was created by God as literally depicted in the Bible's Book of Genesis.

Fortas, Abe (1910–1982)

Fortas, an associate justice of the U.S. Supreme Court, 1965–1969, is best remembered as President Lyndon Johnson's unsuccessful choice to succeed Earl Warren as chief justice. Fortas was one of the few justices in history who was forced to resign from the Court after it was disclosed that he had a financial relationship with a former client who was under federal investigation. Fortas wrote the Supreme Court's majority opinion in *Epperson v. Arkansas* (1968), which overturned an Arkansas law prohibiting the teaching of evolution in the state's schools and universities. Fortas reasoned that the Arkansas law favored the biblical account of creation and thus unconstitutionally breached Jefferson's "wall of separation." It is interesting to surmise how the Supreme Court's decisions would have evolved had Fortas succeed to the post of chief justice.

Fourteenth Amendment

Fourteenth Amendment to the U.S. Constitution. Of the three post–Civil War amendments (Thirteen through Fifteen), the Fourteenth ultimately loomed largest. The Thirteenth Amendment abolished slavery, the Fifteenth gave the right to vote regardless of race or "previous condition of servitude." The Fourteenth Amendment provides a number of protections: "No state shall make or enforce any law which shall abridge the privileges and immunities of citizens of the United States; nor shall any State deprive any person of life, liberty or property, without due process of law; nor deny to any person within its jurisdiction the equal protection of these laws."

Frankfurter, Felix (1882–1965)

Felix Frankfurter, born in Austria, was a close advisor of President Roosevelt who appointed him to the Supreme Court in 1939 to replace Justice Cardozo. Frankfurter served on the Court until 1962. He generally supported New Deal legislation. In later years he usually favored the doctrine of judicial restraint that holds that the courts should not substitute their views for those of the elected legislatures. Frankfurter was one of the true legal scholars on the Court and was called upon to write the Court's opinions in some of the most politically charged cases on the separation of church and state. Frankfurter wrote the opinion in *Minersville School District v. Gobitis* (1940) in which Jehovah's Witnesses asked to be excused from saying the pledge of allegiance. Frankfurter, writing for the Court, held that despite the fact that their religious precepts prohibited reciting the pledge, the government could force schoolchildren to recite the pledge of allegiance to create national unity. The 8–1 decision caused a mass expulsion of Witness children from school and even precipitated mob violence against Witness churches. In an almost identical case heard only three years afterward, the Court flip-flopped, and later Frankfurter found himself writing the minority opinion. There were three new members on the Court and two justices had changed their minds about the issue.

Free Exercise Clause

The First Amendment of the U.S. Constitution prohibits the federal government from making any law "prohibiting the free exercise" of religion. Although the Free Exercise Clause originally applied only to the federal government, the courts have held that it also applies to state and local governments. As public schools are a part of the government, their actions are judged under this clause. Restrictions on religious activities in the schools must be evaluated under the Free Exercise Clause. Freedom of religion and freedom of speech issues sometimes overlap. Some have suggested that whereas the Free Exercise Clause guarantees "freedom of religion," the Establishment Clause guarantees "freedom from religion."

Free Speech

The Bill of Rights—including the First Amendment's Establishment and Free Exercise Clauses—was originally interpreted to apply only to actions of the federal government, not to the actions of state and local governments. Since about 1960, the courts have uniformly held that the Fourteenth Amendment, through its due process require-ment, applies the Bill of Rights to state and local governments as well.

Fundamentalism

Conservative Christianity. The term was first used to describe Chris-tians who subscribed to *The Fundamentals: A Testimony to the Truth,* a series of pamphlets distributed from 1910–1915, espousing religious conservatism and denouncing the theory of evolution. To-day the term generally has a pejorative meaning and is generally used to label certain conservative clergy and their followers. These believ-ers prefer to be referred to as evangelicals.

Inerrancy

The belief that biblical scripture is absolutely and literally true. A person who accepts the absolute accuracy of scripture will regard sci-entific explanations that are at variance with scripture to be false. This includes explanations such as evolution and geological dating of the Earth.

Injunction

An order of the court prohibiting (or compelling) the performance of a specific act to prevent irreparable damage or injury.

Interstate Commerce

Movement of goods or services over state lines. The Constitution gives Congress authority to regulate interstate commerce ("busi-ness"). Originally, this jurisdiction was limited because many activi-ties, such as manufacturing, were considered "local" rater than inter-state. Today nearly all business activities are within Congress' regulatory power, and much regulation is based on the Commerce Clause.

Jefferson, Thomas (1743–1826)

The primary author of the Declaration of Independence, the nation's first secretary of State under George Washington, and John Adams's vice president, Jefferson served as the third president of the United States from 1801 to 1809. A staunch defender of the separation of church and state, Jefferson remains one of the two or three most important influences on the course of religion in the schools of the United States. Although called an atheist, Jefferson was really a deist who believed in God and worshipped regularly. However, even before the American Revolution, Jefferson developed strongly held views on the need for an absolute separation of church and state. In his Virginia Bill for Establishing Religious Freedom, he endeavored to grant religious freedom and equality. At the time, this was a radical proposition and it did not initially pass. Only years later, with James Madison's help was it approved by the Virginia assembly. Jefferson was one of the first influential thinkers to realize that religious freedom required the separation of church and state. His famous phrase *the wall of separation* is still used today to describe the barrier that he wanted erected between the spiritual and secular worlds. Although Jefferson probably did believe that the states could have some involvement in religious matters, he evidently believed that the federal government should have no involvement with religion. As such he could be termed an "absolute" separationist. Unlike his predecessors in the presidency, George Washington and John Adams, Jefferson did not proclaim national days of Thanksgiving, which he regarded as religious exercises. Even James Madison returned to the yearly proclamations when he became president after Jefferson.

John Birch Society

The grandfather of many right-wing groups, the John Birch Society was primarily an anticommunist group. Although named for a slain missionary, the group, led by its founder Robert Welch, called for the impeachment of Chief Justice Earl Warren after the Supreme Court outlawed organized prayer in the public schools.

Judgment

The official decision of a court finally determining the respective rights and claims of the parties to a suit.

Judicial Review

In *Marbury v. Madison* the U.S. Supreme Court arrogated to itself the right of judicial review—the right to determine if a law of Congress is constitutional. If the Court determines that a federal, state, or local law is contrary to the Constitution, then the law will be held invalid. For example, a statute allowing school prayer passed by a unanimous Congress would likely be held contrary to the Establishment Clause and held invalid.

Jurisdiction

(1) The legal authority of a court to hear and decide a case. Concurrent jurisdiction exists when two courts have simultaneous responsibility for the same case. (2) The geographic area over which the court has authority to decide cases.

Jurisprudence

The study of law and the structure of the legal system.

Kennedy, Anthony M. (1936–)

A native of California and graduate of Stanford University, the London School of Economics, and Harvard University Law School, Anthony Kennedy was appointed to the Supreme Court by President Reagan in 1989. He had spent several years in private practice and as a justice of the U.S. Court of Appeals for the Ninth Circuit. Although Kennedy was predicted to be conservative, he surprised many, including Reagan, by siding with the liberal justices in overturning a Texas statute outlawing the desecration of the American flag on First Amendment grounds. Kennedy, a Catholic, found himself writing some of the most important recent opinions on the separation of church and state. He wrote the majority opinion in *Lee v. Weisman* (1992), which forbids school-sponsored prayers at public school graduation ceremonies. Kennedy found that such prayers violate the Establishment Clause because, although they are supposedly voluntary, organized group prayer involves a high degree of indirect coercion that makes it unacceptable.

Ku Klux Klan

In actuality since the 1950s the Ku Klux Klan (KKK) has been made up of a number of related groups, all using the name "Klan" and the trappings of the traditional Klan. The modern Klan was patterned after an earlier group that was formed to battle Reconstruction and freed slaves after the Civil War. It is generally anti-Black, anti-Semitic, and anti-Catholic. Although they are more famous for parading in their white-hooded outfits and burning crosses, Klansmen most recently gained notoriety for erecting a cross on public land as a Christmas display. The Supreme Court decided that this cross had to be removed not because it was erected by the Klan but because its positioning on public property was in violation of the Establishment Clause.

Lee v. Weisman (1992)

A divided Supreme Court outlaws religious benedictions and invocations at public school graduations. Despite the ban, organized public prayer still takes place at some public school events in some districts.

Lemon v. Kurtzman (1971)

The case that devised the "*Lemon* test" in applying the Establishment Clause of the First Amendment to actual cases. This three-prong test was announced in the U.S. Supreme Court case, *Lemon v. Kurtzman* (1971). It is used to determine if a particular law is in violation of the First Amendment's guarantee that the state will not establish a religion. Under the test a law will be upheld only if it meets three tests: the law must be backed by a secular purpose; does not have a primary effect that promotes or inhibits religion; and, does not unduly entangle the government with religion. For example, a law requiring state-funded schools to post the Ten Commandments in classrooms would be judged under the *Lemon* test. Although the *Lemon* case has not been overruled, the Supreme Court has been reluctant to use the test since the mid-1990s.

Litigation

A case, controversy, or lawsuit. Participants (plaintiffs and defendants) in lawsuits are called litigants.

Lynch v. Donnelly (1984)

The Supreme Court, in a 5–4 decision, rules that inclusion of a nativity scene in Pawtucket, Rhode Island, in its annual Christmas display did not violate the First Amendment. The Court felt that display of the crèche alongside Santa Claus and other traditional holiday characters did not constitute even a subtle endorsement of religion.

Madison, James (1751–1836)

Fourth president of the United States and, like Thomas Jefferson, a strong supporter of the separation of church and state. Madison, who was primarily responsible for drafting the U.S. Constitution, is still cited by the courts when they are considering whether a particular religious practice is appropriate in the public schools. Because it was Madison who drafted the First Amendment, including the religion clauses, his views are especially influential as to their original meaning. At the time of the American Revolution, Virginia, like many other colonies, used public funds to support its Anglican church. Madison not only opposed such funding but also agitated for complete religious freedom for minorities. He set out his arguments in his *Memorial and Remonstrance against Religious Assessments* (1785). He agreed with Jefferson that there should be a strict wall of separation between religion and the federal government. Although Madison was a strict separationist, he did proclaim national days of Thanksgiving. His immediate predecessor as president, Thomas Jefferson, thought that proclaiming national days of Thanksgiving violated the doctrine of the separation of church and state.

Magistrate Judges

Judicial officers who assist U.S. district judges in getting cases ready for trial, who may decide some criminal and civil trials when both parties agree to have the case heard by a magistrate judge instead of a judge.

Marsh v. Chambers (1983)

The Supreme Court upholds a state legislature's payment of chaplains who open each day's legislative session and provide pastoral counseling to legislators. The Court reasoned that the practice was traditional and did not conflict with the Establishment Clause. Congress also employs chaplains who fall under this case's protection.

McCollum v. Board of Education (1948)

Vashti McCollum filed a lawsuit objecting to the religion classes being given in her son's school. The students were released early from class and children with parental permission attended religion classes in their own schools. Vashti McCollum did not want her son to participate and sued, arguing the practice was unconstitutional. The U.S. Supreme Court agreed with Mrs. McCollum, holding that the teaching of religion on the school grounds violated the Establishment Clause of the Constitution. Mrs. McCollum's case really set the stage for all of the later cases that banned religious expression by the public schools.

Minersville School District v. Gobitis (1940)

A wartime decision in which the Supreme Court ruled that a public school district can compel children who are Jehovah's Witnesses to pledge to the flag, despite religious objections.

Moment of Silence. *See* Silent Prayer

"Monkey" Trial

The still-famous 1925 Scopes trial in which a Tennessee biology teacher, John Thomas Scopes, challenged a state law forbidding the teaching of evolution in public schools. The trial caused an international sensation as Scopes was represented by the well-known attorney Clarence Darrow and the state by ex-presidential candidate and orator William Jennings Bryan. Although Scopes was found guilty of violating the law and fined (later reversed), most commentators felt the anticreationists gained the most from the case's high visibility. However, laws prohibiting the teaching of evolution persisted in

Arkansas and Mississippi until the mid-1960s. The trial was the basis of the popular movie *Inherit the Wind.*

National Association of Evangelicals

An umbrella group for fundamentalist churches and organizations that functions in the same was as the National Council of Churches. The group claims a membership of over 50,000 churches in the United States, including most of the leading evangelical churches. The organization is politically influential at both the local and national levels, and presidential candidates normally desire to make an address at the association's national meeting. The group has normally supported politicians who support religion in public life.

National Legal Foundation

Conservative public interest law firm that assists litigants in the area of religious freedom and religious expression, including cases that deal with religion in the schools.

Nativists

Pre–Civil War political movement that opposed the presence of immigrants in the United States. In most of the country, the movement has a strong anti-Catholic flavor. The movement is characterized by secret societies whose members, when asked to reveal the society's views, would respond, "I know nothing." The movement became a political party—the "Know Nothings"—and enjoyed considerable success in New York and Pennsylvania. The movement also hatched compulsory education laws aimed at Catholic schools. These laws required all children to be schooled in public schools. The U.S. Supreme Court struck down such laws in *Pierce v. Society of Sisters* (1925).

O'Connor, Sandra Day (1930–)

The first woman to serve on the U.S. Supreme Court. Active in politics, O'Connor was appointed and then elected to the Arizona senate, eventually rising to the position of majority leader. She was next elected a local judge and later appointed to the Arizona Court of Appeals. In 1981 O'Connor was a surprise appointment to the Supreme

Court by President Ronald Reagan. On the bench O'Connor is generally a member of the conservative bloc, sometimes voting against legislation favoring women and minorities. Justice O'Connor has carved out her own test in the separation of church and state area. She will normally find a constitutional violation if the school's action amounts to an "endorsement" of the religious practice. She generally adopts a practical case-by-case approach rather than a doctrinaire one.

Opinion

A judge's written explanation of a decision of the court or of a majority of judges. A dissenting opinion disagrees with the majority opinion because of the reasoning and/or the principles of law on which the decision is based. A concurring opinion agrees with the decision of the court but offers further comment.

Oral Argument

An opportunity for lawyers to summarize their position before the court and also to answer the judge's questions.

Original Intent

Intent of the drafters. Most legal scholars accept that the Constitution's language needs to be interpreted flexibly to enable the courts to deal with developments that were never in the contemplation of its drafters. For example, the drafters of the Constitution could not have envisioned the legal problems posed by the Internet. However, other scholars believe that constitutional provisions need to be interpreted as closely as possible according to the original intent of the drafters. This would typically give the provisions less scope. For example, although the courts currently ban school prayer based on the Establishment Clause, an analysis based on original intent might show that there is no evidence that the drafters desired such a result. If original intent controls, then school prayer might not offend the Constitution.

Paine, Thomas (1737–1809)

Paine, a radical political writer, became an overnight celebrity on the publication of his Revolutionary War pamphlet *Common Sense*

(1776). The first issue of his series of pamphlets called *The Crisis* was so inspiring to patriots that Washington ordered it read to his troops at Valley Forge. Always an advocate of reason and political and individual liberty, Paine is recognized as a leading influence on the age of revolution. He believed in the separation of church and state. Paine wrote, "As to religion, I hold it to be the indispensable duty of government to protect all conscientious profession thereof, and I know of no other business which government hath to do therewith." Many of his ideas were shared or co-opted by Jefferson and Madison.

Panel

(1) In appellate cases, a group of judges (usually three) assigned to decide the case; (2) in the jury selection process, the group of potential jurors.

Parties

Plaintiffs and defendants (petitioners and respondents) to lawsuits, also known as appellants and appellees in appeals, and their lawyers.

People for the American Way

Liberal group that supports cultural pluralism and freedom of expression. The group frequently opposes actions by conservative groups in the matter of religion in the schools. The group publishes an annual "Attacks on the Freedom to Learn," which details the year's attempts to challenge textbooks and library materials because of their supposedly immoral content. The challenges are almost invariably from conservative groups or parents who object to their sexual content, lack of religiosity, or moral relativism.

Pierce v. Society of Sisters (1925)

Supreme Court strikes down an Oregon referendum amending the state constitution to require all schoolchildren to attend public school. This was a victory for parochial and private schools.

Pinckney, Charles (1757–1824)

Charles Pinckney served as one of South Carolina's delegates at the 1787 Constitutional Convention in Philadelphia. Pinckney was a staunch defender of the concept of the separation of church and state. He proposed a motion that would forbid the use of religious tests to qualify for federal office. This proposal is now found in Article VI of the Constitution. Pinckney proposed an amendment on the separation of church and state that was not enacted as part of the final document. The amendment provided that "the legislature of the United States shall pass no law on the subject of religion."

Plaintiff

The person who files the complaint in a civil lawsuit.

Pleadings

Written statements of the parties in a civil case of their positions. In the federal courts, the principal pleadings are the complaint and the answer.

Pledge of Allegiance

Patriotic pledge typically recited by students at the start of each school day. The words *under God* were not inserted until 1954. The pledge has been controversial because several Jehovah's Witnesses prohibit their members from saying the pledge because they believe it to be a worship of a "graven image." Quakers also are uncomfortable with the word *pledge* and an early concession was made. The presidential oath of office allows the president the option to "affirm" or "pledge" to uphold the duties of president. A highly controversial 2002 Ninth Circuit Court of Appeals decision held that the words *under God* should be stricken when the pledge is recited in public school.

Postmillennialism

Belief in the second coming of Jesus Christ after 1,000 years of human progress.

Precedent

A court decision in an earlier case with facts and law similar to a dispute currently before a court. Precedent will ordinarily govern the decision of a later similar case, unless a party can show that it was wrongly decided or that it differed in some significant way.

Premillennialism

Belief in the second coming of Jesus Christ after a period of tribulation on Earth, after which Jesus will usher in a 1,000 year reign on Earth for the righteous.

Record

A written account of all the acts and proceedings in a lawsuit.

Rehnquist, William H. (1924–)

Chief legal council for the Justice Department under President Nixon. William H. Rehnquist Jr. was nominated to the Supreme Court by President Nixon in 1971, and in 1986 President Reagan nominated him to fill the vacancy in the position of chief justice after Warren Burger's resignation. Although a graduate of Stanford, Harvard, and Stanford Law School, there was significant opposition to his nomination as chief justice. On the Court Justice Rehnquist has been a consistent conservative, although often in dissent. This has generally been true in the religion in the school cases as well. For example, Rehnquist was in the dissent in the graduation prayer case (*Lee v. Weisman* [1992]). The chief justice is generally deferential to state laws and would likely allow the states to decide exactly how religion will be dealt with in the public schools.

Release Time

A program in which a public school dismisses students early to attend religion classes away from the public school grounds. Typically, classes will be offered at individual churches and children will attend the classes at the church at which they regularly worship.

Parents may give permission to the public school for their children to be released early for such classes. If permission is not granted, the children are required to stay at the public school. Release-time programs were upheld by the U.S. Supreme Court in *Zorach v. Clauson* (1952). Earlier release-time programs, in which religion classes were taught in public school classrooms during the release-time period, were struck down by the Supreme Court as a violation of the Establishment Clause in *People of Illinois ex rel. McCollum v. Board of Education* (1948). In the *McCollum case,* although the religion teachers were not paid or selected by the public school administrators, they could veto the selection of teachers, and the Supreme Court felt that the "use of the state's compulsory school machinery" to disseminate religious doctrines violated the separation of church and state.

Religious Freedom Restoration Act

Federal law, passed in 1993, and declared unconstitutional by the Supreme Court in 1997, which provided, among other things, that federal, state, and local "Government[s] shall not substantially burden a person's exercise of religion even if the burden results from a rule of general applicability . . . except that Government may substantially burden a person's exercise of religion: if it demonstrates that application of the burden to the person (1) is in furtherance of a compelling government interest; and (2) is the least restrictive means of furthering that compelling interest." The act is intended to deal with the free exercise of religion, not the establishment of religion by the government.

Religious Test

Law requiring public officials to be of a particular religion or barring those of particular religions. Although the U.S. Constitution prohibits such tests, a number of states did employ such tests in the nineteenth century.

Remand

When an appellate court sends a case back to a lower court for further proceedings.

Reverse

When an appellate court sets aside the decision of a lower court because of an error. A reversal is often followed by a remand.

Reynolds v. United States (1879)

The Supreme Court upholds a conviction of a Mormon who was sentenced to two years of hard labor for bigamy (being married to more than one woman at the same time). Although the Mormon Church at the time not only advocated but encouraged multiple wives, the Court felt that the religious belief could not excuse the obvious immorality of bigamy. The Court takes the view that although it cannot interfere with a religious belief, it can interfere with an action. This was the first case in which the Supreme Court examined the Establishment Clause.

Salary Supplement

Amount paid to a parochial or other religious school teacher by the public schools for teaching nonreligious subjects. A few states sought to avoid the ban on aid to public school by providing "indirect" forms of support. Both Rhode Island and Pennsylvania experimented with supplementing the salaries of parochial school teachers on the theory that supplementing parochial school teachers' salaries would be less expensive than educating their students in the public school system. The practice was held to be unconstitutional by the U.S. Supreme Court in *Lemon v. Kurtzman* (1971) because the states were actually paying money to the parochial schools in violation of the Establishment Clause.

Scalia, Antonin (1936–)

A well-known conservative legal scholar and a graduate of Harvard Law School, Scalia was in private practice before becoming a law professor at the University of Virginia. He was head of the White House Office of Legal Counsel in the Nixon administration and returned to teach at the University of Chicago Law School where he enhanced his reputation as a leading conservative legal scholar. President Ronald Reagan appointed Scalia to the very liberal-leaning U.S.

Court of Appeals for the District of Columbia and in 1986 to the Supreme Court. On the Court Scalia has helped forge a solid conservative majority that rejects the judicial activism of the prior fifty years. Like Chief Justice Rehnquist, Justice Scalia gives broad deference to the views of state legislatures in reviewing laws affecting religious practice in the schools. Although he has frequently been in dissent, he wrote the majority opinion in *Employment Division v. Smith* (1990), which held that religious belief could not excuse commission of a crime (use of peyote by Native Americans).

School Prayer Amendment

Proposed amendment to the U.S. Constitution that would overturn the U.S. Supreme Court case *Engel v. Vitale* (1962) and its progeny and would allow verbal, organized prayer in the public schools. Although the proposed amendment has gained ground on a number of occasions, including a strong endorsement by President Ronald Reagan, the amendment has never been enacted.

Scientific Creationism. *See* Creation Science

Scopes, John Thomas (1900–1970)

Tennessee biology teacher who was the defendant in the famous 1925 "monkey trial." Tennessee passed a law outlawing the teaching of evolution in any school or university within the state. Scopes, a high school biology teacher in Dayton, Tennessee, decided to bring a test case challenging the law. The ACLU came to his defense, enlisting Clarence Darrow, perhaps the best-known trial attorney of his day. William Jennings Bryan, the noted orator, was attorney for the state of Tennessee. The trial caught the nation's attention and was also followed closely abroad. William Jennings Bryan, himself a fundamentalist who believed in the literal truth of the depiction in Genesis, railed against Darwin and his theory. Scopes was ultimately convicted and fined $100, although the conviction was later overturned on a technicality and the fine was never paid. The sideshow aspect of the trial tended to discredit the fundamentalist approach and although the supporters of the biblical account won the battle, the supporters of evolution won the war. The Tennessee antievolution law was not repealed until 1967. A similar law in Arkansas remained in effect until struck down by the U.S. Supreme Court in 1968.

Secular Humanism

A philosophical belief system based on the idea of human rationality. Secular humanists embrace rationality, scientific knowledge, and an appreciation for the classics. Although similar to a religion, the emphasis is on the potentialities of humans without the help of God. Fundamentalist Christians apply the term *secular humanist* to individuals or institutions that try to exclude religion from the public schools or public life. Fundamentalists have attacked public school curriculums, labeling them *humanistic,* because moral problems are approached without a discussion of God. The term *humanism* is usually applied to the movement during the Renaissance that stressed the study of classical secular studies and a rejection of medieval religiosity.

Sherbert v. Verner (1963)

The Supreme Court rules that a state cannot deny unemployment compensation to a worker who was unwilling to work on Saturday—her Sabbath.

Silent Prayer (Moment of Silence)

When organized verbal school prayers were outlawed by the Supreme Court, many school districts adopted a moment of silent prayer in their place. Students were instructed by their teachers to either pray or meditate before they started their classroom routines. The U.S. Supreme Court struck down one such law in *Wallace v. Jaffree* (1985). The Supreme Court reasoned that although children could be excused from the classroom, the moment of silence was a disguised compulsory school prayer. Currently, a moment of silence may be acceptable if the law creating it does not create a disguised prayer.

Sodomy

Perceived deviant sexual conduct, usually defined as oral or anal intercourse. Some states limit sodomy to activity between same-sex partners, although others include unmarried partners of the opposite sex.

Souter, David (1939–)

A native of New Hampshire, Souter was appointed to be a judge on the U.S. Court of Appeals for the First Circuit, but after only two months he was appointed by President George H. W. Bush to the U.S. Supreme Court in 1990. The hardworking Souter quickly established himself as one of the intellectual leaders on the Court but with a decidedly moderate bent. At this writing it is difficult to categorize his position on religion in the schools because he has not yet participated in enough separation of church and state cases. His concurring opinion in *Lee v. Weisman* (1992), the case banning invocations at graduation ceremonies, suggests that he will be more of a strict separationist than most of the current justices. In his opinion, Souter wrote that in writing the final cession of the Establishment Clause, the founders wished that the government should refrain from promoting religion in general, not just a particular religion. Although the majority opinion was based on a showing of coercion, Souter felt that there was no need to show coercion at all; the Constitution simply bars all school-sponsored religious ceremonies.

Statute

A law passed by a legislature.

Statute of Limitations

A law that sets the time within which parties must take action to enforce their rights.

Stevens, John Paul, III (1920–)

John Paul Stevens, a native of Chicago, was appointed to the U.S. Court of Appeals for the Seventh Circuit by President Nixon in 1970 after working in private practice for many years. In 1975 he was tapped for the Supreme Court by President Gerald Ford. Although he has been termed a moderate, a more apt description might be a maverick with no ideological agenda. Stevens has been a staunch defender of civil rights and believer in the sharp separation of church and state in the public schools. In recent years Stevens has found himself increasingly dissenting in a number of separation of church and state cases.

The majority of the Court has retreated from the Court's earlier strict separation conception and has tended to allow some exceptions. This approach shifts decision making to state legislatures. Stevens has not agreed with this shift and has remained consistent to the principle of strict separation of church and state that the Court developed in the many school cases that it heard during the 1960s and 1970s.

Storey, Joseph (1779–1845)

Still regarded as one of the Supreme Court's greatest scholars, Storey is also the youngest person ever appointed to the high court. Appointed to the Court by President James Madison, Storey is best known now for his influential *Commentaries* on American law, including one on the First Amendment, which dealt extensively with separation of church and state issues. Like other individuals in public life at the time, Storey assumed that all citizens would ascribe to the tenets of some religious faith, and, like Madison, he saw no problem with official declarations of days of Thanksgiving or invocations asking divine guidance at governmental functions. However, like Madison, he was a firm believer that the federal government should show absolutely no preference toward one sect over another.

Stuyvesant, Peter (1610–1672)

Stuyvesant was the director general of Dutch New Amsterdam (later New York) in the middle of the seventeenth century. At the time, Holland was perhaps the most religiously tolerant country in Europe, and Dutch New Amsterdam was home to a diverse population, including many Jews and Quakers. Stuyvesant, however, imposed strict laws regulating religious practice favoring the Dutch Reformed Church. After complaints from colonists, he was quickly overruled by the directors of the Dutch West India Company, who reinstated their pluralistic approach to religious practice.

Summary Judgment

A decision made on the basis of statements and evidence presented for the record without a trial. It is used when there is no dispute as to the facts of the case, and one party is entitled to judgment as a matter of law.

Temporary Restraining Order

Prohibits a person from an action that is likely to cause irreparable harm. This differs from an injunction in that it may be granted immediately, without notice to the opposing party, and without a hearing. It is intended to last only until a hearing can be held. Also referred to as a "TRO."

Testimony

Evidence presented orally by witnesses during trials or before grand juries.

Textbook Lending

Lending of nonreligious public school textbooks by the government to parochial schools. A few states sought to avoid the ban on aid to public school by providing "indirect" forms of support. One means is to supply textbooks either directly to the parochial schools or to the students themselves. The rationale is that this form of subsidy is still less expensive for the public than educating the students in the public school system. A divided U.S. Supreme Court upheld the practice in *Board of Education v. Allen* (1968), reasoning that the aid went to the students or their parents rather than to the school. The Court has also approved reimbursement of the costs of state-mandated standardized tests but has disapproved of providing free teaching materials other than textbooks.

Tuition Reimbursement

Reimbursement by the government of school tuition at private and parochial schools. The U.S. Supreme Court has held that such reimbursement—whether direct or indirect through tax credits—is unconstitutional (*Committee v. Nyquist* [1973]; *Sloan v. Lemon* [1973]). More recently a closely divided Court upheld a Minnesota scheme that granted a tax deduction for private school tuition (*Mueller v. Allen* [1983]).

Verdict

The decision of a petit jury or a judge.

Vouchers

A voucher system allows the parents of a school-age child to receive a state-paid voucher that can be used to pay tuition in private or religious school. The aid clearly goes to the family, but the family can choose to use the voucher in a religious school. Although the legality of vouchers is still an open question, in *Zelman v. Simmons-Harris* (2002), the U.S. Supreme Court upheld Cleveland's school voucher program, finding it was enacted for a secular purpose and did not have the effect of advancing religion.

Wall of Separation

Phrase originally coined by Thomas Jefferson to describe the proper relationship of religion and the federal government. The phrase is believed to have first been used in Jefferson's 1802 letter to the Connecticut Baptists Association of Danbury, which read, in part, "Believing with you that religion is a matter which lies solely between man and his God, that he owes account to none other for his faith or his worship, that the legislative powers of government reach actions only, and not opinions, I contemplate with sovereign reverence that act of the whole American people which declared that their legislature should 'make no law respecting an establishment of religion, or prohibiting the free exercise thereof,' thus building a wall of separation between church and state."

Wallace v. Jaffree (1985)

The Supreme Court holds that a state-mandated moment of silent prayer in the public schools violates the First Amendment.

Walz v. Tax Commission (1970)

Property tax exemptions granted to religious organizations for churches and other religious uses do not violate the Establishment Clause.

Warren, Earl (1891–1974)

Chief Justice of the U.S. Supreme Court and leader of the influential "Warren Court" (1953–1969) that issued many landmark civil rights and separation of church and state cases. After a career as a crime–fighting attorney general, Warren was elected as a Republican as governor of California in 1942, a post he held for ten years from 1942 until his appointment to the Supreme Court. He was an unsuccessful candidate for vice president in 1948, running with Tom Dewey. Although he sought the Republican presidential nomination in 1952, he withdrew and endorsed Eisenhower, the eventual winner. He was nominated for chief justice by President Eisenhower, who is reputed to have later termed the nomination "the biggest damn-fool mistake I ever made." Although Warren was a Republican, and at least during his early years in office had been a conservative governor, he proved a liberal once on the high court. During his term as chief justice, many of the major cases on religion in the schools were handed down including *Engel v. Vitale* (1962), which threw out a nondenominational school prayer written by the New York State Board of Regents, and *Abington School District v. Schempp* (1963), which banned Bible reading in public schools. Although the Court's desegregation cases raised the ire of many Americans, the school prayer cases caused an absolute furor. An unsuccessful "Impeach Earl Warren" campaign was staged, and he was vilified as a godless villain by politicians and preachers alike.

Williams, Roger (1603–1683)

Founder of the Rhode Island colony, Roger Williams was one of the earliest proponents of religious pluralism in North America. A minister in the Massachusetts Bay Colony, Williams was exiled by the leaders of the colony for advocating the separation of church and state. Such views were considered "dangerous" by the Puritans of the Bay Colony. Williams headed south and founded what is now Rhode Island, establishing a colony based on separation of church and state and freedom of religion—novel concepts in his day. Williams may have been the first to use the phrase *wall of separation* when referring to the division between the spiritual and secular spheres.

Wisconsin v. Yoder (1972)

A divided Supreme Court decides that Wisconsin may not compel Amish families to send their children to public school past the eighth grade. The Court declines to extend the dispensation to compulsory education to any other group.

Writ of Certiorari

An order issued by the Supreme Court directing the lower court to transmit records for a case for which it will hear an appeal.

Zelman v. Simmons-Harris (2002)

The U.S. Supreme Court upholds Cleveland's school voucher system, finding that it was enacted for a secular purpose and did not have the effect of advancing religion.

Zorach v. Clauson (1952)

The Supreme Court upholds New York State's release-time program for religious instruction, observing that it does not take place on public property and does not utilize public funds. This case should be contrasted with the *McCollum* decision four years earlier, which struck down another state's release-time program.

Chronology

1607

English colonists establish Jamestown, the first permanent settlement in what was to be known as Virginia. From the start, Virginia recognized the Church of England as the established church, and dissenters were not tolerated. Although there was no strict separation of church and state in the early days of the colony, about the time of the War of Independence, 170 years later, Virginians were at the forefront of establishing the familiar conception of separation of church and state, a concept that distinguishes life in America.

1620

Pilgrims settle at Plymouth Colony in what is now Massachusetts. Although it is well known that the Pilgrims were motivated by strong religious beliefs, Plymouth Plantation was a curious blend of religious "dissenters" and nonreligious adventurers. The English financial backers of the colony were primarily interested in receiving a return on their investment. The "dissenters"—roughly half the population of the colony—including the familiar Miles Standish and John Aldin, belonged to a group of strict Protestants who "dissented" from the Anglican Church, the established Church of England. An "established church" is a nation's official church. At that time it was normal for each country to have an established Church. In the seventeenth and eighteenth centuries people of other faiths were barely tolerated and even expelled from several countries in Europe. The English dissenters—known as "separatists" and "Puritans"—objected, among other things, that the teachings and practice of the Anglican Church were too close to those of the Roman Catholic Church. The Pilgrims were "separatists" who practiced "Congregationalism"—which replaces church hierarchies by putting each local church congregation in control of its own affairs. These dissenting sects were barely tolerated, and the Pilgrims left England, first settling in Holland, to avoid persecution but also to set themselves up as a religious enclave that would serve as an example to their brethren back in England.

1630

Puritans found Massachusetts Bay Colony. The Puritans were another group of dissenters who founded what is now Boston. Like the Pilgrims, they dissented from the doctrine and practices of the Anglican Church. One group settled in North America to avoid persecution for their beliefs. Ironically, between 1640 and 1660, when the Puritans ruled England under Oliver Cromwell, Richard Cromwell seized power in Massachusetts. Although the Puritans fled England to escape religious persecution, they were not believers in religious toleration for others. The Bay Colony was a theocracy in which church and state were one and the same. Christians whose beliefs differed were not tolerated. Quakers were singled out for particularly harsh treatment.

1635

Roger Williams, exiled from the Massachusetts Bay Colony for his tolerance of other religions, founds Rhode Island, which offered religious freedom to all. In fact, church and state were considered separate in Rhode Island right from the start. Williams was perhaps the first person to use the phrase *wall of separation* when talking about the relationship of the government and religion.

1649

Maryland, founded by Lord Baltimore and a haven for Roman Catholics, passes "Act of Tolerance" encouraging the free exercise of all Christian religions.

1689

About thirty years after the end of the Puritan Commonwealth, the English Parliament passes the Act of Toleration, which allows Protestant dissenters—such as Puritans and separatists—to practice their religions. The act did not apply to either Jews or Roman Catholics, however. Parliament might have been influenced by John Locke's influential "Letters On Toleration," which appeared about this time.

1692

Colony of Massachusetts abolishes the official state church. However, each local government, except the city of Boston, was required to use tax monies to support all churches and clergy. Other New England states follow the practice.

1720

Start of twenty-year period of religious fervor called the "Great Awakening." The movement resulted in a fragmentation of several mainstream religious denominations. American Christianity was now a diverse mixture of many smaller denominations. However, the "established" church in most colonies was still supported by tax revenues, and the other churches generally received no funds. There was no state-run system of public education, although most towns had schools that were often church-affiliated. Early school curriculums included both moral and religious instruction including prayer and Bible reading.

1776

Declaration of Independence signed. Start of Revolutionary War with England.

Publication of Thomas Paine's *Common Sense*. Paine's ideas, including a strong plea for the free exercise of religion, were later incorporated in the Bill of Rights. Although Paine argued that government should protect individuals' right to practice their religion, he also felt that there should be no established church and that the government should avoid active participation in religious subjects. Paine's ideas about religious freedoms were well known to the Founding Fathers and were later engrafted in the First Amendment of the Constitution.

1782

Virginia Bill for Establishing Religious Freedom penned by Thomas Jefferson, prohibited penalties imposed because of religious beliefs or practices and outlawed mandatory attendance or financial support of any religious activity. The bill was not immediately passed by the state legislature. There was substantial resistance to the proposal, especially the idea of withholding funds from an established church. Patrick Henry, another well-known revolutionary leader, firmly believed that it was appropriate for the state of Virginia to use tax money to support teachers of the Christian faith. Henry represented the traditional view that the majority had the right to use tax money to support an established church. Jefferson and Madison, in contrast, felt that supporting an established church not only favored one church over another but also threatened the religious freedom of religious minorities.

1785

In his *Memorial and Remonstrance Against Religious Assessments,* James Madison (later president) attacked a bill that would allow Virginia to financially support all churches. Madison pointed out that although the bill proposed to use tax dollars to support all religions, it also had the potential to allow the state to favor one religion over another. Madison argued forcefully against any "establishment"—in other words an "established church." This idea was later to find its way into the First Amendment. The Virginia proposal was defeated, and the next year Virginia passed Jefferson's Virginia Bill for Establishing Religious Freedom (see above).

1791

U.S. Constitution ratified by a majority of the original thirteen colonies. The document includes the Bill of Rights consisting of ten amendments guaranteeing rights to citizens and states. The document is notable not only for what it includes but also for what it excludes. Unlike all state constitutions, there is no reference to God or a Supreme Being. The Constitution does not provide for an established church or even the furtherance of Christianity. Indeed, the First Amendment includes guarantees that "Congress shall make no law respecting an establishment of religion or prohibiting the free exercise thereof; or abridging the freedom of speech, or of the press; or the right of the people peacefully to assemble, and to petition the Government for a redress of grievances." The first two clauses are called the Establishment Clause and the Free Exercise Clause, respectively. The only other reference to religion in the document is found in Article VI, Clause 3, which prohibits "religious tests" for public office. This clause ensures that the government cannot require an individual to be a member of a particular religion—or any religion at all—as a condition of service. Although the Constitution has a strong separation of church and state flavor, some commentators have suggested that the drafters were merely ensuring that the states, rather than the federal government, would have the power to make laws on the establishment and exercise of religion. In fact, at the time, a few states continued to have "established churches" that were state supported. A few states also had laws that discriminated against members of religious minorities. For example, several states withheld full legal rights from Jews and Roman Catholics. The courts did not apply the First Amendment to the activities of state and local governments until well into the twentieth century.

1800

A wave of evangelistic religious fervor known as the "Great Revival" started around the turn of the century and continued without interruption for several decades. Like the earlier "Great Awakening," the movement was animated by a number of prominent preachers. During this time the Baptist, Methodist, and Presbyterian churches experienced phenomenal growth at the expense of the established "mainline" Protestant denominations. The Great Revival was especially pervasive in the southern states whose citizens to this day have retained their religiosity. Because the South has been more religiously homogenous, pubic life in the South has been less secular. The revival that started in the South and on the western frontier spread to the North. In upstate New York hundreds waited on hilltops after the evangelist William Miller predicted, based on his interpretation of Scripture, that Jesus would return on March 21, 1843.

1810

Congress passes a law ensuring that mail will be delivered and post offices staffed on Sundays. Some states had local laws that banned commercial activity on the Christian Sabbath. During the early 1800s many states passed "blue laws" prohibiting any commercial activity—and even travel—on Sundays, a day devoted to Christian worship. Although many believed that shutting down the mail for religious reasons was a violation of the separation of church and state, Congress succumbed to pressure and Sunday mail delivery was ended. State blue laws persisted into the twentieth century. Jews and Seventh-Day Adventists who recognized Saturday as the Sabbath were forced to abstain from work not only on their own Sabbath but on the Christian Sabbath as well.

1833

Massachusetts—originally founded by the Pilgrims and Puritans—votes to end its status as the last state to give direct financial aid to churches.

1840

With the wave of immigration from Ireland and Germany, many eastern U.S. cities had a sizable population of Roman Catholics. The Catholic Church established its own school systems and colleges in larger cities to help educate these immigrants and also to combine religious and moral instruction in the curriculum. Instruction in the public schools at the time included both prayer and Bible reading. However, Catholics and other minorities recognized that the instruction had a strong Protestant influence. There was a backlash against both immigrants and the Roman Catholic Church, both of which were viewed by many "nativist" Americans as pernicious foreign influences. The aptly named "Know Nothing" movement sought to exclude foreign-born persons from elected office and to require a twenty-five-year waiting period for citizenship. The Native American Party had nationwide support and by 1854 controlled state government in both Delaware and Massachusetts. Friction between Protestants and Catholics over public education remained a problem for the next one hundred years.

1852

Publication of *Uncle Tom's Cabin* by Harriet Beecher Stowe propelled the abolitionist movement into the national spotlight. The movement to eliminate slavery was triggered by the religious revivals of the 1820s and 1830s. Although some abolitionists desired to persuade by moral arguments, others advocated political action. There was a delicate balance in Congress between the "free states" and the "slave states." As new western states were added to the union, proslavery and antislavery advocates jockeyed to tip the balance in their favor. In 1856, John Brown, a deeply religious abolitionist, came to Kansas with his four sons and three friends and killed five proslavery settlers at Pottawatomie Creek. Three years later Brown attacked the Federal Arsenal at Harper's Ferry, Virginia, hoping to incite a slave revolt. Brown was tried for treason and hanged but became a martyr to his cause. The slavery issue caused deep divisions in many churches.

1859

Charles Darwin's book *Origin of Species* challenges the biblical account of the creation. Darwin argued that life on Earth evolved through a process of natural selection. Although some Christians reconcile Genesis and Darwin's theory of evolution, others maintain that the two are irreconcilable. Religious parents who believe in the literal truth of the biblical account of creation believe evolution has no place in the public schools. Those who subscribe to Darwin's theory believe the biblical account should not be taught.

1863

In the middle of the Civil War, President Abraham Lincoln signs an executive order, the Emancipation Proclamation, abolishing slavery in the Confederacy.

1865

The federal government for the first time mints coins with the motto: "In God We Trust."

1868

Post–Civil War amendments are added to the U.S. Constitution, including the Fourteenth Amendment. This amendment, enacted to protect legal rights of ex-slaves and other Black Americans, also extended the reach of First Amendment rights of due process of law and equal protection before the law to the states. In the 1940s, court decisions held that the Fourteenth Amendment also extended other First Amendment protections, including the Establishment Clause and the Free Exercise Clause, to the states. Accordingly, neither the federal government nor state governments could make a law respecting an establishment of religion or prohibiting the free exercise thereof. These rulings ultimately had the result of banning most religious activity in the public schools.

1879

Supreme Court in *Reynolds v. United States* upholds a criminal conviction of a Mormon for bigamy. The Court adopted the view that although the Free Exercise Clause of the Constitution protects an individual's religious beliefs, the Constitution does not stop government interference with religiously motivated actions. The Supreme Court did not fully reverse this view until 1963. The courts are still grappling with the question of whether the Free Exercise Cause protects actions that are religiously motivated or whether they can be prohibited when the action is prohibited by a law of general application. Although Congress seized the Mormon Church's property, the property was returned after the church renounced the practice of polygamy and Utah was admitted to the union upon promising to ban the practice.

1886

The evangelist Dwight Moody establishes was what to become the Moody Bible Institute in Chicago. Moody, a former YMCA worker, was a nationally known evangelist in the 1870s. He was a precursor of more modern twentieth-century evangelists like Billy Graham. Moody subscribed to "dispensationalist premillennialism." Whereas "postmillennialism" predicted Christ's second coming after the millennium of peace and prosperity, "premillennialism" was based on the biblical interpretation that Christ would return to end wickedness before the millennium. Christ's coming and the eventful battle of Armageddon could be foretold by "signs of the times," such as war and apostasy. Moody also preached inerrancy, the literal truth of the Scriptures, which among other things leaves no room for the theory of evolution. Other Protestants believed Darwin and the Bible could be reconciled. They also stressed the "social gospel" over personal redemption. The split between "mainline" and evangelical Christianity continued through both the nineteenth and twentieth centuries.

In *Church of the Holy Trinity v. United States,* the U.S. Supreme Court acknowledges that "This is a Christian nation," upholding a special exemption from immigration laws for the clergy.

1910

Illinois Supreme Court bans in-class reading of King James Bible in Chicago public schools (*People ex rel. Ring v. Board of Education* [1908]). Roman Catholics complained that daily reading from the Protestant Bible in the public schools discriminated against them. The court agreed with the complaining parents that even exclusion of the students from the Bible reading would subject the Catholic students to an unacceptable religious stigma. Although some states followed the lead of Illinois in banning Bible reading, other states let local school districts decide and still other states, mostly in the South, required Bible reading in the schools as a means of moral instruction. Although the U.S. Supreme Court banned all Bible reading in the schools in 1963 as contrary to the Constitution's Establishment Clause, some schools have ignored the ban.

1915

During World War I many states passed laws aimed at Germans or things Germanic. Nebraska passed a law prohibiting the teaching of German or any other foreign language to children not yet in high school. A parochial school teacher at the Zion Parochial School was prosecuted for teaching German to ten-year-olds. The law was overturned by the U.S. Supreme Court in *Meyer v. Nebraska* (1923).

A set of pamphlets, *The Fundamentals: A Testimony to the Truth,* is widely distributed. Besides affirming conservative Protestantism, the booklets also denounce Darwin, Mormons, and Catholics. The term "fundamentalist" starts to be applied to conservative Protestants. By the end of the century many prefer the term "evangelical," leaving the term "fundamentalist" only to those with more "extreme" views.

1920

Eighteenth Amendment to the Constitution outlaws the manufacture, sale, and carriage of alcoholic beverages. Many religious individuals viewed drunkenness as sinful and many states had already outlawed alcohol at the urging of groups like the Anti-Saloon League.

During World War I, Germans and all things German were reviled. Prejudice against beer-drinking German Americans tipped the scale against alcohol sales. Fundamentalist preachers like the popular evangelist Billy Sunday argued that it was unpatriotic to drink "demon rum." Although Prohibition lasted until 1933, the law was widely evaded and benefited organized criminals who smuggled alcohol in from Canada and brewed their own "bootleg" whiskey. Throughout Prohibition the Catholic Church was allowed to use sacramental wine in its services.

1923

During the 1920s fundamentalist Christians, alarmed that the teaching of evolution may threaten their children's faith, lobby for state laws banning the teaching of evolution. Oklahoma passes the first such law. The last such law was to be declared unconstitutional in 1968.

1925

The world watched the "Scopes Monkey Trial" in which noted attorney Clarence Darrow represented high school biology teacher John Thomas Scopes, who was charged with violating a Tennessee law prohibiting the teaching of evolution in the public schools. Religious fundamentalists feel that evolution is contrary to the Bible's teachings. William Jennings Bryan defended the law for the state. Although Scopes was convicted and fined $100, the fine was thrown out on appeal. Bryan, a prime backer of antievolution laws, dies just days after the trial. The movie *Inherit The Wind* is based on the trial.

Oregon voters, alarmed at the growing number of Catholics and Catholic schools in their midst, passed a referendum that amended the state constitution to require all schoolchildren to attend only public schools. Private and parochial schools were to be outlawed. Several private schools challenged the law. A unanimous U.S. Supreme Court, in *Pierce v. Society of Sisters* (1925), held that the Fourteenth Amendment protected students' rights to attend private schools. Although the state of Oregon had authority to regulate its public schools, it could not require all students to attend only the state-funded school system.

1928

Arkansas voters decide to ban the teaching of evolution in the schools.

1939

The evangelist Charles E. Fuller signs a contract with the Mutual Broadcasting System to nationally syndicate his radio program, Old Fashioned Revival Hour. Fundamentalist Christian preachers, who had originally spread their faith on horseback, discovered the power of the media to deliver their message. Radio becomes an important part of evangelists' ministries. Later in the century evangelists like Pat Robertson find that television can be even more powerful than in-person crusades.

1940

U.S. Supreme Court Justice Felix Frankfurter wrote the opinion in *Minersville School District v. Gobitis* (1940) in which Jehovah's Witnesses asked to be excused from saying the pledge of allegiance. Frankfurter, writing for the Court, held that despite the fact that their religious precepts prohibited reciting the pledge, the government could force schoolchildren to recite the pledge of allegiance to create national unity. The date of the case is important. World War II was raging in Europe with the Nazis rolling over much of Europe.

In *Cantwell v. Connecticut* the Supreme Court for the first time announces that the Free Exercise Clause of the First Amendment of the Constitution also applies to the states. Accordingly, it applies to the actions of local school districts. The Supreme Court case involved two Jehovah's Witnesses who sought to pass out religious literature in downtown New Haven, Connecticut. The Supreme Court held for the first time that the Free Exercise Clause was incorporated into the Fourteenth Amendment and so applied to state and local laws. In *dicta* the Court noted that freedom of religion includes the freedom to believe and the freedom to act. Although the first was an absolute right, the second was not.

1943

In *West Virginia State Board of Education v. Barnette,* the Supreme Court invalidates a West Virginia law requiring mandatory recitals of the pledge of allegiance and flag salutes in public school rooms. Jehovah's Witnesses view such actions as worshipping false gods. In *Gobitis,* an almost identical case heard only three years earlier, the Court had upheld such a statute. There were three new members on the Court and two justices had changed their minds about the issue.

1947

In *Everson v. Board of Education,* the Supreme Court upholds a New Jersey subsidy of bus service to parochial schools. The provision of bus service was not a direct subsidy but peripheral or incidental, similar to providing the school fire and police protection. The majority opinion focused on the fact that the aid went to the students or their parents, not directly to the school. The Court found no constitutional problem with "a general program to help parents get their children, regardless of their religion, safely and expeditiously to and from accredited schools." Accordingly, the wall of separation between church and state was not violated. In *Everson* the Supreme Court for the first time announced that the Establishment Clause of the First Amendment of the Constitution also applies to the states. Accordingly, it applies to the actions of local school districts. Justice Black believed that the Constitution's Establishment Clause demanded an absolute wall of separation between church and state. In *Everson,* Black explained his conception of the Establishment Clause, echoing Jefferson's earlier view: "The first Amendment has erected a wall between church and state. That wall must be kept high and impregnable. We [the Supreme Court] could not approve the slightest breach." Surprisingly, Black's opinion held that there was no breach in the *Everson* case in which New Jersey had paid the bus fare of children riding public transit to parochial schools. Although Black would not countenance the "slightest breach" of the wall of separation, he reasoned that the reimbursement of the bus fare benefited the schoolchildren and their families rather than the parochial schools.

1948

The Supreme Court handed down the first in a line of major cases that would change the contours of the United States by largely eliminating religious activities in the public schools. The case, *People of Illinois ex rel. McCollum v. Board of Education,* bans use of public school buildings for release-time religious instruction. The *McCollum* case really set the stage for all of the later cases that banned religious expression in the public schools. Vashti McCollum paid a personal price for her beliefs. She later wrote that she and her family were harassed all during the legal proceedings and she was called an "emissary of Satan, a Communist, and a fiend in human form."

1952

In *Zorach v. Clauson* the Supreme Court upholds a "release time" program taking place outside public school grounds. Release time (also called "dismissed time") is a program in which a pubic school dismisses students early to attend religion classes away from the public school grounds. Typically, classes will be offered at individual churches and children will attend the classes at the church at which they regularly worship. Parents may give permission to the public school for their children to be released early for such classes. If permission is not granted, the children are required to stay at the public school. Justice William O. Douglas's opinion noted that although it was clear that the First Amendment required a separation of church and state, it was equally clear that the Establishment Clause does not require "a philosophy of hostility to religion," which "respects the religious nature of our people and accommodates the public service to their spiritual needs." Three justices wrote dissenting opinions, noting that there was not much to distinguish this case from the 1948 case (*McCollum*) that had disapproved of release-time programs. That in this case the children attended the classes at church rather than in the school itself seemed trivial to the dissenters.

1953

President Eisenhower nominates Governor Earl Warren of California to be the new chief justice of the Supreme Court. Although a conservative Republican, once on the high court, Warren proves to be a judicial activist and is especially eager to strike down laws that violate the separation of church and state such as those allowing prayer in the public schools.

1954

Congress adds the words *under God* to the pledge of allegiance. The change came during the cold war when communism was viewed as a major threat to the United States. The Congress added the language, at least in part, to distinguish the United States from the "godless" Union of Soviet Socialist Republics (USSR), which was officially atheistic.

1956

President Eisenhower nominates William Brennan, a New Jersey jurist, to the Supreme Court. Brennan, a Catholic, proves to be a staunch defender of the separation of church and state.

"In God We Trust" becomes the official national motto.

1961

U.S. Supreme Court in *McGowan v. Maryland* upholds Maryland's "blue law" mandating the closing of businesses on Sundays. Eight justices found no problem in Maryland's declaring the Christian Sabbath as a day of rest for all citizens. Justice William O. Douglas, the lone dissenter, found the law a violation of both the Establishment Clause and the Free Exercise Clause of the First Amendment. The case is interesting in light of what is to happen the very next year in the school prayer case.

1962

One of the most important and far-reaching cases ever heard by the Supreme Court was *Engel v. Vitale* (1962). This case threw out a nondenominational school prayer written by the New York State Board of Regents. The nondenominational prayer had been composed to be inoffensive to those who were compelled to recite it. Justice Black, writing for the Court, felt that it is "no part of the business of government to compose official prayers." Generations of Americans had grown up with school prayer. Religious Americans took the decision as a personal rebuke. The decision also had a tremendous polarizing political effect. Those who supported the rights of minorities—especially non-Christians—hailed the decision as progressive. They pointed out that the decision did not eliminate any student's right to pray silently or aloud in school. It merely banned public schools from composing and compelling the recitation of prayers. Critics of the decision labeled the court and justices as "godless" or "communists."

1963

The Supreme Court heard another major school prayer case, *Abington School District v. Schempp* (1963), and again declared that organized prayer had no place in the public schools. The case went even further than *Engel v. Vitale*, decided the prior year. That case concerned a prayer penned by an administrative body. The 1963 school prayer case banned both the recitation of the Lord's Prayer and Bible reading in public schools. Opposition to the banning of school prayer was swift. Criticism was leveled at the Supreme Court's opinion from politicians and the pulpit. Groups such as the right-wing John Birch Society organized a campaign to impeach Chief Justice Earl Warren, who wrote the majority opinion in the school prayer case.

In *Sherbert v. Verner*, the Supreme Court decides that a Seventh-Day Adventist who celebrates Saturday, not Sunday, as her Sabbath, could not be denied unemployment benefits because she refused to work on Saturday. Two years earlier the court had found against two Orthodox Jews who made a similar argument.

The Creation Research Society is founded by fundamentalist Christians to help combat the spread of the belief in evolution and its teaching in the public schools.

1965

With the Vietnam War escalating, more individuals wish to resist the Selective Service's military draft. In *United States v. Seegher* the Supreme Court decides that the law allows "conscientious objectors"—those opposed to war—to avoid military service if their objection is based on "religious training and belief." There is no requirement that they belong to a sect that itself is opposed to war.

1968

In *Epperson v. Arkansas*, the Supreme Court in a unanimous opinion, struck down an Arkansas statute that prohibited the teaching of evolution. The Court reasoned that the ban was enacted entirely to "aid, foster, or promote one religion over another" and thereby offended the Establishment Clause of the First Amendment. Arkansas could not require that its school curriculum be shaped to conform to the beliefs of the Christian religion. After the U.S. Supreme Court prohibited states from banning the teaching of evolution in *Epperson*, creationists started labeling their body of information supporting the biblical version of creation as "creation science."

In *Board of Education v. Allen*, the Supreme Court allowed a state program that loaned textbooks on secular topics to private and parochial school students. The divided Court upheld the practice reasoning that the aid went to the students or their parents rather than to the schools. The Court has also approved reimbursement of the costs of state-mandated standardized tests but has disapproved of providing free teaching materials other than textbooks.

1970

The Court upholds state tax exemptions for property and income of religious institutions based on historical practices in *Walz v. Tax Commission of New York.*

1971

In *Lemon v. Kurtzman* the U.S. Supreme Court prohibited salary supplements for lay teachers in parochial schools. The majority opinion, written by Chief Justice Warren Burger, noted the religious indoctrination in parochial schools, writing that: "parochial schools involve substantial religious activity and purpose." The case also established a three-prong test to see if a law offends the Establishment Clause. All three prongs must be met.

1. The statute must have a secular purpose.
2. Its primary effect must neither advance nor inhibit religion.
3. It must avoid excessive governmental entanglement with religion.

The "*Lemon* test" was to be used by the Court for approximately twenty-five years and also found its way into the Religious Freedom Restoration Act. It was used to determine if a particular law was in violation of the First Amendment's guarantee that the state will not establish a religion. For example, a law requiring state-funded schools to post the Ten Commandments in classrooms would be judged under the *Lemon* test. Although the *Lemon* case has not been overruled, the Supreme Court has not used the test since the mid-1990s.

1972

In *Wisconsin v. Yoder* the Supreme Court holds it unconstitutional to require compulsory education for Old Order Amish children whose parents object on religious grounds. In *Yoder* (1972), an 8–1 decision, the Court upheld the right of Amish parents to withhold their children from public school despite the state of Wisconsin's compulsory schooling law. Although the state had a strong interest in requiring children to attend school, it did not overbalance the burden on religious freedom of compelling them to attend school. The *Yoder* decision is unusual because it granted the Amish the free exercise of their beliefs despite a clear state law compelling school attendance. It is also a curious decision because it favored one particular religious group.

1973

The Supreme Court in *Roe v. Wade* finds laws restricting a woman's right to abortion unconstitutional. The Court relies on its own precedents in holding that individuals have a right to privacy and a right to make their own medical decisions. The case inflamed not only conservative Protestants but also the Roman Catholic Church, which is not only opposed to abortion but also the use of any artificial birth control devices at all. An earlier case, *Griswold v. Connecticut* (1965), had struck down a state law restricting the right to birth control devices. The Court held that individuals have a basic right to make birth control decisions (*Levitt v. Committee for Public Education and Religious Liberty* [1973] and *Committee v. Nyquist* [1973]).

In *Sloan v. Lemon* the Supreme Court prohibits tax credits and grants to parents of parochial school students. The Supreme Court also struck down a state plan to reimburse private and parochial schools for administering standardized achievement tests. The Court was troubled by the fact that the state could not guarantee that the funds would not be used for religious purposes and that the private school teachers participated in preparing the tests.

1975

In M*eek v. Pittenger* the Supreme Court strikes down state payment of auxiliary services such as the purchase of AV equipment at parochial schools. Curiously, this case involved the same law that was upheld in the 1968 *Allen* case.

1976

In a 5–4 decision the U.S. Supreme Court upholds Maryland's program to provide grants to private colleges including church-supported colleges. The majority finds that this program does not violate the Establishment Clause even though the aid goes to religious organizations.

1977

Supreme Court approves a program whereby the public school employees provided speech and hearing and psychological testing services for parochial school students at their schools. The Court reasoned that such services had no "educational content" and the Court saw no danger in proselytizing (*Wollman v. Walter*). Just two years earlier in *Meek v. Pittenger* the Court had struck down a similar program in part because the services were offered in a parochial school.

The Supreme Court holds that a school district cannot provide instructional materials such as maps, magazines, tape recorders, and buses for field trips to parochial school students even though these are all used for secular, rather than religious, instruction. The Court held that the Establishment Clause was violated because of the "impossibility of separating the secular education function from the sectarian" (*Wollman v. Walter*).

1978

IRS threatens to withdraw tax exemptions from private and parochial schools that were established to avoid court-ordered desegregation.

1980

In *Stone v. Graham* (1980) the Supreme Court banned the posting of the Ten Commandments in public schools even when financed with private funds. The Court found that the purpose was religious and therefore prohibited by the Establishment Clause.

In *Committee for Public Education v. Regan,* the Supreme Court upheld a state-funded program in which the state reimbursed private and parochial schools for the cost of administering standardized tests. The private schools exercised no control over the tests themselves, which the Court felt prevented any forbidden entanglement between church and state.

1981

California Supreme Court in *California Teachers Association v. Riles* holds that "lending" public schools to parochial schools is contrary to the California state constitution, although the U.S. Supreme Court has held the practice is not contrary to the U.S. Constitution.

The Supreme Court holds that a state university cannot deny use of its facilities to a religious club. The Court, in *Widmar v. Vincent,* reasons that it would be a violation of the students' First Amendment rights and would get the university embroiled in excluding groups that the university deemed "religious" but granting use to groups that it perceived as not religious. The equal access language in this case led to legislative action in 1984, when the Louisiana legislature passed a law, "Balanced Treatment for Creation-Science and Evolution-Science in Public School Instruction," which mandates that any school teaching evolution must also provide equal classroom time to the teaching of creation science, based on the biblical account of creation. Although applauded by religious leaders, the law was immediately challenged.

1982

President Ronald Reagan becomes the first president to endorse an amendment allowing prayer in the public schools. Reagan tells Congress that it is time to "allow prayer back in our schools."

The Reverend Jerry Falwell's group, the Moral Majority, becomes a political force advocating traditional values, like public prayer; and opposing abortion, gays in the military, and sex education in the public schools.

1983

In *Mueller v. Allen,* a closely divided Supreme Court upheld a Minnesota law allowing parents of private and parochial school students to take a tax deduction for tuition and other educational expenses. The case is significant because the Court had struck down a similar law. What saved the Minnesota law was that the deduction was also "available" to parents of public school students. The Court conveniently sidestepped the issue that parents of public school students do not actually pay tuition and thereby would not benefit in real terms.

Nevertheless, Justice Rehnquist, writing for the Court, found the tax scheme to be neutral. The fact that the bulk of the benefits would go to the parents of private and parochial school students was held to be irrelevant. The majority opinion stressed the value of supporting private schools not just for those students attending the schools but for the public in general. Rehnquist noted that the public benefited because each student educated in private school reduced the taxpayer's burden of educating the student. Further, the private school system provided a benchmark for the public school system and provided educational diversity.

In *Bob Jones University v. United States,* the Supreme Court upholds the IRS's disallowance of nonprofit, tax-free status to private schools that discriminate against students or prospective students on the basis of race.

The school prayer amendment, supported by both President Reagan and Senate leaders, passes the Senate by a vote of 56–44. Because it lacks the constitutionally required two-thirds vote, the measure fails.

1984

Congress passes the federal Equal Access Act, which prohibits discrimination against student groups on the basis of religious, political, or philosophical views. If a public school allows "noncurriculum related groups," like clubs, to use its facilities, then the school must give equal access to those facilities to religious groups.

The Republican Party platform vows to restore school prayer by constitutional amendment if necessary.

In *Lynch v. Donnelly,* the Court posits that the so-called wall of separation is "not a wholly accurate description of the practical aspects of the relationship that in fact exists between church and state" because the Constitution "affirmatively mandates accommodation, not merely tolerance, of all religions and forbids hostility towards any."

1985

The Supreme Court, in *Wallace v. Jaffree* (1985), invalidates an Alabama law allowing a one-minute period of silence at the start of each school day "for meditation or voluntary prayer." The divided Court (6–3) concluded that this mandated moment of silence amounted to "the State's endorsement of prayer activity" that transgressed the proper wall of separation between church and state. Merely allowing students to be excused was held insufficient to save the law. The Court did say, however, that it was possible for a moment of silence to pass muster if it was not solely for sectarian purposes. The problem with the Alabama law was that it was avowedly for prayer. Presumably, a statute that required a moment of silence for no reason would have avoided the constitutional problems. Of course, the Supreme Court has never prohibited prayer in the public schools. Students are free to pray silently or out loud. However, the school cannot conduct religious ceremonies including the recitation of prayers in the classroom.

The Supreme Court in *Aguilar v. Felton* struck down a program that used federal funds to pay the salaries of public school guidance counselors and teachers providing remedial and clinical help to disadvantaged parochial school students. The Court held that the plan created an excessive government entanglement with religion and therefore failed the *Lemon* test.

In *School District of Grand Rapids v. Ball,* the Supreme Court struck down a school district's program that allowed public school teachers to give secular classes in parochial school classrooms. The majority opinion held that the "symbolic union" of government and religion in one sectarian enterprise entangled the government with religion by implicitly endorsing the church that ran the school. Payment of the teachers' salaries was also seen as a direct subsidy to the parochial school.

1986

Louisiana enacts a "Balanced Treatment" law requiring equal time for the teaching of "creation science" whenever the theory of evolution is taught in school science classes. Only a few states have enacted laws requiring "balanced curriculums," whereas others have rejected such measures. Louisiana's balanced curriculum law was declared invalid by the U.S. Supreme Court in *Edwards, Governor of Louisiana v. Aguillard* (1987).

1987

In *Edwards v. Aguillard,* the Supreme Court invalidates Louisiana's "Balanced Treatment" law, which required public schools to provide equal time for the teaching of evolution and creation science. The Court found that the primary purpose for the law was to promote the teachings of Christianity. This favoritism violated the Establishment Clause.

1988

President Ronald Reagan appoints Anthony Kennedy to replace Lewis Powell on the U.S. Supreme Court. Although he had a reputation as a conservative judge, Kennedy surprises many, including Reagan, by siding with the majority in striking down a Texas law outlawing the burning of the American flag. He goes on to write the majority opinion in *Lee v. Weisman* in 1992, striking down religious invocations at high school graduation ceremonies.

The Reverend Pat Robertson runs unsuccessfully for president but makes a credible showing. A new group, the Christian Coalition, is organized after the election and surpasses Jerry Falwell's Moral Majority as the chief political voice of evangelicals. Religious conservatives become an important wing of the Republican Party.

1989

A federal district court prohibits a local Massachusetts school district from renting space in a Roman Catholic parish center for classroom use. The court holds that the use of church property had the effect of endorsing the Catholic religion (*Spacco v. Bridgewater School Dept.*).

1990

The Supreme Court in *Employment Division v. Smith* held that religious belief could not excuse commission of a crime (use of peyote by Native Americans). Alarmed by the holding that could presumably be applied against any religious practices, such as receiving sacramental wine at communion services, religious groups ask Congress for additional protections. Congress later responds by passing the Religious Freedom Restoration Act (see 1993).

Using the *Lemon* test, the Supreme Court, in *Board of Education of the Westside Community Schools v. Mergens,* upholds the constitutionality of the federal Equal Access Act, enacted to give equal access to public school facilities for religious groups and clubs. The Court held that although there was some involvement of school officials in the appealed case, this did not amount to prohibited "entanglement" with religion nor an endorsement of any particular religion. Clearly, changes of personnel on the Court over the years had made a difference. It is clear that if this case had been brought two decades earlier, the Court would have found the entire act unconstitutional.

1991

President George H. W. Bush appoints Clarence Thomas to the U.S. Supreme Court to replace Thurgood Marshall. Although both justices are African American, Bush denies that race had anything to do with the appointment. Philosophically, Thomas, a staunch conservative, is almost a complete opposite to Marshall, who was the most liberal member of the Court.

1992

A divided Supreme Court, in *Lee v. Weisman,* holds that an invocation at a public school graduation ceremony in Providence, Rhode Island, violates the Establishment Clause. Justice Kennedy, writing for the majority, argues that the public atmosphere created an improper coercion on students, which amount to proselytizing. The majority felt that since the graduation ceremony was a required event, a prayer at the graduation was no more acceptable than a prayer in the classroom at the start of the school day. Justice Scalia wrote a bitter dissent accusing the majority of "laying waste" to traditional nonsectarian prayers at public events and accused the majority's use of the concept of "coercion" of being a "bulldozer of its social engineering."

1993

Religious Freedom Restoration Act becomes law, which provides, among other things, that federal, state, and local "Government[s] shall not substantially burden a person's exercise of religion even if the burden results from a rule of general applicability . . . except that Government may substantially burden a person's exercise of religion: if it demonstrates that application of the burden to the person (1) is in furtherance of a compelling government interest; and (2) is the least restrictive means of furthering that compelling interest." The act is intended to deal with the free exercise of religion, not to the establishment of religion by the government. The act has been challenged on the grounds that it improperly attempts to impose on the courts a substantive role.

The Supreme Court in *Church of the Lukumi Babalu Aye v. City of Hialeah* upheld the right of the Santeria sect to conduct animal sacrifices. Santarians, originally from Cuba, practice a religion that is a mixture of Roman Catholicism and African tribal rites brought to Cuba by African slaves. Santarians sacrifice animals including chickens, doves, ducks, turtles, goats, and sheep at the time of births, marriages, and deaths. The city of Hialeah, Florida, tried to ban the animal sacrifices but the Supreme Court held the city's actions to be a violation of the Free Exercise Cause of the First Amendment.

The Supreme Court found no Establishment Clause violation in *Zobrest v. Catalina Foothills School District,* in which a California school district provided a sign language interpreter for a deaf student at a Catholic high school. The Court reasoned that there was no constitutional violation when the parochial school received only an "attenuated financial benefit" from the educational program that provided benefits neutrally without reference to the student's religious affiliation.

In *Lamb's Chapel v. Center Moriches School District,* the Supreme Court holds that a school district cannot deny access to school facilities to a church group that wants to show a film on child rearing. Although the film was only shown to the church group after school hours, the Court held that any benefit to the group was merely "incidental."

Distribution of Bibles by the Gideons in public school struck down as violation of the Establishment Clause (*Berger v. Rensselaer Central School Corp*).

1994

The U.S. Supreme Court in *Board of Education of Kiryas Joel Village v. Grumet* strikes down New York State's creation of a special public school district to provide state-funded special education services for a community of Hasidic Jews. The community of approximately 8,500, the Satmae Hasidim sect of Orthodox Jews established a private school based on the needs of their religious students, including gender segregation, a special dress code, and speaking Yiddish. In order to obtain state aid to the village's handicapped children, the state legislature allowed the village to establish a separate public school district that would only deal with the problems of the village's handicapped children. The Supreme Court held that this was a violation of the Establishment Clause. Because New York had created the school district along religious lines, it violated the Constitution's requirement that government maintain its impartiality toward religion.

Georgia enacts a Moment of Quiet Reflection that allows public school teachers to begin the school day with an interval of silence. Although the practice was immediately attacked as a "silent prayer," the silent moment was upheld because the law establishing the moment specifically disclaimed any religious purpose. Accordingly, the federal district court held that the law did not violate the Constitution (*Bowen v. Gwinnett School District*).

Mississippi enacts a law allowing student-initiated voluntary prayer at all assemblies, sporting events, commencement exercises, and other school-related events. The law is immediately challenged by the ACLU, and a Mississippi federal district judge upholds the section of the law allowing prayers at commencement exercises but strikes down the parts of the act allowing prayer at assemblies and other school-related events (*Ingebretsen v. Jackson Public School District*).

A Federal court in Florida refuses to order a school district to remove Halloween decorations after a parent complains that Halloween is a pagan religious holiday. The judge determines that Halloween is a secular and cultural holiday and allows the decorations to stay (*Guyer v. School Board of Alahua County*).

1995

U.S. Department of Education issues guidelines on the extent to which religious activity is allowed in public schools. The guidelines allow student prayer and Bible reading by individuals or groups that is not disruptive. The wearing of religious clothing or symbols is permitted, as are limited proselytizing and the distribution of religious literature. Prohibited activities include prayer that is endorsed by a teacher or the school authorities. Teachers may teach about religion but may not teach the tenets of a particular religion and may not encourage either religious or antireligious activity.

The Christian Coalition, headed by Ralph Reed, issues its "Contract with the American Family." One of the ten proposals calls for school vouchers.

The Supreme Court in *Rosenberger v. Rector and Visitors of University of Virginia* (1995) hold that a state university that used student funds to support a number of campus clubs and organizations cannot withhold funds from a religious group to publish their Christian magazine *Wide Awake*. The Court reasons that this is improper viewpoint discrimination. At this time it is unclear how much influence this case will have on the public schools.

1996

A Texas student was a member of her high school's girls basketball team and school choir. She objected to the team policy of praying before and after games, at practices, and pep rallies with the encouragement of coaches. She also objected to the choir's singing of religious hymns. Although the prayers at pep rallies were stopped, the other religious practices continued and she filed suit in federal court. The courts held that the in-school prayers had to stop. However, the singing of traditional choral music was not an endorsement of religion, even though the music was based on sacred themes (*Doe v. Duncanville Independent School District*).

A federal court in Illinois held that the state's policy of closing the public schools on Good Friday violated the U.S. Constitution because Good Friday is a religious day for Christians. Interestingly, the court noted that both Christmas and Thanksgiving had lost their religious significance for many Americans and that school closings on those days had a secular and not entirely religious purpose.

The Wisconsin state legislature expands Milwaukee's voucher program to include private and parochial schools. Parents of school-age children in the city can use the government vouchers to pay for tuition in such schools. The practice was challenged as a violation of separation of church and state and the program was put on hold until court arguments were heard (see 1997).

A movement grows to add a "Parental Rights Amendment" to each state constitution and eventually the U.S. Constitution as well. The amendment would forbid the government—including the public schools—to interfere with or usurp the right of a parent to direct the upbringing of the child of a parent. The amendment would make it easier for parents to challenge classroom material that they find objectionable. Some argue that the amendment would compel the government to pay tuition for parents who want their children educated in church-affiliated schools.

1997

Alabama legislators debate a proposal to seek voter approval for a state constitutional amendment that would require all public schools to set aside time to read prayers from the Congressional Record, and to discuss topics such as the historical significance of the Ten Commandments.

An Ohio state court strikes down the Ohio Pilot Scholarship Program that provided "vouchers" of up to $2,500 to Cleveland public school students to attend private and parochial schools.

The U.S. Supreme Court in *Agostini v. Felton* overturns its 1985 holding in *Aguilar v. Felton* that held that remedial education funded by federal aid under Title 1 could not take place in parochial school buildings.

The U.S. Supreme Court in *City of Boerne v. Flores* overturns the 1993 Religious Freedom Restoration Act. Although the case involved a church that had a zoning dispute with a city, the case may have a major impact on the issue of religion in the schools. According to the overturned federal statute, the federal government was prohibited from passing a law that infringed on the practice of religion. By overturning the law, the Supreme Court opened the door to more regulation of religion by Congress. Opponents of the decision immediately vowed to rewrite the legislation and introduce it in the next session of Congress in the fall of 1997.

2000

Congress enacts the Religious Land Use and Institutionalized Persons Act of 2000. The law, similar to the Religious Freedom Restoration Act, which was declared unconstitutional by the Supreme Court in 1997, was enacted to protect churches from local zoning restrictions. The statute prohibits zoning, which imposes a "substantial burden" on religious exercise unless the government can show that there is a compelling interest in doing so and there is no less restrictive way to further the interest. This is the "compelled accommodation" test from *Sherbert v. Verner* in which the Supreme Court reached perhaps its high-water mark in allowing the free exercise of religion.

When Congress needed to replace the retiring congressional chaplain, a subcommittee recommended a Catholic priest. Republican leaders in the House voiced alarm that a celibate Catholic priest might not be qualified to provide family counseling and that the priest's clerical garb might prove "divisive." Despite claims of anti-Catholic bias, the House appointed a Protestant chaplain, continuing the tradition of only employing Protestant clergymen for the position.

2001

Nationwide the Roman Catholic Church was rocked by dozens of lawsuits alleging that priests sexually abused hundreds of young boys in their parishes. Although the lawsuits against the Boston diocese gained the most publicity, similar lawsuits were filed across the coun-

try. In 2002 a Rhode Island judge ruled that the First Amendment offered no shield to the Catholic Archdiocese of Providence, Rhode Island, which had resisted sharing documents with plaintiffs suing over
sexual abuse by priests. The diocese settled the lawsuits in 2002 for
an estimated $13.5 million. Commentators estimated the potential li-
ability nationwide in the hundreds of millions of dollars. Dozens of
lawsuits are filed by churches under the Religious Land Use and Institutionalized Person Act (RLUIPA). Typical is a lawsuit by the
Freedom Baptist Church of Middletown, Pennsylvania. The city of
Middletown, a Philadelphia suburb, enacted a zoning ordinance that
inadvertently banned churches from commercial zones. Upon dis-
covering that the Freedom Baptist Church was violating the city
zoning ordinance by conducting services in a rented office space, the
city asked the church to move. The church sued arguing that the city
lacked the authority under the RLUIPA. The judge agreed that the
city had not demonstrated a compelling interest so the church did
not have to move. Churches in other states have sued local towns and
cities over unfavorable land use decisions.

2002

In the major case of the year, *Zelman v. Simmons-Harris,* the U.S.
Supreme Court upheld a Cleveland, Ohio, school voucher plan despite arguments that it violates the Establishment Clause. The Ohio
plan gives families a state-paid voucher that can be used to pay tuition in a private or religious school. Relying on precedents in which
the Court has allowed aid to parochial school students, the Court
reasoned that the public money was supporting children and their
parents, not private religious schools. Proponents of vouchers lost
little time in proposing school vouchers in other states. Opponents
of school vouchers argue that vouchers may be unconstitutional under many state constitutions which have more exacting separation of
church and state provisions than the federal Constitution.

In the case *Newdow v. U.S. Congress,* the Ninth Circuit Court of
Appeals rules that inclusion of the words *under God* in the pledge of
allegiance violates the Establishment Clause. Newdow brought suit
against both the local school district and the federal government
claiming that his daughter was injured when she is compelled to
"watch and listen as her state-employed teacher in her state-run

school leads her classmates in a ritual proclaiming that there is a God, and that ours is 'one nation under God.'" Mr. Newdow argued that both the 1954 addition of the words *under God* to the pledge and the daily recitation of the 1954 version of the pledge were violations of the Establishment Clause. The court agreed, saying, "In the context of the Pledge, the statement that the United States is a nation 'under God' is an endorsement of religion. It is a profession of a religious belief, namely, a belief in monotheism. The recitation that ours is a nation 'under God' is not a mere acknowledgment that many Americans believe in a deity." The reaction to the *Newdow* case was swift, sharp, and predictable. Politicians of all political stripes vilified the judges without having read the opinion. However, the reaction was more transitory than the reaction to the school prayer case forty years earlier.

2003

Lower courts uphold the constitutionality of the Religious Land Use and Institutionalized Person Act of 2000. Commentators predict that a test case will make its way to the Supreme Court. Commentators predict that if the present justices hear the case it will meet the same fate as the 1993 Religious Freedom Restoration Act and will be declared unconstitutional as a usurpation of the Court's prerogative to determine an individual's rights under the Constitution.

On the eve of National Prayer Day, May 1, Attorney General John Ashcroft announced that the Justice Department would appeal the pledge case (see 2002) to the Supreme Court. He noted that "our government can acknowledge the important role religion has played in America's foundation, history and character . . ." If the Court accepts the case, it may return to the status quo. Others suggest that if the court of appeals decision is upheld, it will usher in more rigorous enforcement of the separation of church and state.

In June 2003 the U.S. Supreme Court strikes down a Texas law that criminalized sodomy. The Texas statute, like four others, criminalized sexual behavior between same-sex partners. Criminal sodomy statutes in nine other states applied to both same-sex and unmarried opposite-sex couples. Although only a minority of states had similar statutes and prosecutions were few, the decision is significant because of its breadth. The Court holds that governments cannot label gay and lesbian private sexual conduct a crime (*Lawrence and Garner v. Texas*). The three dissenting justices predicted that the case could lead to same-sex marriage, an issue that was not before the Court.

In August 2003 the Alabama Supreme Court orders the removal of a 5,280-pound monument of the Ten Commandments from the state supreme court building. The memorial had been installed by the Alabama Supreme Court chief justice, who viewed the memorial as a "historical" rather than religious display. When citizens protest that the display is a violation of the Establishment Clause, the federal judge orders the memorial removed. When the chief justice defies the federal court order, the remainder of the Alabama Supreme Court votes not only to remove the memorial but the chief justice himself.

Table of Cases

County of Allegheny v. Greater Pittsburgh ACLU, 492 U.S. 573 (1989)

Doe v. Duncanville Independent School District, 994 F.2d 160 (5th Cir. 1996)

Edwards v. Aguillard, 482 U.S. 578 (1987)

Employment Division, Oregon Department of Human Resources v. Smith, 494 U.S. 872 (1990)

Engel v. Vitale, 370 U.S. 421 (1962)

Epperson v. Arkansas, 393 U.S. 97 (1968)

Everson v. Board of Education, 330 U.S. 1 (1947)

Freiler v. Tangipahoa Parish Board of Education, 530 U.S. 1251 (2000)

Goldman v. Weinberger, 475 U.S. 503 (1986)

Griswold v. Connecticut, 381 U.S. 479 (1965)

Guyer v. School Board of Alahua County, 513 U.S. 1044 (1994)

Harris v. Joint School District No. 241, 516 U.S. 803 (1995)

Ingebretsen v. Jackson Public School District, 88 F.3d 274 (5th Cir. 1994)

Jimmy Swaggart Ministries v. Board of Equalization, 294 U.S. 378 (1990)

Lamb's Chapel v. Center Moriches Union Free Public School District, 508 U.S. 384 (1993)

Lawrence and Garner v. Texas, 123 S.Ct. 2472 (2003)

Lee v. Weisman, 505 U.S. 577 (1992)

Lemon v. Kurtzman, 403 U.S. 602 (1971)

Levitt v. Committee for Public Education, 413 U.S. 472 (1973)

Lynch v. Donnelly, 465 U.S. 668 (1984)

Marbury v. Madison, 5 U.S. 137 (1803)

Marsh v. Chambers, 463 U.S. 783 (1983)

McCollum (People of Illinois ex rel. McCollum) v. Board of Education, 333 U.S. 203 (1948)

McGowan v. Maryland, 366 U.S. 420 (1961)

Meek v. Pittenger, 421 U.S. 349 (1975)

Meyer v. Nebraska, 262 U.S. 390 (1923)

Minersville School District v. Gobitis, 310 U.S. 586 (1940)

Mueller v. Allen, 463 U.S. 388 (1983)

Murray v. Curlett, 179 F.2d 698 (4th Cir. 1962)

Newdow v. Congress, 292 F.3d 59 (2002)

Norwood Hospital v. Munoz, 564 N.E. 2d 1017 (Mass. 1991)

Appendix: Supreme Court Justices since 1900

Name	Years Served	Appointing President
Oliver Wendell Holmes	1902–1932	Theodore Roosevelt
William R. Day	1903–1922	Theodore Roosevelt
William H. Moody	1906–1910	Theodore Roosevelt
Horace H. Lurton	1909–1914	William Howard Taft
Charles Evans Hughes	1910–1916	William Howard Taft
*Edward D. White	1910–1921	William Howard Taft
Willis Van Devanter	1910–1937	William Howard Taft
Joseph R. Lamar	1910–1916	William Howard Taft
Mahlon Pitney	1912–1922	William Howard Taft
James McReynolds	1914–1941	Woodrow Wilson
Louis D. Brandeis	1916–1939	Woodrow Wilson
John H. Clark	1916–1922	Woodrow Wilson
*William Howard Taft	1921–1930	Warren Harding
George Sutherland	1922–1938	Warren Harding
Pierce Butler	1922–1939	Warren Harding
Edward T. Sanford	1923–1930	Warren Harding
Harlan Fiske Stone	1925–1941	Calvin Coolidge
*Charles Evans Hughes	1930–1941	Herbert Hoover
Owen J. Roberts	1932–1945	Herbert Hoover
Benjamin N. Cardozo	1932–1938	Herbert Hoover
Hugo L. Black	1937–1971	Franklin D. Roosevelt
Stanley F. Reed	1938–1957	Franklin D. Roosevelt

Felix Frankfurter	1939–1962	Franklin D. Roosevelt
William O. Douglas	1939–1975	Franklin D. Roosevelt
Frank Murphy	1940–1949	Franklin D. Roosevelt
James F. Byrnes	1941–1942	Franklin D. Roosevelt
*Harlan F. Stone	1941–1946	Franklin D. Roosevelt
Robert H. Jackson	1941–1954	Franklin D. Roosevelt
Wiley B. Rutledge	1943–1949	Franklin D. Roosevelt
Harold H. Burton	1945–1958	Harry Truman
*Fred M. Vinson	1946–1953	Harry Truman
Tom C. Clark	1949–1967	Harry Truman
Sherman Minton	1949–1956	Harry Truman
*Earl Warren	1954–1969	Dwight Eisenhower
John M. Harlan	1955–1971	Dwight Eisenhower
William J. Brennan	1957–1990	Dwight Eisenhower
Charles E. Whittaker	1957–1962	Dwight Eisenhower
Potter Stewart	1959–1981	Dwight Eisenhower
Byron R. White	1962–1993	John F. Kennedy
Arthur J. Goldberg	1962–1965	John F. Kennedy
Abe Fortas	1965–1969	Lyndon Johnson
Thurgood Marshall	1967–1991	Lyndon Johnson
*Warren E. Burger	1969–1986	Richard Nixon
Harry Blackmun	1970–1999	Richard Nixon
Lewis F. Powell	1971–1988	Richard Nixon
William H. Rehnquist	1971–1986	Richard Nixon
John Paul Stevens	1975–	Gerald Ford
Sandra Day O'Connor	1981–	Ronald Reagan
*William H. Rehnquist	1986–	Ronald Reagan
Antonin Scalia	1986–	Ronald Reagan
Anthony M. Kennedy	1988–	Ronald Reagan
David H. Souter	1990–	George H. W. Bush
Clarence Thomas	1991–	George H. W. Bush
Ruth Bader Ginsburg	1993–	Bill Clinton
Stephen G. Breyer	1994–	Bill Clinton

---

* denotes chief justice

Annotated Bibliography

Print Resources

Ahlstrom, Sydney E. *A Religious History of the American People.* New Haven, CT: Yale University Press, 1972.

> Historical account of American religious practice and American churches from colonial times until 1970, including the development and application of the doctrine of separation of church and state and the late-twentieth-century Supreme Court cases dealing with religion in the schools.

Allen, Leslie H., ed. *Bryan and Darrow at Dayton.* New York: Russel and Russel, 1925.

> Contemporary account of the famous Scopes "Monkey Trial" pitting William Jennings Bryan against Clarence Darrow. The trial ended in the conviction of John Scopes, a high school biology teacher, for teaching Darwin's theory of evolution in defiance of the Tennessee statute. Includes original source material including a partial trial transcript.

Alley, Robert S. *The Supreme Court on Church and State.* New York: Oxford University Press, 1988.

> A collection of lightly edited U.S. Supreme Court cases on the separation of church and state, most of which involve religion in the schools. The author also provides an analysis of each area.

Barton, Charles D. *America: To Pray or Not to Pray.* Aledo, TX: Wallbuilders, 1989.

> The book chronicles what the author perceives as problems in U.S. society that resulted from the ending of organized prayer in the public schools. The author argues that prayer must be returned to the schools before these ills will reverse themselves.

Beggs, David W., III, and R. Bruch McQuigg. *America's Schools and Churches: Partners in Conflict.* Bloomington: University of Indiana Press, 1965.

This is a dated but useful treatise on cases involving challenges to religion in the schools.

Berg, Thomas C. *The State and Religion: In a Nutshell.* St. Paul, MN: West, 1998.

Written by a leading constitutional authority, this up-to-date book provides coverage of all of the leading cases and many others as well. Because this is a paperback book written for law school students, the emphasis is on law, not politics.

Bollier, David. *Liberty and Justice for Some: Defending a Free Society from the Radical Right's Holy War on Democracy.* Washington, DC: People for the American Way, 1982.

A vigorous defense of the doctrine of separation of church and state, Bollier attacks what he views as the religious right's attack on the the country's pluralistic society and protection of minority rights. Conservative Christians are portrayed for the most part in a very unfavorable light in this book.

Butts, R. Freeman. *Religion, Education and the First Amendment: The Appeal To History.* Washington, DC: People for the American Way, 1986.

Historical background on the separation of church and state in the schools from a strict separationist viewpoint.

Carter, Stephen L. *The Culture of Disbelief: How American Law and Politics Trivialize Religious Devotion.* New York: Basic Books, 1993.

General overview of the secularization of American society including the secularization of the public schools.

Caudill, Edward, ed. *The Scopes Trial: A Photographic Essay.* Knoxville: University of Tennessee Press, 2000.

Although the vintage photographs are featured, this book includes a good discussion of the famous "Monkey Trial' as well as an essay on the trial's effect on Tennessee. This book is well worth looking at for anyone interested in the Scopes trial.

Cord, Robert L. *Separation of Church and State: Historical Fact and Current Fiction.* New York: Lambeth Press, 1982.

Scholarly examination of the Supreme Court's jurisprudence in the separation of church and state area including the Court's controversial decisions on religion in the schools. The author believes that the original intent of the Founding Fathers was not to have strict separation and that the Supreme Court has been selective in quoting Madison and Jefferson and repeatedly ignored sources that prove that the founders never intended a complete separation. The author, a law professor, makes a strong case but the text's tone often tends to be sour.

Costannzo, Joseph, S.J. *This Nation under God: Church, State, and Schools in America.* New York: Herder and Herder, 1963.

Interesting polemical treatment of the subject of religion in the schools by a Catholic priest. The author feels that many of the Supreme Court's decision in the area of church-state separation are clearly wrong and not constitutionally mandated.

Data Research. 1997 *Desk Book Encyclopedia of American School Law.* Rosemont, MN: Data Research Inc., 1997.

Annual encyclopedia that compiles the decisions in both state and federal court cases dealing with school law. A chapter on freedom in religion collects and describes court decisions dealing with religion in the schools. Because it's updated annually, this book provides good current materials for researchers.

Dolbeare, Kenneth, and Phillip E. Hammond. *The School Prayer Decisions.* Chicago: University of Chicago Press, 1971.

Scholarly work that examines a community's disregard of the ban on prayer in the public schools. The authors put this defiance into historical perspective.

Douglas, William O. *The Bible and the Schools.* Boston: Little, Brown, 1966.

Although now dated, this volume is interesting because it was written by one of the Supreme Court justices who took part in many of the opinions. Justice Douglas, a religious man, but also a protector of minority rights, examines the pros and cons of excluding religion from the schools.

Eastland, Terry, ed. *Religious Liberty in the Supreme Court: The Cases That Define the Debate over Church and State.* Grand Rapids, MI: William B. Erdmans Publishing Company, 1993.

This book contains twenty-five edited Supreme Court cases on religion. Most are followed by one or two newspaper editorials commenting on the case that is useful in understanding the popular reaction to the often controversial Supreme Court decisions.

Elwell, Walter A., ed. *Evangelical Dictionary of Theology.* Grand Rapids, MI: Baker Book House, 1984.

General reference work with brief entries on people, doctrine, and religious practices. Useful to those who may be unfamiliar with religious terms.

Engel, David E., ed. *Religion in Public Education: Problems and Prospects.* New York: Paulist Press, 1974.

Collection of essays on religion in the public schools, mainly from a Catholic perspective. The volume includes useful bibliographies.

Finkelman, Paul, ed. *Religion and American Law: An Encyclopedia.* New York: Garland Publishing, 2000.

This is a useful one-volume encyclopedia that includes entries on religions, individuals, major laws, and important court cases involving religion.

Flowers, Ronald B. *That Godless Court?* Louisville, KY: Westminster John Knox Press, 1994.

Scholarly treatment of U.S. Supreme Court decisions on church-state relations. The discussion includes the topics of government aid to church-supported schools and prayer in the public schools. The author is a "strict separationist" who believes in the absolute separation of church and state, although the title might suggest that the author would be taking the opposite approach.

Frankel, F. Marvin. *Faith and Freedom: Religious Liberty in America.* New York: Hill and Wang, 1994.

The author, a famous former federal judge in Manhattan, writes on the issue of religious liberty including religion in the schools. Frankel is a strict separationist although he appreciates the value of religion in American life.

Geisler, Norman, A.F. Brooke, and Mark Keough. *The Creator in the Classroom: "Scopes II" —The 1981 Arkansas Creation-Evolution Trial.* Milford, MI: Mott Media, 1982.

Detailed examination of *McClean v. Arkansas* (1981) in which the Arkansas law mandating that the biblical account of creation be taught in the schools was declared unconstitutional.

Goldberg, George. *Church, State, and the Constitution.* Washington, DC: Regency Gateway, 1987.

Although the scope of this book includes a number of areas under the separation of church and state umbrella, the bulk of the coverage pertains to the issue of religion in the schools. The author makes no attempt at a balanced view and blames the "separationists" for what the author sees as "judicial nonsense" of removing God and religion from the public schools.

Gould, Stephen Jay. *Ever since Darwin.* New York: Norton Press, 1977.

Contemporary examination of the theory of evolution by a well-known science writer.

Hook, Sidney, B.F. Skinner, and Isaac Asimov. *Humanist Manifestos I and II.* New York: Prometheus Books, 1973.

The Bible of the humanists, these works by three of the twentieth century's leading minds are anathema to conservative critics who believe that they promote a godless society.

Jorstad, Erling. *The Christian Right, 1981–1988: Prospects for the Post-Reagan Era.* Lewiston, NY: Edwin Mellen, 1987.

Deals with the political ties of conservative Christians and their efforts to promote their cause through the political process.

Kurland, Phillip B., ed. *Church and State: The Supreme Court and the First Amendment.* Chicago: University of Chicago Press, 1975.

Scholarly legal essays drawn from the University of Chicago's annual *The Supreme Court Review,* which always draws contributions from the nation's leading constitutional scholars. Although the essays in the volume are dated, they provide an excellent scholarly analysis of the school prayer cases of the 1960s and 1970s, which are still "good law." The material is scholarly and may be inaccessible to those without some legal background.

LaHaye, Tim. *The Battle for the Mind.* Old Tappan, NJ: Fleming H. Revell Co., 1980.

LaHaye, a vigorous critic of secular humanism, argues that the real battle for America is taking place in the public schools, pitting the pious against the forces of secular humanism.

———. *The Race for the Twentieth Century.* Nashville, TN: Thomas Nelson, 1986.

LaHaye, a leading conservative critic of "secular humanism" in the schools outlines his theory that America is witnessing a race between secular humanism and conservative Christianity for the hearts and minds of American youth.

Levy, Leonard W. *Constitutional Problems in Church-State Relations: A Symposium.* New York: DaCapo Press, 1971.

Reprint of 1966 issue of the *Northwestern Law Review* dedicated to essays on the religion clauses. Although the material is dated, the essays provide a sound and scholarly introduction to the legal underpinnings of the Supreme Court's Establishment Clause and Free Exercise Clause jurisprudence. The essays may be somewhat inaccessible for those unfamiliar with legal scholarship.

———. *The Establishment Clause: Religion and the First Amendment.* New York: Macmillan, 1986.

Levy, one of the foremost First Amendment scholars and a strict separationist illustrates both the original intent of the founders and current application of the First Amendment in a number of contexts including religious practices in the schools.

Lynn, Barry, Marc D. Stern, and Oliver Thomas. *The Right to Religious Liberty: The Basic ACLU Guide to Religious Rights.* 2nd ed. New York: ACLU, 1995.

American Civil Liberties Union handbook covering the role of religion in many facets of public life including the public schools. The handbook is arranged in question-and-answer format and is referenced to the many court cases in the area.

Manwaring, David R. *Render unto Caesar and Religion.* Chicago: University of Chicago Press, 1962.

Scholarly examination of the legal disputes that arose when Jehovah's Witnesses refused to recite the pledge of allegiance to the flag in the public schools. Very detailed treatment of an issue that is now largely forgotten.

Martin, William. *With God on Our Side: The Rise of the Religious Right in America.* New York: Broadway Books, 1996.

This book provides a detailed account of the growth of conservative Christianity in the last half of the twentieth century and how it has shaped the debate over religion in public life. The book also details how the religious right discovered and used political power in advancing its views.

Marty, Martin E. *Pilgrims in Their Own Land: 500 Years of Religion in America.* Boston: Little, Brown, 1984.

As the name suggests, this volume provides an overview of American religious history. The volume is especially useful in gaining an understanding of different faiths.

Matriscana, Carly, and Roger Oakland. *The Evolution Conspiracy.* Eugene, OR: Harvest House, 1991.

This book presents a conservative Christian defense of the biblical account of creation and criticizes evolution as only an unsubstantiated theory.

McCay, Mary, ed. *Equal Separation: Understanding the Religion Clauses of the First Amendment.* Westport, CT: Greenwood Press, 1990.

Essays based on a panel discussion by scholars in the area of separation of church and state.

McWhirter, Darien A. *The Separation of Church and State.* (Exploring the Constitution Series). Phoenix, AZ: Oryx, 1994.

Well-written, current reference text that presents both analysis of the area and heavily edited U.S. Supreme Court cases. Although the subject of the book includes many topics in addition to the education area, many of the cases presented involve religion in the schools.

Menendez, Albert J. *School Prayer and Other Religious Issues in American Public Education: A Bibliography.* New York: Garland, 1985.

Very thorough bibliography on religion in the schools to 1985.

Moe, Terry M. *Schools, Vouchers, and the American Public.* Washington, DC: Brookings Institution Press, 2001.

This is a scholarly review of the voucher issue, including the politics behind the "school choice" movement. The emphasis is on education and politics rather than law.

Numbers, Ronald L., ed. *Creation-Evolution Debates.* Hamden, CT: Garland Publishing, 1995.

This volume reproduces original source documents from the 1920s defending and attacking the theory of evolution. The collection includes an essay by Williams Jennings Bryan, the attorney who won the famous Scopes "Monkey Trial" upholding Tennessee's antievolution law.

Pfeffer, Leo. *Church and State in the United States.* Boston: Harper and Row, 1964.

Although now almost forty years old, this work remains one of the better sources in detailing religious freedom from a legal viewpoint. Of course there is no coverage of many important recent cases.

———. *God, Caesar, and the Constitution: The Court as Referee of Church-State Confrontation.* Boston: Beacon Press, 1975.

A leading separationist scholar, Pfeffer describes the role of the Supreme Court in umpiring the line between church and state, including the role of the Court in protecting minority interest in the public schools. Although the text is somewhat dated, the analysis remains perceptive.

Provenzo, Eugene F., Jr. *Religious Fundamentalism and American Education: The Battle for the Public Schools.* Albany, NY: SUNY Press, 1990.

This paperback examines a number of issues concerning religion in the schools including classroom materials, the teaching of creationism, and school prayer. The tone is generally critical of conservative Christian beliefs.

Rice, Charles E. *The Supreme Court and Public Prayer.* New York: Fordham University Press, 1964.

This book presents the argument, from the Catholic viewpoint, that the Supreme Court's school prayer decisions were incorrect and that prayer and other religious practice should be returned to the schools.

Rosenblum, Nancy L., ed. *Obligations of Citizenship and Demands of Faith: Religious Accommodation in Pluralist Democracies.* Princeton, NJ: Princeton University Press, 2000.

This a collection of essays dealing primarily with the issues surrounding how far the law should go in allowing members of minority faiths to practice their religion when this practice conflicts with the law.

Sherrow, Victoria. *Separation of Church and State.* New York: Franklin Watts, 1991.

Well-researched and accessible work on separation of church and state issues including the topic of religion in the schools. The author makes a number of interesting insights, but there is little legal analysis. Appears to be written primarily for high school audience.

Stokes, Anson Phelps, and Leo Pfeffer. *Church and State in the United States.* Westport, CT: Greenwood Press, 1964.

The basic scholarly volume on church and state relations including the school prayer cases. The text is now dated.

Tribe, Laurence H. *God Save This Honorable Court: How the Choice of Justices Can Change Our Lives.* New York: Random House, 1985.

Written by Laurence Tribe, a Harvard Law School professor and leading constitutional scholar, this popular book illustrates how individual personalities on the Supreme Court have influenced the Court's decisions, including those dealing with religion in the schools.

Utter, Glenn H., and John W. Storey. *The Religious Right: A Reference Handbook.* 2nd ed. Santa Barbara, CA: ABC-CLIO, 2001.

Handbook on the religious right with an emphasis on conservative Christians. The volume is a current sourcebook for studying the many individuals and groups composing the religious right. The book describes both the theological development of the religious right and their political agenda, including the return of religion to the public schools.

Wills, Gary. *Under God: Religion and American Politics.* New York: Simon and Schuster, 1990.

Although it provides an overview of the politics behind First Amendment issues, this work is most useful in understanding the issue behind the movement to ban the teaching of evolution.

Internet Resources

There is a wealth of legal resources available on the Internet, and the number of web sites is growing exponentially. Accordingly, the list in this book, although current when written, will be outdated by the time you read it. Although many sites listed below contain current information, other sites are seldom updated. Unfortunately, web site addresses change frequently. All of the addresses listed here were active when the book was written, but if the address does not work, try searching for the name of the organization or the name of the site to find the new address. Luckily, most web sites contain links to similar sites. If you find a good site there will be a number of links to current sites on the same and related topics.

The following selected web sites include material on the separation of church and state and legal issues facing religion. Some of the sites contain primary source materials while others offer opinion pieces. Be aware that many sites advocate either a "strict separation" or "accomodationist" approach. Accordingly, users should be aware that many sites provide material advocating one side of the issue or the other.

General Legal Web sites

FindLaw
http:/www.findlaw.com/casecode/
This is an easy-to-use site that provides access to both current and historical material. The site has a convenient search engine to help with your research. The site includes Supreme Court cases and the U.S. Constitution.

GPO Access
http://www.gpoaccesso.gov
The official web site of the federal Government Publications Office provides access to both federal laws and court cases. The site contains its own search engine, which can be used in looking for specific items or topics. Use the first box to find the file "Supreme Court cases" then use the search box to find a particular case or topic. The Supreme Court cases can be downloaded in full or in summary form.

Indiana University
http://www.law.indiana.edu/v-lib
　　The law school at Indiana University maintains this excellent site, which is another virtual law library that provides a large number of links to outside web sites. This is definitely worth a look.

'Lectric Law Library
http://www.lectlaw.com
　　This is a fun site that provides a vast amount of legal information that can be easily accessed. The site is organized as a "library" with various "reading rooms" that contain different subjects. Supreme Court cases can be accessed here. This award-winning site also has several less serious nooks and crannies that can provide some diversion.

Legal Information Institute
http://www.law.cornell.edu
　　This site, maintained by Cornell University Law School, is one of the premier electronic law libraries available. A "virtual law library," it contains both recent and historical U.S. Supreme Court cases. The site has its own search engine that can help pinpoint material. The full text of court cases is available, and they can be downloaded in text or in Wordperfect word processing format. This site contains useful links to other legal research sites.

Villanova Law On-Line
http://www.law.villanova.edu
　　This site provides an excellent source of legal materials including full-text legal cases. The site has its own easy-to-use search engine and is somewhat easier to use than many of the other legal sites.

Yahoo
http://www.Yahoo.com
　　Yahoo is one of the most popular sites on the World Wide Web because of its unique search feature. Yahoo's editors check cites for relevancy first, which results in very efficient searching. Use Yahoo's search feature to find relevant links. Of course, Yahoo is scarcely limited to either religion or legal matters.

Specialized Law and Religion Web sites

American Civil Liberties Union
http://www.ACLU.org
　　Excellent "strict separationist" site detailing religious liberty issues.

Americans United for the Separation of Church and State
http://www.au.org
　　This organization is one of the more visible proponents of maintaining a strict separation of church and state in all areas of public life. The organiza-

tion's web site reflects this approach, but it is a good source of basic material on church-state matters.

Antidefamation League
http://www.adl.org/main_religious_freedom.asp
Site maintained by the Antidefamation League of B'nai B'rith. Takes a strict separationist viewpoint. Contains both Q and As, essays, and links.

Baptist Joint Committee on Public Affairs
http://www.bjcpa.org
This web site is a good source of recent legal activity. The organization is a defender of separation of church and state. The site contains an excellent set of links to other sites.

Baylor University
http://www3.baylor.edu/Church_State/
Sponsored by the Truett Seminary on the campus of Baylor University in Texas, the site has an extensive section on religious freedom issues including links to other useful sites.

Becket Fund for Religious Liberty
http://www.Becketfund.org
This excellent site is maintained by a Christian legal defense fund. This is one of the best sources detailing current lower court cases dealing with religious freedom issues, particular in the zoning area.

Christian Coalition
http://www.cc.org/search2html
This is a large web site that contains material on a number of issues including many pertaining to religion in the schools. The Christian Coalition is an advocacy group that supports accommodation of religion in the schools. The site is so large that it contains its own search engine that will help the user navigate through the large library of materials.

Christian Legal Society
www.clsnet.org
Pro-Christian advocacy site that contains lots of current material on freedom of religion issues from a legal perspective.

First Amendment Center
http://www.firtamendmentcenter.org
Although this site contains a variety of material on the First Amendment, it is a good place to look for freedom of religion information. This is a good source of information on recent lower court cases because the site is frequently updated.

First Amendment Cyber-Tribune
http://w3.trib.com/FACT/
Award-winning site sponsored by the Casper, Wyoming, *Star-Tribune* includes much separation of church and state material along with other First Amendment materials. The site contains documents, Supreme Court rulings, and First Amendment information.

Freedom Forum
http://www.freedomforum.org/
A Christian political organization maintains this site that has an "accomodationist" viewpoint. The site deals with many current issues. Includes a number of useful links.

People for the American Way
http://www.pfaw.org
The site is maintained by an organization opposed to the religious right. The web site's content reflects this view. The site includes a discussion of prayer and religious activities in the schools, attempts at censorship, teaching of creationism, and vouchers.

Pew Forum On Religion and Public Life
http//www.pewforum.org
Comprehensive web site on religious issues including freedom of religion and legal issues.

Return of the Separation of Church and State
http://www.members.tripod.com/~candst/tnppage/tnpidx.htm]
This site is a good place to start your research. Although the site itself is not extensive, it contains a listing of links to other church-state separation web sites. The site was created and is maintained by three individuals who advocate strict separation of church and state. However, the site also contains much politically neutral source material. Topics include an overview of the debate, the case for separation of church and state, what the Founders believed about separation, answering the religious right, misquoting by the religious right, the case against government-sponsored prayer, the case against school vouchers, important establishment cases, timely articles, and separationist documents. The site also includes "links of importance" that also advocate the separationist view.

Rutherford Institute
http://www.Rutherford.org
This site is maintained by a conservative political organization that has been involved in a number of high-profile legal cases including the Paula Jones case against President Clinton. The institute is especially interested in religious liberty issues. At this point the web site is still somewhat sketchy.

Virginia Wesleyan College
http://www.vwc.edu/academics/csrf/
   Strong site on religious freedom. This site contains numerous useful links.

Witherspoon Society
http:www.witherspoonsociety.org
   Maintained by the conservative Witherspoon Society, this site contains a variety of current information on separation of religion and church government issues.

Audiotapes

May It Please the Court
Type: audiocassette
Length: 8 hours
Source: Earl Warren Bill of Rights Project
      University of California at San Diego
      San Diego, CA
   Original recordings of important twentieth-century Supreme Court cases, including the attorneys arguing before the Court and questioning by the Supreme Court justices. The set includes both *Abington v. Schempp*, the 1963 case that struck down Bible reading in the schools, and *Edwards v. Aguillard*, the 1987 case that struck down Louisiana's "balanced treatment" law that allowed equal time for the teaching of evolution and "creation science" in the state's public schools.

Videotapes

Books Our Children Read
Type: 1/2" videocassette
Length: 28 min.
Source: Insight Media
      2162 Broadway
      New York, N.Y. 10024
      (212) 721-6316
   Film examines book banning and censorship of classroom material in a small Ohio town. Parents, teachers, and students express their opinions about the process.

Darwinism on Trial
Type: 1/2" videocassette
Length: 120 min.

Source: Reasons To Believe
      P.O. Box 5978
      Pasadena, CA 91117
      (818) 335-1480
    This film, based on work by the conservative Christian Philip Johnson, upholds the biblical account of creation.

Education and the Founding Fathers
Type: 1/2" videocassette
Length: 60 min.
Source: Wallbuilders
      P.O. Box 397
      Aledo, TX 76008
      (817) 441-6044
    Created by conservative Christian David Barton, the video presents the religious beliefs of several of the Founding Fathers including George Washington, to support the idea that religion should be returned to the public schools.

First Amendment Freedoms
Type: 1/2" videocassette
Length: 30 min.
Source: Insight Media
      2162 Broadway
      New York, NY 10024
      (212) 721-6316
    Interviews with political scientists and other constitutional experts about the status of religious freedom as guaranteed by the First Amendment. Although the film is primarily about freedom of religion, it also includes discussions about freedom of the press and the right to peaceable assembly.

For The People
Type: 1/2" videocassette
Length: 60 min.
Source: Films for the Humanities and Sciences
      P.O. Box 2053
      Princeton, NJ 08543-2053
      (800) 257-5126
    Film discusses the impact of three important Supreme Court cases, including the Supreme Court's landmark school prayer case (*Engle v. Vitale*). The other two cases involve academic freedom and homosexual sodomy.

God and the Constitution
Type: 1/2" videocassette
Length: 60 min.
Source: Films for the Humanities and Sciences
        P.O. Box 2053
        Princeton, NJ 08543-2053
        (800) 257-5126
    A part of the "In Search of the Constitution" series with Bill Moyers, the film presents Martin Marty and Leonard Levy, two constitutional scholars specializing in religion in the schools, who discuss school prayer, religious symbols on public property including the schools, and tax-exempt status for religious institutions.

Inherit the Wind
Type: 1/2" videocassette
Length: 130 min.
Source: Movies Unlimited
        6736 Castro Avenue
        Philadelphia, PA 19149
        (800) 523-0823
    Hollywood version of the Scopes "Monkey Trial," made in 1960, pitting William Jennings Bryan and Clarence Darrow against one another, with Spencer Tracy and Fredric March in the title roles.

Religion, Politics and Our Schools
Type: 1/2" videocassette
Length: 90 min.
Source: American Humanist Association
        7 Hardwood Drive
        Amhurst, NY 14226-0146
        (716) 839-5080
    Video presents a discussion of separation of church and state as it pertains to the public schools.

Vista: A Battle for Public Education
Type: 1/2" videocassette
Length: 11 min.
Source: People for the American Way
        2000 M Street, NW
        Suite 400
        Washington, DC 20036
        (202) 467-4999
    Documentary describing a California town's reaction to a religious right takeover of a local school board.

Index